An Endless Trace

An Endless Trace

THE PASSIONATE PURSUIT
OF WISDOM IN THE WEST

Christopher Bamford

Codhill Press
NEW PALTZ, NEW YORK

Copyright © 2003 Christopher Bamford
Foreword© 2003 Philip Zaleski

Published by Codhill Press, Inc.
1 Arden Lane
New Paltz, NY 12561

Book design by Will Marsh
Title Page Illustration: Rosicrucian design from the title page of Robert Fludd's
    Summa Bonum, The Highest Good, Frankfurt, 1629
Chapter opening illustration by Glynis Oliver

Library of Congress Cataloging-in-Publication Data

Bamford, Christopher, 1943-
  An endless trace : the passionate pursuit of wisdom in the west /
Christopher Bamford.
      p. cm.
Includes bibliographical references.
  ISBN 1-930337-07-8 (alk. paper)
  1. Spirituality--History. 2. Wisdom--Religious aspects. I. Title.
  BV4490.B36 2003
  291.4'09--dc21
                            2003046156

10 9 8 7 6 5 4 3 2 1

Printed in the United States of America

To the Master

To my friends & teachers

To Betsy

and Noah, Ceridwen, Sarah, Julia, Amber, Luke, & Alex

But you, o divine one, resounder to the end,
When the swarm of unrequited maenads fell upon you,
O beautiful one, you oversung their cries with order,
Your edifying song rose from the destroyers.

No one was present who could crush your head and lyre
No matter how they struggled and rested, and all the sharp
Stones they threw at your heart
On touching you became tender and gifted with hearing.

Finally they tore you, impelled by vengeance,
while your sound still lingered in rock and lions,
in trees and birds. You still sing there now.

O you lost God! You endless trace!
Only because in the end hate divided you
are we now nature's mouth and listeners.
—Rilke, *Sonnets to Orpheus,* I, 26

Contents

Foreword

by Philip Zaleski

The great task of rediscovering one's true self, which lies at the heart of Christian life—and indeed, of all spiritual paths—should be, on the face of it, a simple matter. The operative verb, after all, is *rediscover;* we have no need to carve a new identity or cross a new frontier. "Be renewed in the spirit of your mind," writes St. Paul (Ephesians 4:23). The renewal or *metanoia* of which he speaks is a regeneration, a recollection of our original state, golden and pure, that innocence that once was ours and which we have heedlessly misplaced. "Except ye be converted, and become as little children, ye shall not enter into the kingdom of heaven," said Christ; and he meant exactly what he said.

So things appear at first glance. But recovering one's true self is, as any seeker soon discovers, the most arduous and painful of tasks. We are encrusted by fear, error, and endless hungers, by what our elders, who spoke more bluntly and accurately than we, called sin. We wear a mask of deceit, molded by desire and glued on by self-love. It will take more than a fervent wish, or even a wish and a valiant struggle, to remove that veil and let our true face shine through. It will take knowledge and experience, longing and prayer, effort and endurance—in a word, wisdom. And more than all these good qualities put together, it will take the grace of God. Without grace nothing will happen; we will spin in endless circles, never breaking out into the upward spiral that becomes, at last, the flight to Truth.

No small task, then, this process of stepping out of oneself and into oneself; out of the false ego and into the true being, out of "I" and into "Not I, but Christ liveth in me." Nonetheless, countless men and women have accepted the challenge, made the effort, and achieved the goal, and have become thereby models for the rest of us, teachers at whose feet we may sit, guides whose steps we may follow. The most renowned of these perfect exemplars are the saints—Francis,

Catherine, Augustine, Thérèse, John, Teresa, Thomas, and all the rest, *ora pro nobis*—and their names will be remembered and their lives emulated until the end of the world. There are many others, however, who have not been and will not be canonized, but who nonetheless serve as helpmeets and mentors, and whose work brings illumination, hope, and joy.

These figures fill the book that you hold in your hands: Pythagoras, Paracelsus, Marsilio Ficino, Angelus Silesius, Pico della Mirandola, Christian Rosenkreutz, Novalis, Goethe, Johann Georg Hamann, the Troubadours, a galaxy of proto-Christian and Christian pioneers who have labored, for the most part, on or beyond the outermost reaches of the great orthodox mainstream of the Church. These men and women constitute a second river of Christian thought, the hermetic or esoteric, allied in some mysterious yet undefined way with the mainstream. Their field of study is the inner life and how best to awaken it. Their tools are the alchemist's retort, the musical scale, the grammar of symbols, the open road. Their methods are arcane, their doctrines heterodox, but their devotion to Christ is unwavering. As Pico wrote, "I bear on my brow the name Jesus Christ and would gladly die for the faith in him.... It is Jesus whom I worship, and his cross I bear upon my body."

Christopher Bamford has given us a great gift by exploring the lives and teachings of these men and interpreting their work, often opaque to modern intellects. He makes it clear that the hermetic tradition, despite its obscure (and sometimes obscurantist) language, aims at the simplest and most profound of goals: the return of the human being and of the entire cosmos to native purity and innocence. Whether examining the nature of food as sacrifice and offering, the mission of Pythagoras, the lyrical holiness of the Celtic Church, the mysteries of the Rosy Cross, the relationship of walking to prayer, the love mysticism of the Troubadours, or Goethe's thoughts on the evolution of consciousness, the same vital notes can be heard: longing for God, transformation through Christ, the construction on earth of a heavenly society, insofar as that is possible in this fallen world.

I have had the privilege, for more than twenty years, of reading and relishing Christopher Bamford's writings on esoteric themes. He penetrates the most difficult materials with clarity, and brings to all his compositions admirable insight and grace. People who write with understanding about the deep mysteries of the spirit are increasingly rare; those who do so in prose worthy of the subject are rarer still. Christopher Bamford is one of the few who can wed sagacity and beauty. Anything that flows from his pen is well worth reading, and in this book you have among the best of his essays. Reading a text like this sets the heart on fire with love of God and gratitude for those who have devoted their lives, with whatever measure of success, to the myriad paths of the Christian life. Here Christopher Bamford plants seeds for that transformation of the human being and the cosmos toward which all creation yearns. Let us rejoice and work together toward the consummate harvest.

Preface and Acknowledgments

The essays making up this book arose in the course of a more than twenty-year affair with the wisdom tradition of the West. I say "affair," but that is not quite true, especially if "affair" were to conjure up something secondary and illicit. Simply put, they are the fruit of love. It was not, however, love at first sight. It was more like discovering a childhood sweetheart in later life and finding her radiantly different, transformed, more complex and beautiful than one had imagined she could be. And so was born a second love, more passionate than the first.

As a young person growing up in Scotland, I loved nature and was deeply moved in subterranean ways by the stark outlines of the Christian mystery austerely limned by dour Presbyterian ministers. I was a solitary child. My companions were wind and rain and endless pages of books. I roamed the moors and let my imagination run wild in the mansions of literature. I took culture for my bride and sought to understand the paradoxical reality of how such depth and beauty could have led to horrors like Auschwitz and Hiroshima.

In 1967, I brought this riddle to America. Amazingly, I thought I might find an answer in graduate school! More amazing still, I found one. I encountered the work of Gregory Bateson, the anthropologist-philosopher, who pointed out that all our problems—social, psychological, and ecological—were problems of epistemology, of how we think. He taught that we get the world we think. He also taught that there are other ways of thinking—that we can change our thinking. This led me on a fourfold search: How do we think? How did we come to think as we think? Are there truly other ways of thinking? How can we change our thinking? (Is it possible to change one's thinking?) To begin to answer these questions led me on an intensive interdisciplinary course of autodidactic study in philosophy, history of science, anthropology, psychology, and religion.

By then, around 1972, I was part of William Irwin Thompson's Lindisfarne Association, a sort of "New Age" think tank dedicated to just such questions, pursued consciously in a context of the practice of spiritual disciplines. It was the time of interreligious dialog; we conducted our search with the aid of meditation teachers from different religious traditions—Buddhist, Hindu, Sufi, as well as Christian and Jewish. Besides practicing (more or less superficially, I must confess) with these masters, I studied the classics of the different traditions. Then came a key moment when I realized that what I really loved was my own tradition, the Christian West. I therefore chose an author from that tradition, the Celtic Christian sage John Scotus Eriugena. I determined to work with him as seriously and with the same sense of immediacy and relevance as my Buddhist friends worked with Dogen, my Sufi friends with Ibn 'Arabi, or my Hindu friends with the great Vedantic saint, Sankara. The die was cast. I became Christian and immersed myself in the practices of Christian theology, mysticism, philosophy, and history. Traces of what I found make up this book.

Many people, living and dead, have helped me on my way. Some provided the occasion for the original versions of these chapters. I think of them and thank them as friends, patrons, mentors, and godparents.

—William Irwin Thompson for "Orpheus's Perpetual Return: Homage to Pythagoras" and "Romanticism and the Evolution of Consciousness," which originated as talks at Lindisfarne conferences.

—Kathleen Raine for "The Magus of the North" and "Becoming Novalis," the first of which was a talk at a Temenos conference, while the second was written for *Temenos: A Review Devoted to the Arts of the Imagination.*

—Ralph White for "The Mystery of Celtic Christianity," "What Ails Thee?" and "The Meaning of the Rose Cross," all of which originated in Open Center conferences. Ralph also provided a home for a version of "The Way of Sophia" in the Open Center magazine, *Lapis.*

—Robert Sardello and Cheryl Sanders for "The Way of Sophia" and "Deserts and Gardens," which originated as talks at their School of Spiritual Psychology Sophia conferences.

—Philip Zaleski and David Appelbaum, editors at different times of *Parabola,* for "Our Daily Bread" and "Washing the Feet," as well as earlier versions of "The Troubadours and the Cultivation of Eros" and "Deserts and Gardens."

—David Fideler for another earlier version of "The Troubadours and the Cultivation of Eros," published in his journal *Alexandria.*

—Robert and Deborah Lawlor for "The Hermetic Tradition," originally written as an introduction to R. A. Schwaller de Lubicz's *Nature Word.*

There are many others without whose conversation, support, and friendship over the years these texts could not have come into being:

—Thomas Moore, who introduced me to archetypal psychology and whose Institute for the Study of Imagination provided a forum where some of these ideas first saw the light.

—Alice O. Howell and her late husband Walter Andersen, at whose home and in whose company Sophia rejoices, communes, and "conjoins all."

—Fred Paddock, lunch companion and librarian *extraordinaire,* who built up the Rudolf Steiner Library into one of the finest esoteric libraries.

—William Manning and Ruth Mickelsen, whose support at a critical moment encouraged the creation of this book.

—Mary Giddens, Stephan O'Reilly, and Gene Gollogly, colleagues at work, whose unfailing support and friendship make possible more than I can say.

—Will Marsh, editor and friend, without whom—literally—this book would not have come into being.

—Owen Barfield, whose conversation on the evolution of consciousness was always helpful.

—Georg Kühlewind, whose radiantly pure Christianity and understanding of attention and consciousness permeate everything I do.

—Among the dead, I thank and acknowledge above all Rudolf Steiner.

—Finally, David Appelbaum, my publisher, without whose vision and confidence in me these chapters would never have been gathered.

—And my extended family and children, whose presence in my life is my greatest blessing.

1

The Way of Wisdom

THIS BOOK SEEKS TO CELEBRATE SOPHIA, Divine Wisdom, to walk her ways and invoke her capacity for new creation. Before we do so, however, we must first find her, which is not easy, for it is Wisdom's nature to hide, to be elusive, and indefinable. Like all spiritual realities, she resists explanation, demanding instead to be embodied, enacted, performed. Do me, she commands, and you will know me!

Often, we first come upon her as if it were by chance, almost without knowing it. She finds us when we are not even looking for her. We feel her touch like a feather on our cheek. For a moment, our senses become alive. We feel her approaching at the edges of our thinking; and then—just as we anticipate finding her—she slips away, returning to her sanctum which in retrospect seems closer to us than our own jugular vein and yet remains inaccessible. Anyone who has been moved by beauty, or caught the glance of another and found one word rising on two pairs of lips, knows what it means to sense her presence. If you have felt someone else's suffering as your own, or have been with a group of friends and suddenly sensed a new unity descend and thoughts manifest that had not been thought before, you will know what I mean. One feels lifted out of the daily grind of linearity and mechanical causality into a preserve, a sacred enclosure of the heart one can describe only as "wisdom." Enveloped by wonder, filled with love, we feel solidarity with the Earth in its struggles, joys, and pains. It is a moment of identity in which we know with certitude, confidence, and humility that we are open, universal, cosmic beings—children of heaven, united with the Earth, whose destiny is our own.

Many people today have such premonitions, or intuit that such experiences could fulfil their deepest need to be whole and fully human. That is why *Sancta Sophia,* the feminine divine, Holy Wisdom, is on everyone's lips. Wherever we turn, we find traces of her coming. We see her in the crumbling of the old patriarchal social order. We see her dawning in the light rays breaking through the setting sun of patriarchal dominance in ways of knowing. Much that has been suppressed or repressed in our history is reentering the light of consciousness, demanding that we rethink who we are and where we have come from. We are beginning to realize that our history is quite different than we have been led to believe. The monolith is being dismantled. Feminist philosophers of science, for instance, have shown us that, from the beginning of modern science, a magical, holistic, participatory alternative to reductive, mechanistic science has always existed. No less pioneering, feminist historians have uncovered whole lineages of philosophers, mystics, and theologians whose recovered contribution is forcing us to rethink the entire meaning of Christianity and Western civilization.

At one level, the recovery of the feminine divine Wisdom or Sophia is part of this general revisionism.

But there is more to it than that. There is a new mood abroad. It is a kind of heart's need for a renewal of religion, a yearning for what religion should and once did provide, a seamless vessel of meaning within which to live, move, and have our being. Those who experience their lives as empty or meaningless are beginning to recognize that to oppose spirit to matter, locating all our problems in "materialism" does not work. Pursuing a "spiritual" path in a void leaves the world untouched. We need a context. The world and we are indivisibly one. Walking a path in isolation from the world ultimately leaves us untouched too. Thus, the realization dawns that "secularism"—the lack of the sacred—is a more useful description of our state than "materialism," because secularism gives us an ethical directive. It calls us to resacralize—consecrate—the world and our lives. "Everything that lives is holy," said Blake. When we seek Sophia, it is the presence of this renewing, sacramental vision that we seek.

We can become aware of Sophia in other ways. Around 1910, Father Pavel Florensky, the polymath theologian and sophiologist who later disappeared in a Stalinist labor camp, moved into a lonely house to lead a solitary life of prayer and meditation. He had no furniture, not even a bench to sit on. It must have been late fall or early winter, for it rained a great deal. The rain, he wrote, "would fall in sobs.... The roof would sob in ultimate despair and desolation." Every so often, Father Pavel would think he heard a knock on the door; but nobody was ever there. He felt abandoned. Desolate, he could neither work nor pray. His soul shuddered with a great, unnamable fear. Suddenly, filling him with new life, the memory of his old teacher returned to his heart. For a moment, in his heart's eye, Isidore stood before him, "gracious and made beautiful by grace…, the most solid, the most undeniable perception of a spiritual person I have had in my entire life." The perception was undeniable because of the wisdom, beauty, compassion, and love that Father Isidore radiated. He united the objective and subjective aspects of these qualities. He emanated their power and reality. He was not only beautiful to contemplate but his beauty transformed the world around him into a new life. Seeking to understand how creation could be born anew in beauty, love, and wisdom, Florensky was led by the memory of Isidore to an encounter with Sophia. Sophia, he discovered, was and made possible these things.

We have all met such truly good and wise people or, if we have not, can imagine them. More and more today we are emerging from the thick pall cast by the nineteenth century on the true nature of the human being. We are beginning to sense a different possibility of what it means to be human than that taught in our textbooks. As for Father Isidore, we are lucky enough to have a description of him in Florensky's own hand, written before his experience in the cabin.

Father Isidore, Florensky writes, "blossomed like a flower,… shone like a small clear sun." Everything about him caused one to marvel— his love; his meekness; his modesty; his impartiality; his straightforwardness; his independence; his unpretentiousness; his selflessness; his poverty; his clarity; his peacefulness; his lightness; his playfulness; his quiet smile. Seeming to be in the world, but not of it, he could destroy all conventions with a single glance because he was above the world and enjoyed complete spiritual freedom. When you visited Father Isidore in his tiny cell, you felt you were entering another world. Everything was simple and poor, but filled with inner warmth and cheerfulness. The place seemed alive. As you entered, every nook and cranny looked at you with loving eyes. Meeting them, you were carried into deep worlds of wisdom. For all things around Father Isidore were symbols, resonant images of infinite depth. Everything was deeply cared for. There was a little garden, about five feet square, that Father Isidore called his "desert." Here he kept company with toads and mice, weeds and herbs, all planted in old tin cans, dusted and neatly arranged.

Father Isidore welcomed whoever visited as though they were kin. He was available to all. He loved everyone he met. He blessed and kissed each with absolute and transforming love and never sent anyone away without a gift. Then, too, his life was joyful, full of fantasy and fun. He never had much to offer, but he would always concoct something no one else ever thought of—his famous jam, for instance, a conglomeration of old cherries, dried figs, cranberries, rye beer, and turnips! With his old crates around him, he felt he had the finest furniture in the world. There was not an ounce of egotism or selfishness in him. He loved outcasts and the downtrodden especially. After all, he said, are we not all one family? And not only people, of course: he was kind to all living creatures He had a special love for plants, grass, and flowers: everything the earth gives birth to. He kept reptiles, frogs, mice, and rats. He loved his cat. Asked, "Don't the mice bother you?" he replied, "No. I feed them lunch and supper." When the Bishop came to visit him, Isidore announced, "I have a guest with me and no longer live on my own," and then he introduced the Bishop to a frog, who had taken up residence in his "desert." Then, too, there were always miracles—a magical atmosphere.

Such virtues or "soul qualities," which we recognize instinctively as inherently right and human, are Sophianic. Father Isidore's beauty, wisdom, and love are, above all, "soulful," of the soul. Isidore lives in the world and with the world. He does not leave the world for the peaks of transcendent experience but transforms it with childlike clarity, gentleness, depth, humility, humor, simplicity, and purity. Like St. Thérèse, the Little Flower, Father Isidore practices the little way that is available to all, no matter how small or imperfect. He transforms the world from within, out of the infinite depths of his own inwardness, in little things. He has cultivated his soul so that it can become a place of the spirit. He holds the spirit, as it were, always in his soul. His first gesture is always the archetypal gesture of the soul: affirmation, active receptivity, trust, absolute surrender, a great Yes. His heart has become one with the heart of the world and, from this deep center of infinite, selfless feeling, he embraces all that he encounters.

The contemporary urge to recover soul—to protect and nurture inwardness and the integrity of psychic life—is a premonition of and a preparation for Sophia's coming. For the soul is the ground and *sine qua non* of the spirit's presence in the world. If the soul is not prepared, made ready, lived with, worked, purified, exalted, and transformed, the spirit cannot manifest. Where the soul is not prepared, the gods become diseases, as Jung taught. But where the soul is ready, the spirit is already there. Perception, consciousness, even matter are transformed. Soul and spirit, world soul and the divine, are two sides of a single activity, distinguishable, but not divisible. The call for soul-work is really preparing for a new spiritual reality, a new kind of knowing—which is to say that wisdom is of the soul. We think that intelligence gives birth to wisdom, but in fact it is the other way around, wisdom gives birth to true intelligence. No civilization in recorded history has been as clever, as intelligent as our own. We are drowning in the products of intelligence in the form of information and ever more sophisticated technological applications of it. But how much wisdom do we have? We are beginning to realize that wisdom is something else, a quality of being we must have in order to survive and continue to evolve as human beings. We are recognizing that to be human, which, as all the sacred texts teach, is the most blessed seed state, has to do with qualities, virtues, that we have ignored, cast away, and despised, as the alchemists used to say of the matter of their work. Now we seek it again, wherever we can find it.

The history of Sophia's relationship to humanity and the gods is difficult to trace because she is so intimately involved with both that it is impossible to view her dualistically. She is the relationship itself. Where human beings and the divine interact, she is there. Her story is difficult to tell because—like all good stories—it begins with the beginning of all things, the very beginning, hence also our own beginning, the mystery of our creation.

We meet Sophia first as Hochma, Wisdom, in the so-called Wisdom books of the Old Testament associated with Solomon—Proverbs, the Wisdom of Solomon, and so on. We find her as the cosmogonic companion of the Creator, "set up from everlasting, from the beginning, or ever the Earth was." She was always with the Creator, participating in the acts of creation—witnessing, accompanying, helping—providing joy, playfulness, and delight. She is called the wisdom in the inward parts of all things, measuring the rhythms and distances of the heavens, binding the influences of the Pleiades and loosening the bands of Orion. She provides the raven with its food and the lily with its glory. She knows when the wild goats bring forth their young and how the infant grows in the womb. Delighting in all things, her special delight is humankind. It was Wisdom who kept guard over Adam when Adam alone had been made. She saved him after his fall, and gave him strength to master all things. Created before time, she accompanies time and will endure to its end. Splendid and beautiful, brightly shining, she spans the world from end to end, gently ordering all things wisely. One, yet many, subtle, free-moving, lucid, spotless, clear, inviolable, she pervades and permeates all things. In the words of Solomon, "Like a fine mist she rises from the power of God, a pure effluence from the glory of the Almighty.… She is the brightness that streams from everlasting light, the flawless mirror of the active power of God and the image of his goodness. She is one, yet can do everything. Unchanging, she makes all things new. Age after age she enters into holy souls and makes them God's friends and prophets, for nothing is acceptable to God but the person who makes his home with wisdom …" in the Temple that Wisdom has hewn with seven pillars.

Complex though her image is, she is clearly an intermediary. It matters little whether we call the two terms she mediates Heaven and Earth, God and humanity, or God and creation. She is in-between, a veil that conceals and reveals. She partakes of both created and uncreated. From her perspective, creation is not *ex nihilo,* from nothing—where there is a radical discontinuity between God and creature—but is theophany or revelation. What she means is suggested by the mystics of Islam who meditated deeply on the saying Mohammed attributes to the Creator: "I was a hidden treasure and yearned to be known. Therefore I produced creatures, in order to be known in them." Here the Creator suffers the solitude, the sadness of not being known. And this sadness—this anguish at being unknown because unnamed, unseen, unembodied—this desire to be known, which is the secret of the Creator's creativity, unfolds in a "sigh of existentiating compassion," an all-surrounding cloud that, like a mirror, receives and gives beings their form. Henry Corbin calls it "the absolute unconditioned Imagination," the creative, active theophanic Imagination. Solomon, too, spoke of Wisdom in just such terms as "a fine mist ... a pure effluence from the glory of the Almighty ... the flawless mirror of the active power of God and the image of his goodness."

Sophia is thus simultaneously matrix and imaginatrix, mediatrix and workshop of creation—its place and its process. She is Imagination, the intermediary between the world of mystery and the visible world. In her, incorporeal beings take body and sensuous things are "dematerialized." Through her, spiritual beings enact the evolutionary drama of the world. From this perspective, Sophia is the first image of the Godhead, its first emanation, the image of what is deepest in the Godhead. In her, the Godhead contemplates the secret of compassion—the liberation of beings by being known and loved in them. In this Sophia, as Corbin points out, the feminine is not opposed to the masculine, but combines the aspects of receptivity and activity. She is Sophia-Creatrix.

Here is a great secret. The place of creation—Imagination or Wisdom, the veil between created and uncreated reality, the divine feminine Creator—has another name. Sophia's other name, revealed since the Mystery of Golgotha, is primordial cosmic human nature itself. That is why, as the Gnostic Valentinus taught, when the angels were creating humanity they stopped in fear when the creature they had made uttered a cry greater than its creation seemed to justify. For the angels realized that the one above had invisibly deposited in this human being a seed of itself, thereby revealing the hidden nature of the ground of all being. This nature, concealed since the foundation of the world, was *Anthropos,* the cosmic archetype of the human being. The new revelation proclaimed openly that *creation is creation in human nature.* The world is brought forth from human nature. It fell through human nature, and through human nature in the end, when the hidden treasure will be known, it will return to God whence it came. According to the likely story, taught secretly in the initiatory temples of Egypt, and practiced as the heart of their sacred science,

God created all things in the mirror, the cloud, of archetypal human nature in order to be *known* or—in Christian terms—*all in all*. God's primordial divine intent has never changed. It is the true meaning of the microcosm-macrocosm analogy. The human being is not a little cosmos; the cosmos is a big human. Cosmic evolution is therefore the progressive unfolding, transformation, and mutation of the seeds planted in the original human archetype.

It is, of course, a fantastic idea that all creation, all nature, is human nature; that human nature is the only "nature" there is. To be understood it must be lived. At the same time, potentially, we are more than nature, for, as Sophia, it is we who must mediate between what is created and what is uncreated.

We may call this view "spiritual anthropomorphism." Ancient humanity dimly intuited it. Remnants of it remain in so-called primitive animism. It explains at once humanity's profound grief over the fall and the understanding that, just as human nature had lost its original state so, too, the world now embodied wisdom only in signs and symbols, and that even these were confused. Original Wisdom was felt to have withdrawn from human beings. For Plato, Wisdom belonged only to the gods. The best a human could aspire to was to be a "friend of Wisdom," a philosopher. Wisdom—original human nature, the Tree of Life planted in Paradise—was felt to be far away. For the Greeks, Sophia became an increasingly distant being to be glimpsed only after lengthy purification of the soul in contemplation of the heavenly movements of the stars, the still, silent harmony of the spheres. Consciousness was experienced as falling into dualism, multiplicity, and otherness. Wisdom, on the other hand, as Heraclitus taught, was not many things but one.

The writers of the Wisdom books understood that Sophia, who had dwelt with God—helping in the work of creation—had lived with humanity and been rejected by it in pride and arrogance. They knew that Sophia had gone away. They understood, too, that she was approaching once again. They sensed her coming; they wooed her; they felt her preparing her ways. Sophia would come to help human beings build her Temple once again. As the angel said to Ezra, "The present is for those now alive, the future for those yet to come.... You, Ezra, should direct your thoughts to yourself and the glory awaiting those like you. For all of you, paradise already lies open, the tree of life is planted, the age to come is made ready,… the city is already built, rest from toil is assured, goodness and wisdom are brought to perfection."

With Ezra, we reach a critical moment in our search for Sophia. Certainly, we can find many manifestations of the divine feminine and "Sophianic" female divinities in pre-Christian times. We need think only of Ishtar, Isis, Maat, Nut, Demeter, Persephone, Athene, and so on. But the mythology and lived presence of Sophia, the Divine Wisdom, is only called "Sophia" with the coming of Christianity. Christianity, of course, has to do with Christ, the Word and Son of God, God with God, sacrificed and freely given out of love for the sake of the world. This God, for Christians, enters creation, penetrates to its very depths, even to those parts that had turned utterly away from God, uniting God's own destiny with that of human nature and the Earth, so that God's original intent, that he be all in all, be made possible once again. In other words, Christianity is founded upon a divine cosmogonic act of creation—the deed of Christ is a new creation—rather than upon a revelation or a teaching.

The heart of Christianity is thus a being, the being of Christ. The presence of the Christ being in our world means that human nature and divine nature, God and cosmos, are no longer two but, potentially at least, one. Oneness, unification, is the meaning of the Incarnation. By uniting with human nature, God entered the earthly, evolutionary world. The Word became flesh. But not only the Word because, as the early Christian Fathers recognized, the Persons of the Trinity—the Father, the Son, and the Holy Spirit—though distinct, are indivisible. The Three cannot be separated. Through the incarnation of the Son, the entire Godhead entered the stream of world evolution. God entered the world so that now there is no longer any transcendent outside. The transcendent is omnipresent in *this* world. As the Rosicrucians said, *Ex deo nascimur; in Christo morimur; per spiritum sanctum revisicimus.* From God we are born; in Christ we die; through the Holy Spirit we come to life again.

That God is no longer outside the world means the world is now engodded. The Creator entered creation so that creation could become creative. Creation turned inside out. The outside is now inside, but with this difference, that there is no longer any outside. This is why now, and for the past two thousand years—witness Mahayana Buddhism—the sacred is in the commonplace and the ordinary is the potentially divine. Earth, air, fire, and water; salt, water, stone, star, darkness, light—the inner rhythms of all things—await only our love to be gathered up again into their abundance, wholeness, and beauty. Though we would never suspect it, we now live in a non-exterior world that awaits only our realization of it. We need no longer seek causes or explanations outside what we can experience. There is no beyond. Each thing in our experience can open to infinite depth and height. Humanity—which is the world—potentially contains all. This is why the "Mystery of Golgotha" is a cosmic, universal event, not a local human one. "The whole of creation groaned and travailed in pain until now," wrote St. Paul. All of creation awaits only the manifestation of the children of God to be delivered into glorious liberty— raised up into its wholeness—from the bondage of separation, isolation, meaninglessness, and death.

To try to practice this is to walk the way opened by the Incarnation. It is not easy. Inertia and old habits militate against it. Christianity, furthermore and justifiably, has a bad name. Much that is horrible and inexcusable has been committed in its name. But the Christianity I am talking about here is larger, indeed quite different, from the religion we have been taught. Generalizing, one may say that before the Incarnation—before the Godhead entered bodily into the world— worship, devotion, walking the way of the gods, was an activity directed outward. The gods were other, and lived in a realm apart, even distant. The mystic, the shaman, the priest had to leave this world, leave behind their bodies and their earthly members, and "travel" to the other world which was wisdom, beauty, truth, light, and so forth. Since the Incarnation, the divine—the gods—are nowhere else but here. Walking a spiritual path no longer means going anywhere else. The task is now to render the divine present in this earthly life. It even means *building it*.

We see this new way clearly in the teachings of St. John. For John, God is not something or the doer of something, but a doing, an activity. God does not generate love in us; rather, our loving generates God. "No man hath seen God at any time. If we love one another, God dwelleth in us, and his love is perfected in us" (1 John 4:12). Our loving makes God present. Once God is present, anything is possible. As John repeats, "God is love and whoever abides in love, abides in God and God in him." God is not to be identified with any faculty. God is what we do when we do God. This is to say, finally, that to be born of God means to bear God. "Let me be Mary and give birth to Christ," says Meister Eckhart. He could have said, "Let me be Sophia and give birth to Christ."

When the events of the Incarnation occurred, few people noticed them beyond the small circles of the disciples and the women and friends around Christ. Fewer still understood. The first people to try to understand the significance of what had happened out of their own spiritual experience were early Gnostics like Valentinus. In doing so, it was they who encountered and named Sophia for the first time. We will not now go into the complexities of Gnostic mythology, but we cannot avoid taking note of what the Gnostics had to say of Sophia, for they were the first to greet her in her new being.

The Gnostic picture fits with much that we have already found. They saw creation and redemption as the drama of Christ and Sophia. They begin with an account of an emanation. The first couple, incomprehensible Depth and ineffable Silence, create the first seed, from which arise the first pair, Conscience and Truth. From these gush forth the other Aeons—Reason and Life, Anthropos and Community, and so forth down—always in pairs. The last to arrive is Sophia, the youngest of the Aeons, unpaired.

Sophia, like the other Aeons, enjoys the fullness of all life. But she feels far removed from the Source. Impetuous and impatient, her passion gets the better of her. Refusing to wait to know the ineffable One from whom she sprang, she rushes forward. Much happens to her, many adventures, and perhaps she would have reached her goal, but she met *Horos* (limitation). Horos separated Sophia from her passion—dividing her—and exiled that passion (now called *Achamoth* or Lower Sophia) from the spiritual world. Expelled from the spiritual world, Sophia brought forth Jesus, as a remembrance of it. But he would not stay with her. He returned to the spiritual world. This was before creation or the fall, as we know it.

Left alone, cast out, Achamoth-Sophia suffered agonies of fear, despair, passion, and ignorance. Her suffering was not ineffective. It produced a false, alien, aborted world whose very matter, soul, and spirit mimicked that of the Truth. Valentinus says, "Ignorance of the Father brought about anguish and terror. And the anguish and terror grew thick like a fog, so that no one was able to see. For this reason error became powerful; it fashioned its own matter.... It set about making a creature, with all its might preparing in beauty as substitute for the truth."

Meanwhile, above, the heavenly Sophia, together with Jesus and all the Aeons, looked down with pity, sadness, and compassion as the Sophia below, born of passion, labored in ignorance, suffering, and anguish. Finally, at the last moment, they decided to rescue her. They sent the celestial bridegroom Christ, "a being of perfect beauty, the very star of the spiritual world, its perfect fruit," into the world she had made.

None of these Gnostic insights into the cosmological place and role of Sophia in the Christian path of redemption became part of orthodox Christian tradition. Perhaps it was because the power of the Gnostic mythological imagination obscured the reality of the Incarnation, with the result that they exalted Sophia-Mary Magdalene and ignored Sophia-Mary the Mother of Jesus. These two ought to be seen as two faces of a single being. Both are figures of Sophia. Mary is the deep bow, Magdalene, the deep turn. Though it has always been difficult to accept the teachings of the Gnostics as a whole, the light of their insights helps us understand Sophia's place.

From the Gnostics, we learn that Sophia is threefold. First, she is present with God before the creation. In a sense, she is uncreated creation itself in God. Secondly, she aids the creation and—this is the Gnostic insight—partially falls with it, so that the suffering of the world, as it falls out of Paradise and hurtles further and further away from direct participation in divine wisdom, is the suffering of Sophia herself. Finally, there is renewed, redeemed Sophia. Rooted in, and reunited with, the divine as the source of the divine-human relation, Sophia now works at the new creation in time. She is the New Jerusalem, a new Heaven and a new Earth—at once the preexistent and eternal and built in time. These three, who are one, are made one through the collaboration of Christ and Sophia.

These different images of Sophia—the way of Wisdom—show us how important it is not to literalize her in a specific formation. We must begin to understand Sophia-Wisdom as an activity that we can embody and participate in. The guiding image for this has always been Mary. But we must understand this Mary not only as the Virgin Mother of Jesus Christ, transparent to the Holy Spirit, but as coextensive both with Jesus' human bodily nature and with the body of Christ. Christ's body is that invisible body built up by its members through their love, namely, by all those who walk the way of love of Sophia-Mary-Jesus. It is the interpenetrated, interconnected solidarity of love, the *Ecclesia,* which is not any political institution but is coextensive with the universe itself.

Mary stands for virtues like faith, kindness, compassion, purity, humility, inner attentiveness, joy, sincerity, patience, and the ability to wait and to hold in active openhearted receptivity. She embodied them in the midst of a long daily life that stretched from birth and childhood, through the experiences of the Incarnation, to her last earthly days in Ephesus with the beloved disciple, John.

There is a letter, purporting to be from St. Ignatius of Antioch to John in Ephesus, which tells us a great deal about Mary, if perhaps in an unusual way. Ignatius writes: "Many of our women desire to see Mary, Mother of Jesus, and try every day to run to you to touch her breasts that fed him—and hands that gave him food to eat and stroked his hair—and to ask more intimate questions. Salome, who was Mary's guest in Jerusalem, and others who know her personally tell us that Mary is full of all grace and all virtues, that she is like a virgin fruitful with virtue and grace. In persecutions and sorrows, they say, she is joyful; she does not complain when needy; she thanks those who insult her, rejoices at pains, and feels immediately with anyone who is unhappy or persecuted, coming to their aid as soon as she can.… She is said to be the teacher of our new faith; the helper of all the faithful. Devoted to the poor and humble, she is all the more humble herself when she meets with true devotion. We glorify her as much as the scribes and Pharisees revile her. Much else is said of her, but we do not dare believe everything. Of those whom we can believe, we learn, above all, that Mary, the Mother of Jesus, combines in a remarkable way human nature with the nature of angelic holiness." Such was the way the Mother of Jesus formed the body in which the Son of God would pitch his tent.

In a vision, the second-century visionary Hermas saw this body, which is the community of those who love, being built. He saw a vision of a woman clothed in a beautiful garment, who was first aged, then younger, finally completely youthful. He was told this was an image of the Church—old in the first vision because preexistent and older than time, and young because it was now youthful in its building. The woman then showed him another vision of a Tower being built by angels and supported by women. These women represented the virtues (faith, abstinence, simplicity, innocence, modesty, and love) that would build up the body. Commenting on this, Pavel Florensky writes: "If we look attentively, we can notice that all the virtues are nuances of a single, chief virtue, which—in contrast to fragmentedness and distraction—could be called integrity or chastity of soul: *simplicity.*" Lack of guile. It is this primary virtue, writes Florensky, that makes possible all the others necessary for the building up of Sophia. The Shakers knew this when they gathered to sing and dance.

> 'Tis a gift to be simple, 'tis a gift to be free,
> 'Tis a gift to come down where we ought to be,
> And when we find ourselves in the place that is right,
> We'll all be in the Valley of Love and Delight.
> Turn, turn will be our delight,
> Till turning, turning we come round right.

The words of the whole song are a marvelous Sophianic hymn. They invoke Mary Magdalene in the "turning" and Mary the Mother of Jesus in the "bowing and bending."

> When true simplicity is gained,
> To bow and to bend we will not be ashamed,
> To turn, turn will be our delight,
> Until turning, turning we will come round right.

Such simplicity, writes Dumitru Staniloae, a contemporary Romanian, means one has overcome all duality and pretense. Those who possess this virtue have passed beyond the struggle between soul and body, good intentions and works performed, deceitful appearances and hidden thoughts, between what they pretend to be and what they actually are. They have become simple because they have given themselves up wholly—which is why they are also able to give themselves up wholly to others.

Building up the invisible community that is Sophia is not just an image. The practice of these virtues, the walking of this way, has an ontological reality. Each action creates a stone of being and thus the edifice of integral nature rises. We must realize, too, that such ethical virtue or soul gestures transform the world. Effected properly, they can transform matter itself, for the practice of such virtues roots us in the very metaphysical substance of the world. Athanasius draws a comparison with the ancient habit of great kings to place their name on every stone of which their mighty palaces were built. Walking the way of Sophia we begin to place her name on every stone raised up to build Christ's body. We begin to recreate the world in immaculate purity, holiness, and beauty. From this point of view, Sophia's activity —her place—is the beginning and center of redeemed creation: *the heart*. Like can only be known by like. Pavel Florensky knew this:

> Purity of heart, virginity, immaculateness is the necessary condition for seeing Sophia-Wisdom, for acquiring citizenship in Heavenly Jerusalem—the mother of all. It is clear why this is so. The heart is the organ for the perception of the heavenly world. The primordial root of a person, his angel, is perceived through the heart. Through this root, a living link is established with the mother of the spiritual person, with Sophia, understood as the guardian angel of creation. In Sophia, a person is given perception of God as love, a perception that gives bliss: for the pure in heart are blessed, they shall see God. They see God by their purified heart and in their heart. Purity cuts away the excrescences on the heart, bears its eternal roots, and clears the path by which the ineffable light of the Spiritual Sun penetrates into human consciousness. Then the whole inner being, washed by purity, becomes filled with the light of certain knowing and the bliss of clearly experienced truth.

The way of Sophia is the way of the heart—the attentive, tender, sensitive, actively receptive heart purified of all hardness, indifference, prejudice, and hatred, which is traditionally the center of the soul. Sophia's way is the intuition that what we need is a "culture of the heart"—a culture that serves and valorizes the heart, not in any sentimental manner, but as the organ of wisdom and love. Rudolf Steiner, for one, spoke of the need for hearts to begin to have thoughts. These thoughts, he pointed out, would not, like head-thoughts, aspire to a pure, cold mathematical objectivity in which the thinker's experience counts for nothing. Heart-thoughts would have a subjective objectivity, a personal character, for they are the fruit of whole experience forged, in James Joyce's phrase, "in the smithy of the soul" and raised into individual consciousness.

John Keats spoke from experience when he wrote: "I am certain of nothing but the holiness of the Heart's affections and the truth of Imagination. What the Imagination seizes as Beauty must be truth—whether it existed before or not—for I have the same Idea of all our Passions as of Love, they are all in their sublime, creative of essential Beauty." Keats, of course, is the poet who gave the world the name of "the vale of Soul-making." "I say Soul-making," he wrote,

> Soul as distinguished from an Intelligence—There may be intelligences or sparks of divinity in millions—but they are not Souls until they acquire identities, until each one is personally itself.... How then are souls to be made? How are these sparks which are God to have identity given them—so as ever to possess a bliss peculiar to each one's individual existence? How but by the medium of a world like this?... Do you not see how necessary a World of Pains and troubles is to school an Intelligence and make it a Soul? A Place where the heart must feel and suffer in a thousand diverse ways! Not merely is the Heart a Hornbook: it is the Mind's Bible; it is the Mind's experience; it is the teat from which the Mind of intelligence sucks its identity.

The saints have always known this. "What can one say of a soul, a heart, that is filled with compassion?" writes St. Isaac the Syrian:

It is a heart that burns with love for every creature: for human beings, for birds and animals, for serpents and for demons. The thought of them and the sight of them make the tears of the saint flow. And this immense, intense compassion, which flows from the heart of saints, makes them unable to bear the sight of the smallest, insignificant wound in any creature. Thus they pray ceaselessly, with tears, even for animals ... and for those who do them wrong.

To say heart is to say love. It is love that, lifting the veil from creation reveals its true beauty, wisdom, and truth. Sophia known through the heart is love. Not love in any privative, exclusive, selfish sense, but a cognitive love that is wisdom and imagination and creative of what is not yet. In this sense, the heart, love, is what draws us into the future; it is how the future reaches into us so that we can be co-creators of its coming.

All those who have loved greatly are our teachers in the way of Sophia. The Greeks had four words for love: *eros, philia, storge,* and *agape. Eros* pierces the veil, giving us a momentary total passionate identification with the object. *Philia,* friendship, one of the deepest mysteries, has to do with the cultivation of intimacy, interpenetration, closeness, common feeling. *Storge* is the love of mothers for children—for the Greeks it means a calm and permanent love in the depths of the being, tender and organic, overflowing, and radiating an aura of continuous protection. *Agape,* the most difficult to understand, meant for the Greeks a kind of mutual moral warmth, respect, estimation, and cordiality. To cultivate all and any of these is to cultivate the heart—even, to seek the heart—which then becomes at once the organ for the perception of Sophia and her place as well.

While paying lip service to it, the dominant, outer exoteric stream of Western culture has persistently devalued and marginalized love and the heart, as it has devalued and marginalized the feminine. Both Greek and Latin cultures were deeply resistant to it, finding the essence of what it means to be human in the head, in rationality. From an evolutionary point of view, this was perhaps necessary. It has given us our individuality, our strong sense of self. Nevertheless, the centrality of the heart was obscured, and we now live in a world that is

dominated by mechanical self-feeling, abstraction, dualism, and literalism. To recover the heart, the soul, is to recover the possibility of
wholeness, of Sophia, as a way of being in the world that does not separate and oppose spirit and matter, mind and body, religion and psychology, science and art. Through the heart—through knowing with
the heart—these can become whole again and Sophia can once again
work in us in her caring, imaginal, creative way.

There has always been a tradition of those who have loved and
whose love was knowing and creative. I am thinking of the great
women mystics of the Middle Ages, the sages of the School of Chartres
who renewed the soul realm of the imagination where the Goddess
Natura, the Seven Liberal Arts, and the Muses were beings once again;
of the alchemists, the Troubadours, and the Grail seekers, and even,
more recently, the visionaries and poets of the Romantic era. All of
these recognized with Novalis that "the heart is the key to the world
and life." All of these can be our teachers.

This heart is not the biological pump we can have replaced thanks
to modern surgery. It is a new heart, the supernatural center of our
being, a sacred vessel wherein the divine can manifest and lived meanings sacramentalize the world. It is the place where all things come
together in harmony, beauty, and wisdom. Ibn ʿArabi, a great Sophianic witness, one of the faithful in love, knew this when he cried out:

> O marvel! A garden among the flames ...
> My heart has become capable of all forms.
> It is a meadow for gazelles and a monastery for Christians,
> A temple for idols and the pilgrims of the Kaʿaba,
> The Tables of the Law and the book of the Koran.
> I profess the religion of love, and whatever direction
> Its steed may take, Love is my religion and my faith.

The spiritual heart is found and nurtured above all by prayer—not
petitionary prayer, but rather prayer that is a kind of alchemy. In the
mystical sense, the heart is a kind of flame or fire. To begin with it is
only a tiny spark, a smoldering coal barely noticeable beneath and
within the dank morass of memories, fears, desires, anxieties, trau-
mas, and preconceptions that make up our ordinary inner lives. The

alchemists—who were also pray-ers—knew this barely glowing coal could be separated from the morass, contained in stillness, and carefully tended into a steady, transforming fire of love and imagination. The old Desert Fathers, too, knew this and spoke of "the prayer of the heart," meaning by this the union of the mind and the heart. Neither mind nor heart, they felt, could be left alone in prayer. Prayer of the mind alone became cold and inflationary. It led to a kind of spiritual egotism. But prayer that came only from the heart led either to sentimentality, which is a kind of egotism of feeling, or to a kind of cosmic oceanic immersion in feeling. The true way was to unite the mind and the heart. Not by bringing the heart into the mind but by a descent of the mind into the heart, so that the heart becomes knowing, a sensorium with eyes and ears, taste, touch, and smell. In the new heart, as in a deep mirror, the old monks saw that all their ideas of the world—of divine, angelic, and human natures, of animals, plants, trees, minerals, and the starry heavens—were living realities. All around them were beings, fellow players in the great drama of creation. They saw the world differently. And it *was* different. It was a new world. That is why the monks were often thought to possess the philosopher's stone that could transmute common metals into gold. Those coming from the outside world to visit them found the world miraculously transformed, and went away wondering. These early monks called their practice "working the earth of the heart." This is what Novalis meant when he said, "We are on a mission; we are called to cultivate the earth." Putting it another way, Novalis asked, "Is it not understandable that in the end all will become poetry—will the world in the end not become soul?" It is what Rilke meant when he wrote:

> Earth, is it not this that you want: invisibly
> to resurrect within us. Earth, is it not your dream
> one day to be invisible—Earth! Invisible!
> If this transformation is not your mission, what is?

To do this work, to cultivate the Earth in all these senses, is to walk the way of Sophia and join in her task of uniting Heaven and Earth.

2

Our Daily Bread

Our experience in the world of visible nature is always paradoxical. Born with the intuition of unity, of the singleness of the universe, we find ourselves divided and confused by the discovery that we are distinct from the world. As soon as seamless reality splits into outside and inside, the first obscures the second, while the second hides behind the first. The realization that unless these two split parts become one we cannot, in Rilke's words, become "reliably at home in our interpreted world" comes only later and marks the first stage of spiritual awakening. The initiatory path of transformation—the work of esotericism—is the movement from outer to inner. It is the way of love, by which two are made one.

Many traditions begin the path with the contemplation of death, which is all around us. Living in transient, outer nature, we do not seem wholly to belong to her. Ambiguity masks our relationship with what surrounds us. We find ourselves tragically cut off and alien. Nature sustains us; our body is assembled from her elements and maintained according to her laws; but she is indifferent to us. When we "die," the innocent necessity of her laws takes over our body, reducing it to dust. Yet the elements that make up the body are never destroyed and would seem to live on forever. In that sense, as children of physics and chemistry, we are immortal and nature is our place; but insofar as we aspire to the freedom of self-knowledge, nature's mother-womb seems a prison or a trap.

The Gnostic injunction is to leave this world of exile. Many teaching stories portray the human soul as a pilgrim, a stranger, a homeless traveler. Jesus said, "My Kingdom is not of this world." It is true. When we consider nature with our ordinary minds, we are surrounded by mortality. Whatever is externally visible, including our own body, is transient and forever dying. Death, infirmity, disease—mortal nature with its needs and passions—is the cosmic condition. Human life, history, is carnage and pain. Yet deep within us we dissent. We abjure that reality. We know it cannot be right. Such suffering must be evidence of a pervasive sin or wrong. Our dissent affirms that it is not ours essentially. We know in our bones that we have been made for something else. Yet we love her, our Earth; we know that she was made for us, and we for her. "Our mother, the beauty of the world." She intimates our paradise, our most perfect nature, our true home. Because we intuit her meaning and beauty, we feel responsible for her. We sense her participation in another reality. Without sharing in nature, we know that we share in her nevertheless, as she does in us. We realize that humanity and Earth are united, that our fate is one, we are Earth and she is us—that, in the phrase of Scotus Eriugena, nature is human nature.

More astonishingly still, confirming this, each morsel and drop of outer, visible nature, every sensorial perception, feeds our inner being. The dying world, from which we feel apart, paradoxically sustains our inner being. Visible, mortal food is transformed in us, in mortal nature, into food for immortality. Surely this is a great mystery. "Nature" uses "nature" to resist and overcome "nature." In the celebrated sentence of the ancient alchemist Ostanes: "Nature delights in nature, nature overcomes nature, nature dominates nature."

Nineteenth-century science spoke of the conservation of "matter," its indestructibility. Nothing was lost, nothing created; there was only matter in transformation. Thinking centered on utilizing it. Health, nutrition, and agriculture became synonymous with the utilization of quantified elements. However, while biological transmutation—true transmutation of elements—may be the rule in nature, in human beings what can only be called a *resurrection* of "matter" into "consciousness" occurs. This indicates that, rather than speaking of the conservation of matter or energy, one ought to speak of its (and the world's) continuous creation or resurrection—out of nothing.

The symbol for continuous creation is food. In the words of the Taittiriya Upanishad: "I am food, I am food, I am food. I am the food-eater, I am the food-eater, I am the food-eater. I am the combining agent, I am the combining agent, I am the combining agent. I am the firstborn of the world-order, earlier than the gods, in the center of immortality. Whoso gives me, he surely does save thus. I, who am food, eat the eater of food. I have overcome the world. I am brilliant like the sun."

As always, the question arises: Who am I, to what world, where do I belong? Where are human beings at home? Visible, outer nature seems to exclude us. As we perceive her, she is death and we know nothing of her. The being of things escapes us and we find ourselves always outside. As Rilke says:

> And we: spectators, always, everywhere,
> looking *at* everything and never *from!*
> It floods us. We arrange it. It decays.
> We arrange it again, and we decay.
> (*Duino Elegies,* "The Eighth Elegy")

The first, paradigmatic transmutation is thus the overcoming of "outsideness"—the overcoming of the world of mortality and its transformation into food for immortality.

For Angelus Silesius, life is the Christ light of human beings. True food is true knowing, as the Father knows the Son and the Son the Father.

> The bread is not our food. What feeds us in the bread
> Is God's eternal Word, is spirit and is life.
> (Angelus Silesius, *The Cherubimic Wanderer*)

Writing of the meaning of "supersubstantial"—as in the Lord's Prayer, "Give us this day our *supersubstantial* bread"—Origen confirms that our true bread is incorporeal, spiritual, living food which comes down from Heaven. For Origen, it is the bread of angels, so that whoever receives it becomes an angel and feeds upon contemplation of the truth. But one cannot become an angel—a being of perfect inwardness—unless one already is an angel. These are not metaphors. Henry Corbin has shown how, gnostically, anthropology must become angelology. Nor was St. John being metaphorical when he spoke of

God's Word, the *Logos* in the beginning, as "Bread." The *Logos* is the foundational activity of creation. Sharing in it, we become children of the unity of the origin, but sharing in the dragon, as Origen says, we become serpents of the fragmentation of subjective, psychological time. Food therefore comes in two kinds. Origen writes: "Since the Son of God exists substantially, as the Adversary also does, there is nothing incongruous in either of them becoming the food of this person or that. Why then do we hesitate to admit that in the matter of all powers, good and evil, each of us can be nourished by them all?" For Origen, to eat is to think. We live by our thoughts.

It has often been said that by our thoughts, feelings, and desires, we nourish superhuman entities, angelic beings, but less frequently alluded to is the equally plausible circumstance that by these same thoughts, feelings, and desires we *feed on* what is superhuman. The relationship, the connection, is primary. It is an eating world. Feeding, we are fed; eating, we are eaten. We become what we eat and what eats us. This is our intrinsic food-nature. Realizing it, the organic health of the one true world is maintained. In the Christian tradition, all of us, as many as we are, form one Body because we partake of one Bread. It is only a question of doing so.

Dionysius the Areopagite begins his work on the celestial hierarchies with a quotation from St. James: "Every good gift and perfect gift is from above and cometh down from the Father of Lights." Dionysius goes on to explain that every procession of radiance "fills us anew, as with a unifying power, by recalling us to things above." Such food is heavenly. Eating it, we are led into unity, and the "outer world" drops away. For Dionysius, the process of unification is by means of hierarchy, which is a holy order of sacrifice. It is both knowledge and activity, at once purifying, enlightening, and perfecting. By its means all beings, animate and inanimate, harmoniously conform in the divine cooperation, the theophany by which what is mortal becomes immortal and what is immortal becomes all in all.

Dionysius enjoins three interdependent activities as the means by which to partake of divine food. The first activity, called *Seraphic,* indicates the primacy of self-sacrificing love or devotion: the laying down or surrender of all one is for another. By this unconditional sacrifice, absolute openness, the living warmth of true life is generated.

The warmth is light, and by it transmission and reception of *Cheru-bimic* gnosis are made possible by the reciprocity of the three. For Seraphim and Cherubim rest in *Throne*-like immobility, the place of all that is itself no place.

To understand this hierarchical process of transmutation we may consider the first celestial order, that of the Seraphim, the Cherubim, and the Thrones. By their ceaseless activity, the Cherubim "kindle or make hot" those below them with a purifying, energetic flame. The Cherubim or "Streams of Wisdom," lost in contemplation and filled with love, bounteously outpour on those below the wisdom bestowed upon them. Meanwhile the Thrones rest immovably and perfectly in Immanence. Theirs is the purity, the power, and the steadfastness of divine presence. This first celestial order provides the foundation of the whole creation. Each feeds each. As a tri-unity—below and above in this case denoting not direction but a Trinitarian relationship—they feed the whole. Of this first order, which we may take as exemplary, Dionysius says: "They are filled with the divine food which is manifold through the first given outpouring and yet one through the unific oneness of the divine banquet; and they are deemed worthy of communion and co-operation with God by virtue of their assimilation to him."

The threefold sacrificial process is paradigmatic. The two other orders that are intermediary to human beings repeat it. Humanity constitutes a fourth (celestial) hierarchy. Only the connection is missing. Should human beings enact a similar sacrificial process then—here is the foundation of *gnosis*—sensible, outer reality would be translated into intelligible symbols, the bearers of the primal source-reality. By the sacrifice that is self-knowledge, mortal food becomes immortal manna. By self-knowledge, which is communion and transformation, interiorization and appropriation by sacrificial action, creation subsists.

Vedic tradition is clear. Sacred science is sacrificial science, the science of sacrifice. The cosmos is a sacrificing one. Sacrifice is the path of the gods, the link between temporal and eternal, outer and inner, nature and spirit. Sacrifice is the primordial deed or bond that unites and distinguishes. As in eternity the primordial sacrifice of dismemberment gave rise to the names and forms of creation, so now, in time, sacrifice re-members all names and forms in a single embodied moment. The Eucharist likewise is an *anamnesis,* or recollecting, and affirms the unity of the two sacrifices—creation in eternity and redemption in time. Sacrifice is the single effort that integrates what is fragmented. It is the effort that counts, spiritual food being received according to labors performed. More precisely, as Swedenborg notes, it is received according to the degree that we transform the past into the present, that we live in the present. That is the labor for which we receive our *daily* bread, for "*daily* signifies ... a continual glorification of the God Messiah, so that the moments are continuous without differentiation." As Swedenborg says, such bread cannot be kept until tomorrow, for worms breed in it, as in manna. To sacrifice is to be present, in the present.

In the Vedas sacrifice is central, but it is the context, the sacrificial hymn, that makes the sacrifice efficient. "The gods created the hymns first." The divine food—*soma*—grows through the hymns. The hymns themselves, however, born as they are on the breath, depend upon and are themselves the first sacrifice. For one cannot speak truly without laying oneself down in recognition of the primacy of the Other, the Open. True speech, song, spun on the airy threads of breath, is synonymous with sacrifice—each breath, each word, selflessly, rhythmically, perfectly laying itself down for the next. This is the weaving power of *maya,* made possible by the affirmation of each moment—the great "yes" which is prayer, unmediated presence, and union. The author of the Bhagavad Gita knew this.

> Except for the action engaged in as sacrifice,
> This world is subject to the bondage of action.
> For the sake of that, Son of Kunti,
> Perform action free from attachment as sacrifice.
> Long ago Prajapati created creatures together with sacrifice, and said:
> By sacrifice shall you prosper,
> Let this be the milch-cow of your desires.
> By this nourish the gods and may the gods nourish you;
> Thus nourishing each other, you will attain to the supreme good.
> For the gods nourished by the sacrifice
> Will give you the enjoyments you desire.

To be fed by the world, to feed our immortal being in the world, by our activities in it and our perceptions of it, we must overcome our attachments. That much is obvious. But what of the suggestion that sacrifice is primordial and fundamental to creation; that creatures were created by sacrifice for sacrifice; that sacrifice is the rule of life, the cosmic law, by which all is food, that is, life?

Traditionally, creation is separation and reunion, difference and relation, fall and redemption. Unity is trinity. It abides, proceeds, returns. First, there is nothing, nonexistence. Nothing, desiring, polarizes—it sacrifices itself to itself. Duality arises: an infinite non-existence, nothing—and indefinite existence, something. But this indefinite something also desires. It desires to be measured. Thereupon the third arises: rhythm, relationship, harmony, the pattern that connects—consciousness. Hence transformation, life, food: the cosmic web. Consciousness connects: it is the ternary, to-gethering power, carrying back what has been carried apart. Consciousness—itself sacrifice, separation, and reunion—sacrifices itself. The Cosmic Human, total being-consciousness, offers itself on the altar of itself and becomes *Anthropocosmos,* the archetypal human universe, perfect nature. With the "fall"—the descent—cosmic consciousness of total reality enters incarnation. Consciousness, life, food, begins its complex journey into visibility, unfolding and opening, analyzing the implications implicit in its seed or principle, Divine Humanity, the *Anthropos.*

What sufferings this descent of the Anthropos into visibility has involved! No wonder the privileged images are sacrifice and crucifixion. For incarnation is just that: limitation, fixation, concretization. Cosmic consciousness is sifted and analyzed, measure by measure, sacrifice by sacrifice, from realm to realm, until the moment of present earthly humanity. We are the last, the deepest materialization, the outermost visualization: the point of inversion or return. To us, outer nature no longer seems a home, but the home we must leave behind. Or rather: take it with us and leave it behind as cosmic humanity in its unfolding has always taken all with it and left all behind. What else is the meaning of transformation?

But who or what is cosmic humanity? Who or what evolves? Rumi gives an answer, and more, when he writes:

I died as a mineral and became a plant,
I died as a plant and became an animal,
I died as animal and I became a human being.
Why should I fear? When was I less by dying?
I shall die once more as a human, to soar
With the blessed angels; but even from angelhood
I must pass on: all except God perish.
When I have sacrificed my angel soul,
I shall become what no mind ever conceived.
Oh, let me not exist! For Non-existence
Proclaims in organ tones, "To him we shall return."

Before Abraham was I AM. The true I, the Logos-being who is cognition, sacrificing itself again and again, unfolds its cognitive powers in the marvelous visual display we call "nature." Tearing itself apart, it dies from realm to realm. What suffering, what sacrifice! By which we understand that this being divides, measures, specifies itself; purifies itself; unites itself with itself; assimilates itself to itself; exalts itself: *a perpetual offering to itself.* Schwaller de Lubicz writes: "Suffering is the only stylus whose nature corresponds to the substance on which imperishable consciousness is inscribed. This is because suffering is of the same nature as consciousness; for both depend upon the realization, the conjunction, of opposites."

Today humanity finds itself increasingly outside, opposite nature. Nature is turned inside out. What was outside is now inside—or rather, there is no longer any outside. Containing all within himself, the prodigal son prefers the path of duality, spending his substance and power in the husks of illusion and trompe l'oeil creations. *Maya,* the creative power of true Imagination, what Paracelsus called "the Star," has become a mere fantasy, a will-o'-the-wisp. We are entranced by our creations; technology seems to have the upper hand. Nevertheless, there is an underlying uneasiness. We fear death, set life against death, and thereby make a mockery of both. We abuse ourselves, isolate ourselves, so that like nature—the nature we have created—we languish in the deep sleep of ignorance.

Archetypal humanity, entranced by its own image, fell face first into nature's arms. Now, having struggled from realm to realm to raise

ourselves up, we, upon whom much depends, do not realize that it is
for us to raise nature up, insofar as she is who we are—imperishable
consciousness. That is what feeds us in the bread—the sacrifice of
consciousness. "The human being is the Messiah of nature," wrote
Novalis, who also said: "If God could become human, then he can also
become stone, plant, animal, and element, and perhaps in this way
there is a continuous redemption in nature." Put another way: "The
stone has suffered for the plant, the plant has suffered for humanity,
and humanity has suffered for Redemption" (Schwaller de Lubicz).

In his marvelous letter to Witold von Hulewicz, Rilke affirms:

> Nature, the things of our intercourse and use, are provisional and
> perishable; but they are, as long as we are here, *our* property and
> our friendship, co-knowers of our distress and gladness, as they
> have already been the familiars of our forebears. So it is important
> not only not to run down and degrade all that is here, but just
> because of its provisionalness, which it shares with us, these phe-
> nomena and things should be understood and transformed by us
> in a most fervent sense. Transformed? Yes, for it is our task to
> imprint this provisional, perishable earth so deeply, so patiently
> and passionately in ourselves that its reality shall rise in us again
> "invisibly." *We are the bees of the invisible....* The earth has no way
> out other than to become invisible: *in* us who with a part of our
> natures partake of the invisible, have (at least) stock in it and can
> increase our holdings in the invisible during our sojourn here—*in*
> us alone can be consummated this intimate and lasting conversion
> of the visible into an invisible no longer dependent upon being vis-
> ible and tangible, as our own present destiny continually *grows at
> the same time* MORE PRESENT AND INVISIBLE *in us.... We are
> the transformers of the earth; our entire existence, the flights and
> plunges of our love, everything qualifies us for this task.*

Having become visible, outward, we must become invisible,
inward. We must make the world inward. This transformation is true
sacrifice, true making-sacred. It is to give back to the world what it has
given us. Giving back, which is the laying down of our petty ego-
power and its objects, is the food that renews life for gods and humans

alike. Once nature—stars and planets, trees and mountains—seemed ensouled, animate, divine. Now, like Pascal, we shudder at the infinity of empty space and the litter of dead matter. But what once lived still lives, if only we give it life. In the Kingdom of Heaven, the stars are divine. By overcoming the outwardness of the visible world, in the form of our attachment and our desires, another energy, another food, becomes available. For, unlike the exterior world, the not-outer world is a "moral" world of goodness, truth, and beauty, as well as courage, humility, and steadfastness. Such ideals produce true work long after physical energy is exhausted. True health, as Plato knew, is the cultivation of this moral world. To "know" the virtue of Mars within oneself benefits a person infinitely more than any outer voyage in a spacecraft. The same is true of all aspects of our sundered nature. Let them rise invisibly within us. Thus we overcome them and unite with them. This is the work against nature, *opus contra naturam*— against necessity, animality, objectification. The sacrifice of these is true food for human beings, daily bread in the spiritual sense.

Swedenborg writes that the food and drink that nourishes spirits and angels is spiritual and lies in their continual desire to know. Spiritual hunger is for *knowing, for meaning,* and knowledge by identity— inner and outer made one in a living act of being—is daily bread for human beings as spiritual beings. More specifically, Swedenborg writes, "The food of celestial angels is love and, at the same time, the intelligence of truth and good by which especially they are gladdened." By love, which repeats the original and creative sacrificial gesture of unconditional openness, the living bread of knowledge that comes down from Heaven (and rises to it) is made manifest.

3

The Hermetic Tradition

Hermes *saw* the totality of things. Having seen, he understood. Having understood, he had the power to reveal and show. And what he knew, he wrote down. What he wrote, he mostly hid away, keeping silence rather than speaking out, so that every generation on coming into the world had to seek out these things.

—*Kore Kosrou (The Virgin of the World)*

So go, then, my child, to a certain laborer and ask him what he has sown and what he has harvested, and you will learn from him that the one who sows wheat also harvests wheat, and the one who sows barley also harvests barley.... Learn to comprehend the whole fabrication, *demiourgia,* and generation of things and know that it is the condition of man to sow a man, of a lion to sow a lion, of a dog to sow a dog.... See, there is the whole of the mystery.

—Isis the Prophetess to her Son Horus

And he said unto them, Go ye into all the world, and preach the gospel to every creature.

—Mark, 16:15

DERIVING PRINCIPALLY FROM EGYPT and sharing a common origin with Pythagoreanism, Platonism, Neoplatonism, and some manifestations of Gnosticism—not to mention Kabbala and the Mosaic teachings of the Old Testament—the so-called *Hermetic* tradition became, during the last two thousand years, the cosmological complement of the Christian revelation.

Christianity, as a metaphysical and earthly historical event, needed a cosmology or sacred idea of nature for its complete embodiment.

Hermetic tradition provided this natural theology. Hermetism, for its part, found in Christ not only the initiatory effusion necessary for its survival but also a supernatural justification and natural consummation of its "great work" of cosmic divinization. As cosmology, Hermetism, cast off from Egypt, needed a ground from which to derive and a goal toward which to aspire, a theology. The Christian Mystery as revealed by the Trinity and the Incarnation was providential, above all because the revelation of Christ unveiled the divine ground of the "Human Mystery" and it was precisely the "human" world that was the Hermetic or cosmological one, mediating and reconciling celestial and terrestrial realms. From the Hermetic point of view, the Christian Mystery revealed the divine unity of humanity and the cosmos and vindicated Hermetism, which was founded upon this certitude, as an authentic Christian esotericism or spiritual practice. Thus the Hermetic science of alchemy, evolving into a sacramental science whose object was the eucharistic divinization of the entire cosmos, taught that "The Stone is the Christ." At its heart lay the revelation of the *Anthropos*, whose Resurrection Body was at once the Body of God, Nature, and the Human Being.

That such ideals could be dangerous if misunderstood or assimilated without due preparation goes without saying. One may understand the attitude of the Church Fathers in wishing to conceal the truth upon which these ideals were founded. Nevertheless, for those who have eyes to see, the human mystery of Christ was clearly proclaimed by Scripture and particularly by St. John and St. Paul. The veil of the Temple had been rent, and lo! The Human Being found itself. The Word in the beginning was shown to have been made flesh. "And there are others," wrote Irenaeus, the second-century Bishop of Lyons, of certain Valentinian Gnostics, "who assert that the Forefather of all things himself, the Pre-beginning and Pre-unthinkable, is called 'Man' [*Anthropos*]. This is the great and hidden mystery, namely, that the power that is above all and embraces all is termed 'Anthropos.' And because of this the Savior designates himself Son of *Anthropos*."

Modern science, insofar as it is cosmological, is still "Hermetic" and anthropocentric. But, by virtue of its claim to be autonomous and self-constituted, rather than open to, deriving from, and expressive of mystery, it is not. From the Hermetic perspective, it may be viewed both as a loss of orientation and as the chaotic but nevertheless perhaps necessary precondition for a new birth. One may speak with Gaston Bachelard of a possible mutation of spirit or "epistemological rupture." By this account, scientific method, having developed faculties of reasoning and intellectual honesty, has reached its limits, and by virtue of the paradoxes generated by these limits, opened the possibility for the development of new faculties of knowing based upon these very contradictions. From this perspective, the whole movement of thought and philosophy in the twentieth century has been toward the necessity of learning to think without objectifying and of discovering, upon the basis of such thinking, a new theory of truth and a new science. This science would once more be true science from a Hermetic point of view. It would be a unifying science of causes, not facts, penetrating the mystery presiding over material phenomena, rather than objectifying phenomena into a "system."

To understand this, we must distinguish science and scientific thinking from technology and technological thinking. The modern age—"The Age of the World Picture" as Martin Heidegger terms it—represents not so much the ascendancy of science as that of technology and the machine. Scientific thinking has become technological thinking. "Nature" is objectified as a fixed, self-contained, atomized spatiotemporal picture or system, whose parts operate according to abstract, predominantly statistical laws—"the laws of nature." These are clearly definable, usually in terms of mathematics, and are verifiable within the projected framework, where they may be manipulated and calculated in terms of work or energy. Nature has become a "system," conceivable and graspable as a picture within limits defined by the senses. Truth meanwhile has become the comforting certainty of the shared representation, rather than the disclosure of the Real as a certainty revealed and experienced in the individual soul. This science of the "picturable" makes exact research possible and penetrates every level of contemporary life.

We should note that the picture depends entirely upon what is given by the senses or by mechanical extensions of these. It is organized according to a logic that is sense-based. Since Aristotle, Western thinking has rested upon two fundamental "laws." First, *the law of contradiction:* "The same attribute cannot belong and not belong to the same thing at the same time in the same respect." Second, *the law of the excluded middle:* "B cannot be both B and not B." Consequently, present-day consciousness is permeated by the loneliness and suffering occasioned by the twofold impenetrability of space and time.

Unfortunately, both what it means to be human and more particularly an understanding of the twofold reality of consciousness and matter fall outside the sensory limits. They are not represented in the picture. This is what Coleridge referred to as "that despotism of the eye" which derives from the assumption that the spatial world exists objectively, whereas in fact it is projected by the rational consciousness working in isolation from other centers or fields of knowing. Coleridge spoke of "that Slavery of the Mind to the Eye and the visual Imagination or Fancy under the influence of which the Reasoner must have a *picture* and mistakes surface for substance." Such people, he added, "consequently *demand* a *Matter* as a *Datum.*" However, "As soon as this gross prejudice is cured by the appropriate discipline and the Mind is familiarized to the contemplation of matter as a product in time,… the idea of *Creation* alone remains."

Traditional Hermetic science, based upon just such a discipline of mind and body, was very different. Rather than the objectification and control of the known by the knower, it sought unification and identity—to transform the knower and thereby the known as perceived and experienced. The "object" was conceived of as a *symbol*. Hermetic science strove for a qualitative, unifying exaltation of the relation of the knower to the known in the symbol *through the act of knowing*. Knowledge was how the human being participated in and contributed to an "evolution," whose end was the coming-into-unity of the whole. Humanity was called to be the means of the coming-into-unity, just as by its "fall" it had been the means of multiplicity— of unity's unfolding or self-articulation into a multiplicity, not of objects, but of relations. Such unity and multiplicity, however, must not be thought of in opposition, but as the polarization of "two forces of one power," as Coleridge put it.

Hermetically, knowledge and evolution are one and founded on the primacy of humanity as life and consciousness. Hermetists, finding themselves in a sense-based, psychological consciousness of multiplicity—which *separates*—and bearing within themselves the memory of original unity, are called upon to transform the one by the other. Hermetic science is the way and contemplation of this process. Methodologically, it is a way of posing and articulating this unity, for unless each perception or act unifies, "things" (the consciousness that separates) cannot not be seen as interconnected, nor life *(bios)*, soul *(psyche)*, nature *(physis)*, or human being *(anthropos)* understood.

The assumption of Hermetic science is that the whole universe is sacramental, embodying and proclaiming the process of the revelation of unity—of unity as *identity*, however, rather than as nonduality. The Christian teaching of the Trinity, particularly as contained in the Prologue to the Gospel of St. John, is the key: *"In the beginning was the Word, and the Word was with God, and the Word was God. The same was in the beginning with God."* The Identity of the Unspeakable Unity is revealed as *mediated*. It is at once Origin, Word, and *With*—as a thing that is identical is the same *with respect to* itself, is returned *toward* itself. St. John then goes on to assert that an identity exists between the innate, total consciousness that is the Human Being, for which the entire human bodily structure is the instrument, and the Life that is the Universe. "All things were made by him; and without him was not anything made that was made. In him was life; and the life was the light of men." This is the unitary vision, subscribed to by all the great medieval men and women of "knowledge" (who were not those anonymous technologists whose thinking gave rise to the great inventions), and it is founded not upon a sensory material unity of nature, but on a spiritual unity.

The Prime Matter of the alchemists is not sensory matter. It is the water of life, the unmediated Divine Presence as the feminine element in nature, even the Holy Spirit. "If God could become human," wrote Novalis, "then he can also become stone, plant, animal, and element, and perhaps in this way there is a continuous redemption in Nature." From the perspective of a hierarchy of aspects of *consciousness*, the shift from science to technology may be seen not only in terms of a movement from unity to multiplicity or spirit to matter, but also, as Schwaller de Lubicz indicated, as *the degeneration of Love into utility*.

To confuse utility with love is a fundamental loss of orientation. Hermetically, creation as well as the knowledge of it, is Love. Pherecydes of Syros, by tradition a teacher of Pythagoras, taught that "Zeus, when about to create, changed himself into Love; for in composing the order of the world out of the contraries, he brought it to concord and friendship, and in all things he set the seed of identity and the unity which pervades everything." Pherecydes is "Hermetic" because he was learned in the Prophecies of Ham and the secret books of the Phoenicians, whose revelation is attributed to *Thoth* or *Hermes*—"the master," according to Horopollo, "of the heart and reason in all human beings." According to another text, Hermes or Thoth is "the great, the only God, the Soul of Becoming." He is the mediator through whom the world is brought into manifestation, the master of creation, of every aspect and level of the formal world.

Hermes is thus the patron of science and knowledge, the judge and equilibrator of polarity and relation. He is *Hermes Trismegistus,* Thrice Great, the Master of the Three Worlds. All knowledge in the ancient world was ascribed to him. As Archetypal Human Being, he is the primordial culture-bringer, the institutor of all arts, crafts, and sciences. He is healer, master architect, and founder of agriculture, smelting, and mining. His temple was called the "House of the Net," which indicates cosmology or the weaving of the world fabric or garment, each knot representing a conjunction of life and death, impulse and resistance, contraction and expansion. From this point of view, Hermes-Thoth is one with Enoch, Idris, Quetzalcoatl, and Odin— leaders of Humanity in the celestial world from which they guide and sustain terrestrial manifestation.

We may also note, in connection with the idea of Archetypal Humanity or Perfect Nature, that Hermes-Thoth also suggests the idea of the Celestial Witness or the Philosopher's Angel. The Witness or *Daimon,* illuminator of "the knowledge and mysteries of Creation, causes of Nature, and origins and modalities of things," is simultaneously, as Henry Corbin has shown, "the one who gives birth and the one who is born." "The seeing through which I know Him is the same seeing through which He knows me," wrote Meister Eckhart. In the *Corpus Hermeticum,* the treatise called "the Mind of Sovereignty" (the *Poimandres,* Witness or Shepherd) states: "I know what you wish, for I am with you everywhere;

keep in mind all that you desire to learn and I will teach you.... Learn my
meaning ... by looking at what you yourself have in you."

The *Corpus Hermeticum*, the primary source for Hermetic teaching, is a collection of Hellenistic "gnostic" texts, purporting to derive
from Egypt and to represent a *summa* of Egyptian cosmology. Parallels to and amplifications of the doctrine it contains abound throughout the literature of the period. Parallels may be found in Orphic-
Pythagorean and Platonic literature, Egyptian mythology, the *Enneads*
of Plotinus, and certain Gnostic and alchemical texts such as the
Megale Apophasi and those attributed to Pseudo-Demokritus, Zosi-
mos, Kleopatra, Maria the Jewess, and Olympiodorus. Study of these
reveals that the cosmos is a unity of consciousness and life:

> The Kosmos is an instrument of God's will, and it was made by Him
> to this end, that, having received from God the seeds of all things
> that belong to it, and keeping these seeds within itself, it might
> bring all things into actual existence. The Kosmos produces life in
> all things by its movement; and decomposing them, it renews the
> things that have been decomposed; for, like a good husbandman, it
> gives them renewal by sowing seed. There is nothing in which the
> Kosmos does not generate life; and it is both the place in which life
> is contained and the maker of life. (*Corpus Hermeticum* IX)

Again, in Book XIII, Hermes says that the cosmos "is one mass of
life, and there is not anything in the Kosmos that is not alive." However, the cosmos is not itself the source of life. The source of life is the
Good, which is "full of immortal life."

In Plato's *Timaeus*, the Demiurge sought to make the universe a
single, visible, living being—an organism—with body, soul, and
intelligence. He did so in the model of the most completely perfect
synthesis and seed of all intelligible things: "the perfect living creature." The latter, Proclus tells us in his *Commentaries*, is the first-
begotten threefold archetypal Human Being of Light called *Phanes*
(Shining), *Erikepaios* (Power, male), and *Metis* (Wisdom, female). In
the words of the Orphic Hymn, "Erikepaios, seed unforgettable,
attended by many rites, ineffable, hidden, brilliant scion, whose
motion is whirring, you scattered the dark mist that lay before your

eyes, and, flapping your wings, you whirled about, and throughout this world you brought pure light."

Phanes, also called Eros and Dionysius, is born of the Cosmic Egg, which is formed by the polarization (doubling) of *Chronos*, the Principle of Principles, into *Aether* (a male principle of Limitation or Distinction) and *Chaos* (a female principle of Unlimitedness). Since mutual love, or affinity, draws Male and Female into One, the original division—scission or severance—is, at the same time, the original union. "Great is the mystery of marriage," says the Gnostic *Gospel of Philip*, "for without it the world would not have existed." In Pherecydes' cosmology, too, there is a Primal Triad—*Chronos, Zas, Chthonie*—and the world arises out of the "wedding" of Zas and Chthonie. Socrates, in the *Philebus*, puts it thus:

> There is a gift of the gods—so at least it seems evident to me—which they let fall from their abode, and it was through Prometheus, or one like him, that it reached humankind, together with a fire exceeding bright. The human beings of old, who were better than us and dwelt nearer the gods, passed on this gift in the form of a saying. All things, so it ran, that are ever said to be consist of a one and a many, and have in their nature a conjunction of limit and unlimitedness.

Plato accordingly describes the Soul as formed out of the Same and the Different, two principles that become the Fire and Water, Sulphur and Mercury, of medieval alchemy. The primordial complements exist in perpetual struggle, but find their fulfillment in union or matrimony, symbolized by the interpenetrating triangles of the hexagram. Thus the doctrine asserts the mutual interdependence of the Unity of Consciousness and the Multiplicity of Existence, of Transcendence and Immanence, of the Divine and its Presence. Phanes, the Egg—"the original Human Being in the *Fiat Lux*"—is Light and Life, illuminating, animating all things in it. Phanes, Seed of seeds—the life of all things, in their essence as in their unfolding—is born through polarity and conjunction.

"What is not Life that really *is*?" wrote Coleridge. In the identity of the two counter-powers, which for Coleridge were "gravitation" and "light," life subsists. In their reconciliation it at once dies and is born again into a new form.

The Hermetic universe is alive and is a unity. Both life and unity arise out of a conjunction or identity of complements. A manuscript of the *Goldmaking* of Kleopatra expresses the idea to perfection: a serpent with its tail in its mouth, the Ouroboros, encloses the motto *En to Pan*, One the All. Another ancient text states: "One is the All, and thanks to it the All, and by it the All, and if the All did not contain the All, the All would be nothing." The circle is closed. The universe is a uni-verse; there is nothing else. It is one-only, non-exteriorized, and everything is connected to everything else. The *Corpus Hermeticum* (XVI) says, "If any one attempts to separate all things from the One, taking the term 'all things' to signify a mere plurality of things, and not a whole made up of things, he will sever the All from the One, and will thereby bring to naught the All." Likewise, Ostanes, in the earliest alchemical formula, affirms, "Nature rejoices in Nature, Nature triumphs over Nature, Nature dominates Nature."

What is involved is not a theory, nor any kind of reductionist, monist speculation. Rather it is a matter of *experience*—the experience of a state of consciousness in which the opposition between subject and object, inside and outside, observer and observed, is transcended to reveal the spiritual unity and creative interdependence of humanity and the cosmos. The Hermetic universe, the Hermetic work, and the human subject are *one and the same*. "Everything is the product of one universal creative effort," wrote Paracelsus; "the Macrocosm and the human being (the Microcosm) are one. They are one constellation, one influence, one breath, one harmony, one time, one metal, one fruit." Hermes teaches in the *Asclepius* that "the human being is all things; the human being is everywhere." This is the teaching that, when it emerged in the fifteenth century, was to inspire the Renaissance:

> None of the gods of heaven will ever quit heaven, and pass its boundary, and come down to earth; but the human ascends even to heaven, and measures it; and what is more than all beside, he mounts to heaven without quitting the earth; to so vast a distance can he put forth his power. We must not shrink then from saying

that a man on earth is a mortal god, and that a god in heaven is an immortal man. (*Corpus Hermeticum* X)

This is the great postulate: the first, the seed of all, was the *Anthropos,* the divine human being. To realize this was and is the great mystery, the Christian Mystery foretold by "pagan" Hermetism and practiced by Christian Hermetism. To know it is to be saved. It is knowledge, the beginning of science, but to know in this way is to be born again: begotten by the will of God, through a seed that is the true God, conceived in silence, in a womb that is wisdom. Reborn in this way, as in the famous Hermetic "Treatise Concerning Rebirth," one comes to perceive "not with bodily eyesight, but by the working of mind," and a new science of revelation becomes possible: "Father, now that I see in mind, I see myself to be the All. I am in heaven and on earth, in water and in air; I am in beasts and plants; I am a babe in the womb, and one that is not yet conceived, and one that has been born; I am present everywhere" (*Corpus Hermeticum* XIII).

If one would know God, one must become like God. Only like may know like. Becoming like God to know God, one comes to know like God. The knowing with which one comes to know God is the knowing with which He knows. As all things are in God, so they must also become in the human being. Since they are not in God as in a place, or space, corporeally, but rather invisibly, beyond space and time, the human being must withdraw from space and time, matter and motion. Outside space and time, consciousness is all. There are no continents in mind, nor elephants, nor any distance or time between galaxies or aeons. With each thought, as the *Corpus Hermeticum* (XI) says, we *are* there. There is only the present. This is the teaching:

If then you do not make yourself equal to God, you cannot apprehend God; for like is known by like. Leap clear of all that is corporeal, and make yourself grow to a like expanse with that greatness which is beyond all measure; rise above all time, and become eternal; then you will apprehend God. Think that for you too nothing is impossible; deem that you too are immortal, and that you are able to grasp all things in your thought, to know every craft and every science; find your home in the haunts of every living creature;

make yourself higher than all heights, and lower than all depths; bring together in yourself all opposites of quality, heat and cold, dryness and fluidity; think that you are everywhere at once, on land, at sea, in heaven; think that you are not yet begotten, that you are in the womb, that you are young, that you are old, that you have died, that you are in the world beyond the grave; grasp in your thought all this at once, all times and places, all substances and qualities and magnitudes together; then you can apprehend God. But if you shut up your soul in your body, and abase yourself, and say, "I know nothing, I can do nothing; I am afraid of earth and sea, I cannot mount to heaven; I know not what I was, nor what I shall be"; then, what have you to do with God? Your thought can grasp nothing beautiful and good, if you cleave to the body, and are evil.

To realize the vision requires a radical transformation of consciousness or perception, a change in the way we know and perceive, "for all things which the eye can see are mere phantoms and unsubstantial outlines; but the things which the eye cannot see are the realities" (*Corpus Hermeticum* VI).

The tradition is unanimous. Plato in his *Timaeus* refers to the distinction between knowledge *(episteme)* and opinion *(doxa)*. The one is apprehensible by "intelligence with the aid of reasoning," while the other remains "the object of opinion and irrational sensation." Paracelsus forcefully contrasts knowledge *(Wissen und Erkantnuss)*, which is experience *(Erfahrung)*, with pseudo-knowledge or *logica,* which is a figment of the rational mind, "a foreign doctrine." This, he says, is "the leaven of the Pharisees who move about in the schools, who break the power of nature and follow neither Christ nor the natural light." The Pharisees are "the dead who bury the dead; there is no life in what they do, for there is no light for them in which they can learn anything."

The *Corpus Hermeticum* (X) puts it this way:

Then only will you see it, when you cannot speak of it; for the knowledge of it is deep silence, and suppression of all the senses.... Knowledge differs greatly from sense perception. Sense perception takes place when that which is material has the mastery; and it uses the body as its organ, for it cannot exist apart from the body. But knowledge is incorporeal; the organ which it uses is the mind itself.

What is implied is a schooling of the senses—a cleansing of "the doors of perception," so that, instead of being "stuffed up with the gross mass of matter" and "crammed with loathly pleasures," they may become *active* organs of true vision. Once this is achieved, one may "see with the heart him whose will it is that with the heart alone he should be seen." Later students will term this faculty *Imaginatio Vera:* True Imagination, the Star in the Human Being.

Sensory phenomena appear to exist independently of us in time and space. Yet the world lives only to the extent that it speaks in a language we can understand. Its meaning becomes alive only to the extent we assimilate it in experience. If we were aware (awake) and could direct our habitual responses—could see through our eyes rather than with them (realizing that an eye never saw anything)—we might realize that in each perception it is we who bring meaning and life to bear upon the world. At the level from which meaning derives, of which our intuition of meaning is a recollection, there is no inside and outside. There is only one world of Archetypal Imagining, outside time, where each thing *is,* without any comparison. Perception is remembering, and we stand toward the spiritual world as toward a forgotten actuality. It is only our sensory apparatus and how we use it that divides the world into inside and outside, giving to time and space an outerness they do not have.

We need not infer that the sensory function itself is in any way unnecessary or prone to error. On the contrary, it is the source of knowledge. "The knowledge of human beings comes from the greater world, not from themselves," states Paracelsus, adding paradoxically that these two—the greater world and the human being—are "one thing and not two."

What he means becomes clear when we realize that by knowledge he means experience, which he contrasts with "experiment," the latter being "accidental." Experiment may teach the "fact" that a certain herb, *Scammonea,* purges, or rather that there is a virtue or knowledge in the *Scammonea* that teaches it how to purge, just as there is a knowledge in the pear tree that teaches it how to grow pears. Objective observation, "experiment," apprises us of the fact, but truly experienced knowledge is union with the knowledge in the *Scammonea*. "When you overhear from the *Scammonea* the knowledge which it possesses, it will be in you just as it is in the *Scammonea* and you have acquired the experience as well as the knowledge."

Knowledge, then, is the nonobjectified understanding of the way in which, as Walter Pagel puts it, "any particular natural object fulfills itself and thereby attains perfection—its inborn and sure instinctive 'knowledge." In other words: "That 'knowledge' is 'correct' which enables an object to realize its specific aims."

We may go further and compare the two kinds of knowing with two ways of "perceiving." In the first, ordinary sense perception, the object is immediately transformed or abstracted into a representation, while in the second the perception is not abstracted or transformed but rather, as it were, allowed to germinate in the soul. As Rudolf Steiner notes, we may compare perception to a grain of wheat, which may be either eaten or planted in the soul: "Whenever a seed of corn is processed for the purposes of nutrition, it is lifted out of the developmental pattern which is proper to it, and which ends in the formation of a new plant; but so also is a representation, whenever it is applied by the mind in producing a mental copy of a sense perception, diverted from its proper teleological pattern."

To plant a perception in the soul is to allow it to complete itself, to reveal its "knowledge," whereas to fix it in a representation, a "picture," is to reduce it to mental fodder. Rather than catching the bird in flight and flying with it, we shoot it down and so kill it. Hence we live with dead thoughts, not living ones. True sense perception not only works to recall the inner sense to its spiritual archetype, but also permits the exaltation of phenomena through individualized self-knowledge, now revealed to be none other than world knowledge under an individualized aspect. "True imagination," writes Maurice Aniane in an extremely perceptive essay on alchemy, "actually 'sees' the 'subtle' processes of nature and their angelic prototypes. It is the capacity to reproduce in oneself the cosmogenic unfolding, the permanent creation of the world in the sense in which all creation, finally, is only a Divine Imagination."

Such a philosophy of perception is at once a philosophy of symbols, a symbolism or "symbolic method," and a phenomenalism. All phenomena are symbols. They are the necessary representations of the knowledge they contain—the knowledge being that which makes them what they are, the principle according to which they function. Each thing in nature—bird, tree, and flower—is a question containing its own potential answer, meaning, and explanation. All phenomena—light, color, and sound—and all natural processes— germination, growth, digestion, and fermentation—contain the power to evoke, in the prepared observer, the true response that is their meaning. This Hermetic doctrine of the reciprocity of human being and world is well represented by Goethe when he writes, "One knows oneself only insofar as one knows the world, becoming aware of it only within oneself, and of oneself only within it. Each new subject, well observed, opens up within us a new organ of thought." In this philosophy lies the foundation of a true science of phenomena, a science of the commonplace, essentially dispensing with all instrumentation and relying on consciousness alone—for consciousness is everything. Goethe says, "The best of all would be to realize that every fact is already theory. The blue of the sky shows us the principles of color. We need not look for anything behind phenomena: they themselves are the doctrine." Hermetic science is able to understand such phenomena as life, light, space, time, matter—which our science cannot fathom—because it is able to experience phenomena as such, as God himself knows them.

We must go beyond the idea of a single, unique act of creation and assume as well a "creative state" of continuous creation, metaphysical in nature, outside space and time. Creation is continuously unfolding, and consciousness may always know its states by virtue of the principle whereby "the One is the All." Hermetically, to know a god is to penetrate to a specific creative phase or relationship. As Hortulanus says, "Our Stone is made in the same way that the world is created." The world is not continuous as our senses present it to us. There are moments of eternity, gaps or openings in perception, which our senses conceal. For the Hermetist, it is by means of these "gaps" that causality—out of time—is effected by the gods who are themselves the "causes." Causality is vertical, for in the realm of phenomena—the horizontal plane—there are only connections without cause.

Since "the path up and down is one and the same" as Heraclitus said, continuous creation is, and contains, the mystery of Resurrection. Creation is theophany; theophany is theosis: "I was a hidden treasure, I yearned to be known. That is why I produced creatures, in order to be known by them."

It is not difficult to see why Hermetic alchemy has been called "the science of the symbol," in contrast to modern science, which is rather "the science of representation." If knowledge of creation depends upon the ascent of the soul then, as Corbin says, imagination and theophany, the way up and the way down, are but other terms for what is called in Islamic esotericism *ta'wil*. *Ta'wil* is the spiritual exegesis whereby things, natural objects as well as scriptural meanings, are "led back" from their outerness, their letter, to their innerness or spirit—a process that can take place only in the soul. *Ta'wil* becomes therefore a word for the "continuous ascent of the soul" through the world hieroglyphically conceived as constituted of symbols and images. Phenomena are twofold, ineffable *coincidences of opposites,* conjunctions of inner realities and outer facts, visible and invisible worlds—all of which implies an irreducible polarity, bidimensionality or reflexivity of being itself, and of consciousness and life.

"All things are but two," states the *Corpus Hermeticum* (XIV), "that which is made and that which makes. And the one cannot be separated from the other; the Maker cannot exist apart from the thing made, nor the thing made, apart from the Maker. Each of them is just that and nothing else; and so the one can no more be parted from the other than it can be parted from itself." So, too, it is with male and female, heavenly and earthly. "When you make the two one," Jesus said, in the Gnostic *Gospel of Thomas,* "you will become the sons of man, and when you say, 'Mountain, move away,' it will move away." A Greek alchemical text makes all this a little clearer: "One becomes Two; Two becomes Three; and by means of the Third the Fourth realizes Unity. Thus the Two no longer form but One." From the Hermetic point of view, this is the King, the perfect union of Creator and Creature, Spirit and Soul, Sun and Moon, the Perfect Human Being.

Here is the true end of Hermetic science—to give birth to a Child of God—in contradistinction to contemporary science, whose end is its own methodology. However, although the knowledge may be one and unchanging, people and times change, and the knowledge must each time be won anew, because knowledge is attainable only through profound personal experience, suffering, and sacrifice. Although a study of great spiritual works of the past helps—it is one of the two great "aids" in the Work, the other being the study of nature—true Hermetic knowledge is achieved only through deep inward realization and effort. Thus each student of the Hermetic speaks in his or her own voice, from personal experience. Nature and Scripture may have been one's guides, but the only justification for speaking is that one knows.

The perenniality of the Hermetic tradition having been affirmed, something should be said, however briefly, of its history, or evolution, as this is not unconnected to our present situation. There are several possible histories, but the likeliest began in Egypt, in a hierarchical society in which all activity derived from, and received its form and substance from, the Temple. The arts, crafts, and sciences were ritualized, initiatory embodiments of the metaphysical and theological knowledge realized by the priestcraft. Under priestly guidance, Egypt achieved a unique level of perfection in which functions and languages—myth, theology, hieroglyphs, and geometry, for instance—were interconnected. At the shift of the world age at the time of Christ, the connections were broken. The wisdom of Egypt was cast haphazardly into the creative ferment of Hellenism, and Greco-Roman alchemy, at once craft, philosophy, and religion, was born.

The earliest "alchemical" texts available to us (such as the Leyden Papyrus and the Holm Papyrus) derive from this period and contain only recipes, *aides memoires* for the craftsman. Appearing at the same time as these are other texts, more Neoplatonic, Neo-Pythagorean, and Gnostic in character, in which the metaphysical principles are more openly stated. The texts are not works of philosophy so much as they are manuals of "inner work" and self-initiation, harking back, as Jack Lindsay says, to an ancient unity of craft-process and metaphysical principle. But the period—that of the political foundation of Christianity—was not propitious for freedom of individual thought and research, and as this progressively diminished—was progressively repressed—alchemical, philosophical, and hermetic thinking moved eastward, through Syria, into Persia. On the way, in an act of cultural transmission that has been compared by Henry Corbin to the transmission of Mahayana Buddhism from Sanskrit into Chinese, an enormous number of texts, the patrimony of the ancient world, were translated. The transfer was providential, for it meant that the fully flowering fruit of Hellenistic science and philosophy lay ready to be received by Islam. The result was that, within 150 years of its founding, Islamic alchemy had reached its height with Jabir, whose immense oeuvre includes more than three thousand treatises.

Jabir is particularly interesting because of his use of the so-called *Emerald Tablet* in his *Second Book of the Element of the Foundation,* discovered by E. J. Holmyard in 1923. Until Holmyard's discovery, this epitome of alchemical philosophy was known only in medieval Latin versions. More recently, another Arabic version has been found, ascribed to Apollonius of Tyana. According to tradition, The *Tabula Smaragdina* or *Emerald Tablet* came from Egypt via Greece and Persia, as we would expect.

From Islam, Hermetic alchemy traveled to the medieval West, the first work to be translated, *A Testament of Alchemy* of Morienus, arriving in 1144. Other translations followed. Soon original works began to be written in Latin, with Artephius, Albertus Magnus, Thomas Aquinas, Roger Bacon, Raymond Lull, Arnold of Villanova, and Nicholas Flamel continuing the tradition of bringing what is imperfect into perfection. Apart from such a work as John Scotus Eriugena's *On the Division of Nature,* alchemy in the West lacked any real metaphysical foundation except as embodied in its own techniques and in Scripture. Mention must be made of the School of Chartres, which in its own way—through its Platonized Hermetism—laid the ground for the Renaissance and the explosive influence of Marsilio Ficino's translations. These, beginning with the *Corpus Hermeticum* in 1463 and including Plato, Plotinus, Iamblichus, Porphyry, Proclus, and the Chaldean Oracles, enabled Hermetism to flower once more as "Renaissance Hermetism" in the life and work of, for instance, Paracelsus, Bruno, the Rosicrucian Brotherhood, Van Helmont, Basil Valentine, and Jacob Boehme.

What is interesting is that with the Renaissance alchemy and related Hermetic sciences emerged into the open and actively sought to gain ascendancy in the emerging scientific age. Hermetists were turning "outward," not only in the sense of becoming more "engaged" socially, but also in that they turned their attention more consciously to "nature."

In the final analysis, the sudden availability of texts, of course, is more a symptom than a cause of the revolutionary moment we call the Renaissance. What the Renaissance represents may in some sense be said to have matured slowly throughout the entire historical course of what the great Quaker historian Rufus Jones called "Spiritual Religion." By this he meant that invisible Church founded by St. John (but taught also by St. Paul), whose basis is: "That which is born of the flesh is flesh; and that which is born of the Spirit is spirit. Marvel not that I said unto thee, Ye must be born again. The wind bloweth where it listeth, and thou hearest the sound thereof, but canst not tell whence it cometh, and whither it goeth: so is everyone that is born of the Spirit" (John 3:6–8).

The seeds, revolutionary then as now, germinated slowly, gradually giving rise to the consciousness of a human spiritual unity, a Cosmic Humanity, united in the "inner light" with God and all beings—a Spiritual Being in whom all participated. Its task was to create a New Jerusalem, a spiritual city without walls, an invisible Temple whose altar was the human heart and whose name was the Universe.

The historical course may be traced both from Plato and Plotinus and from St. John and St. Paul. Passing by groups of Gnostics and other "heretics," gaining strength through St. Gregory of Nyssa and Dionysius the Areopagite, it entered the medieval West. There it gave birth not only to that great movement of mystics such as Eckhart, Suso, Tauler, Ruysbroek, Nicholas of Cusa, the Friends of God, and the Brethren of the Common Life, but also to the "heresies" of the Cathars and the Waldenses. Then, with the Renaissance proper, this current of mystical spirituality, within which had been forming the new being (the "human being") that humanity was to become, merged with the now readily available Hermetic and Platonic teachings. Exoterically, the result was the Reformation; esoterically, it was the renewal, the interiorization of the ancient view of the universe as a sacred, initiatory Temple—a Temple transformed and reborn through the saving work of Christ.

In this spirit, *The Chemical Wedding of Christian Rosenkreutz* begins on an "evening before Easter-day" and ends, the wedding consummated—Sun and Moon, Spirit and Soul perfectly united—with the formation of the Order of the Golden Stone. This is accompanied by the presentation of a golden medal bearing on the one side the inscription *Art is the Servant of Nature* and on the other *Nature is the Daughter of Time.* Knowledge must follow nature, imitate her in her mode of operation according to the alchemists, listen to her needs, and attend her will. But nature, the world of becoming, is herself but an offspring, a moment of time, the finite fruit of an infinite evolutive faculty. Within nature there is no time. Nature *is* time, time *is* nature. It is an inseparable, identical process. Having learned this, the new Knights are given their articles, enjoining them to ascribe their order "only to God and his handmaid Nature," to overcome their lower natures, and to place themselves fully at the service of humanity for the sake, and in the reality, of the Spirit. Finally, they sign their names, Christian Rosenkreutz appending to his the motto *Summa scientia nihil scire*—"The height of knowledge is to know nothing."

Outwardly, the story of the origins of modern science is complex and not easily understood. Suffice it to say that Hermetic, Platonic, and Rosicrucian influences were continuously at play in the formation of the new scientific attitude. Ficino, Bruno, Paracelsus, Dee, Fludd, Van Helmont, and other representatives of the tradition worked openly to create a "new world," a new science, art, and religion—a new society. But the old order recoiled, persecuting the "new men" as fanatics, madmen, and heretics. Materialism and mechanism won the day. What was actually at stake was much more complex: a new state of *consciousness.* What the Renaissance, in its mystics and Hermetists, modestly proclaimed was the need for (and hence possibility of) a new "initiation," a new and powerful science of nature based upon a transformation of consciousness, a new way of knowing. Something that had previously been the exclusive province of the saint, monk or hermit was now taught to be the birthright of every human being, attainable with the aid of God alone by virtue of the "inner light" of human consciousness. Rufus Jones, for instance, writes of the Quakers:

One comes back from a study of the Quaker literature of the seventeenth century with the profound impression that these Children of the Light did actually have a fresh revelation of God. The most remarkable thing about the movement is not that its leaders founded a new state, or worked out a new and, I think, an extraordinarily happy form of religious organization, or discovered a new principle of social fellowship, or inaugurated a new type of human service; it is, rather, that they came into a new experience of the present reality and the living presence of God. They passed from a religion based upon the accumulated deposit of other men's faith, and on the authority of books and creeds, to a religion based on their own vision of God, and tested by their own experience of His transforming power.

After the first pulsation in the Renaissance, the impulse died away, went underground, only to return with renewed vigor and a new form, as Romanticism or the "romantic" path to higher knowledge. Goethe, Coleridge, Blake, Keats, Novalis, Lamartine, de Nerval—and even the philosophers Fichte, Schelling, von Baader, and Hegel—are manifestations of the "symbolic method," which is Hermetism. The Romantics too, like their predecessors, tried to proclaim a new science of the spirit. But the impetus toward materialism was set and not yet ready to be transformed. Theirs was a prophetic mission, one only able to come to fruition in our own time, when, in the words of Owen Barfield, referring to Rudolf Steiner, "Romanticism comes of age." He may as well have said, "The Renaissance comes of age."

Today not only Rudolf Steiner, but also others like R. A. Schwaller de Lubicz, constitute a third call, renewing the summons to a science of the spirit first sounded by Paracelsus and Ficino, the original Romantics. Perhaps now, finally, the stage is set. Certainly philosophers such as Nietzsche, Bergson, Whitehead, Heidegger, Gadamer, and Ricoeur have begun to dismantle the fortress of Cartesian consciousness and replace it with a consciousness open to the mystery of revelation and the process of existence, in which human beings participate by the mediation of signs, the surrender to which discloses truth. In science, too, physicists such as Einstein, Heisenberg, de Broglie,

Bohm, and von Weizsacker, logicians such as G. Spencer Brown, and the whole emerging paradigm of self-organization in biology and the origin of life, have brought contemporary thinking uncannily close to the Hermetic.

The issue is quite clear. Everyone agrees about the need to learn to think in a new way. But how is this to be achieved? For Heidegger, philosophy has become "thinking otherwise," but, tragically, "the greatness of what must be thought remains too great" and no thinker appears great enough "to bring thought before its proper business immediately and in resolute form." His conclusion is that "Only a god can save us now." Gregory Bateson, too, realized the life-and-death necessity of learning to think in a new way; but when it came to making that way of thinking habitual he was pessimistic about the possibility. Other instances could be cited to show that modern science and thinking have reached a limit—the limit of a sense-based rationality—and that, in the face of this limitation, they are not sure how to proceed. A leap, a reversal, is necessary. For science and knowledge to be reborn they must first die. The consequences of such a position, the implications of turning thought against itself in this way, are enormous. But they are on the side of Life; on the side of Truth, Beauty, and Goodness; on the side of Freedom, Humanity, and Responsibility. Given today's state of affairs, we would do well to study closely the work of the students of Hermes.

4

Orpheus's Perpetual Return: Homage to Pythagoras

> All such disciplines, theories, and scientific investigations,
> as truly invigorate the eye of the soul, and purify the intel-
> lect from blindness introduced by studies of a different
> kind, so as to enable it to perceive the true principles and
> causes of the universe, were unfolded by Pythagoras to the
> Greeks.
>
> —Iamblichus, *Life of Pythagoras*

ALCMAEON OF CROTON, who lived in the old age of Pythagoras, said
that "human beings die because they cannot join their beginning and
their end." It is especially fitting at this time of beginnings and end-
ings to reconsider Pythagoras because he is, in so many ways, the presiding genius of our culture and the originator of so many of its
governing principles. Not only does much that we consider of value
derive from his enigmatic spirit, but the whole epoch whose end we
are witnessing may be said to begin with his birth and represent a still
continuing metamorphosis of his teaching.

Simone Weil for one made it clear: Pythagorean thought is the
seminal mystery of Greek civilization and recurs everywhere, impreg-
nating almost all religion, poetry, philosophy, music, and architecture, not to mention the "sciences," which are still those of today. And
not only ancient Greece. Every critical moment in the development of
Western civilization has witnessed a revival of the principles of
Pythagoras. At each turn—at the time of Christ, in the twelfth century, during the Renaissance, in the Romantic period, and now
today—Pythagoras is invoked. When we consider him, we consider

the destiny of our culture—the culture, for better or worse, whose vessels of transformation we are.

To render homage to Pythagoras is to ask who we are, whither we have come, and where we are going. It is to seek our culture's meaning, and an answer to Joseph Needham's question in *Science and Civilization in China:* "Why did modern technological science develop only in the West?" Not for nothing was Pythagoras assimilated to Apollo, whose injunction "Know Thyself" he taught to the fullest degree.

My first guide in these matters was the poet Charles Olson, who taught the need and possibility of thinking the Earth and its history whole. By the old Pythagorean principle that "a one is only if it produces a one," Olson showed that the world, the Earth, was knowable, sizable, single, and *our* thing. If the universe is a whole, it must produce a whole, and we are it—*imago mundi, anima mundi.* We can know it. Myth for Olson became history in the sense of a finding out for oneself, as the way we human beings, estranged from that with which we are most familiar, namely ourselves, could return to ourselves and find ourselves at home.

Following Olson, Gregory Bateson gave me a more philosophical, epistemological way of thinking about the universe—as mind. Bateson taught the dynamic, recursive, self-organizing pattern-nature of the mental world of relations and differences, which is the world we live in, we are. He called his path or approach Pythagorean and gave it a lineage: Pythagoras, the Gnostics, the alchemists, Goethe, Blake. He also made it very clear that if we do not understand and fully achieve this way of thinking the consequences will be appalling.

I studied the tradition he proposed. At the same time, having learned the valuable lesson that epistemologies or worldviews, though deeply embedded, are not irrevocably unchangeable, I found myself led to the "traditionalist" school of René Guénon and Frithjof Schuon. I turned with equal passion to scholars, philosophers, and spiritual teachers like Henry Corbin, Martin Heidegger, Owen Barfield, Rudolf Steiner, and R. A. Schwaller de Lubicz. All showed me that the so-called Pythagorean thinking that Bateson sought to recover was common, at least in its epistemology, to all the world's spiritual traditions. It was in the very nature of things. This, in turn, led me to the study of nature and of Christianity.

What remains most elusive is the actual mission, meaning, and contribution of Pythagoras himself. Pythagoreanism, with a small *p* and in the broadest possible sense, is an easily graspable notion. We know what it is. We can talk about music, number, pattern, form, relationship, and geometry, as primary. In the process, we can invoke the great traditions of Egypt, Vedic India, and Islam, and find apparent echoes among such contemporaries as seem to inquire after pattern rather than substance. But what Pythagoreanism with a capital *P* is, what the man himself stands for, is more obscure. The closer one examines the Western lineage of pattern seekers, from the early Neo-Pythagoreans and Neoplatonists on through, the harder it is to grasp the origin. One traces the evolution of an ecology of ideas, but the central idea disappears in the process. This is because Pythagoreanism, though revolutionary, is not original. Just as its history shows evidence of a continuous change of form or understanding—a changing framework of application of the principles—so Pythagoras himself only instituted such a change. As we are the seeds generated from the plant that sprang from Pythagoras, so Pythagoras is also a seed sprung from another plant.

To discover what it is that we are destined to carry into the future—should we have one, by which Alcmaeon would mean, should we be able to join our beginning and our end, our seed and our fruit—we must examine the past. The problem is that the past is obscure. It is uncertain and ambiguous. Our memory is defective. Things are forgotten. They are confused and misattributed. It is difficult to recall what we are trying to remember. By circling around the point of oblivion, now turning this way, now that; by connotation, not denotation; by waiting, as Heidegger would say, not pointing, the point we seek will come to meet us.

Though Pythagoras traveled and learned much of God, nature, and humanity in Egypt, Babylon, and Crete (and perhaps India), what he taught and practiced—as far as the Greeks were concerned—was a form of *Orphism*. From early on, a number of Orphic texts were attributed to him, confirming his Orphism and suggesting the nature of Orpheus to be an angelic, initiatory state similar to that of Hermes Trismegistus. To understand the riddle of Pythagoras we must begin to decipher the prior riddle of Orpheus, from whom tradition asserts

Pythagoras derived most of Pythagoreanism, including the study of numbers. Iamblichus writes: "If anyone wishes to learn what were the sources whence these men derived so much piety, it must be said that a perspicuous paradigm of Pythagoric theology according to numbers is in a certain respect to be found in the writings of Orpheus. Nor is it to be doubted that Pythagoras, receiving auxiliaries from Orpheus, composed his *Treatise Concerning the Gods* ... [which] contains the flower of the most mystical place in Orpheus."

According to this "sacred discourse," Orpheus, learning from his mother on Mount Pangaeum, said that the eternal essence of number is the most providential principle of the universe, Heaven and Earth, and the realm in between. As Syrianus says, "The Pythagoreans received from the theology of Orpheus the principles of intelligible and intellectual numbers, assigning them an abundant progression and extending their dominion as far as sensibles themselves." Not only numbers, but the entire religious framework of Pythagorean study, from the Greek point of view, was Orphic. We find the whole of Pythagorean number theory in Orpheus, but it is embodied in mythological, symbolic, religious language.

This view serves to remind us that, for the Greeks, Pythagoras was a "religious" teacher. Aristoxenus, a pupil of Aristotle and friend of the Pythagoreans of his day, wrote of them: "Every distinction they lay down as to what should be done and not done aims at conformity with the divine. This is their starting-point: their whole life is ordered with a view to following God, and it is the governing principle of their philosophy."

Note the identity of philosophy with "following God." Pythagoras, who traditionally was the first to call himself a philosopher, clearly meant something different by it than we. Human beings come into life, he said, as into a festival. Most come to buy and sell and compete in the many competitions offered, but some come simply to observe, revere, and contemplate the order, beauty, and purpose of what is occurring. Their focus is the golden unifying thread of essential wisdom that binds all together. As Heidegger suggests, the philosopher is one who loves, *philein*, this wisdom, *sophia*. Love of this kind connotes amity, harmony, correspondence—Platonic *friendship*—rather than either the yearning that is *eros* or the realized spiritual identity that is *agape*. Though these three loves are all one Love, the Greek can distinguish without separating. Nevertheless, *philein* definitely has a friendly feeling of cooperation and community, of familial affection between equals and codependents. The philosopher who is the friend, the intimate, of wisdom holds amicable discourse with her. We may recall Philolaus' definition of harmony as the common thought of separate thinkers or the agreement of disagreeing elements, the reciprocal unity or third in which two things are brought together.

The philosopher is one whose thinking is in accord or harmony with wisdom, and whose practice of philosophy is devotion and dedication to it. This is why Heidegger says that *philein* here means *homolegein*, to speak in accordance with wisdom, which, for Pythagoras—since only like can know like—is itself a harmony and a *philia*. Philosophy, in other words, has to do with the wisdom that is the Kosmos, which is that divine, true, and beautiful order held together harmoniously by bonds of amity, reciprocity, and affection or sympathy. Pythagorean philosophers strove to align their being, unite their thinking—though these are one, not two—with the thinking and being sources of the Kosmos, i.e., the gods, numbers, or archetypes.

What Pythagoras taught was assimilation to the divine and an imitation of it by the practice of a *way*. He called it *philosophy*, meaning a right relationship with the universe and with God. This is the famous "Pythagorean way of life." Its teaching is "religious" rather than scientific or philosophical, though for Pythagoras these are one, distinguishable perhaps but certainly not divisible. By the same token, all three—religion, science, and philosophy—are quite different from what we usually consider. That Pythagoras brought these together, in a new way, with a social and artistic vision, is what from ancient times accorded him the specific status of a religious, prophetic genius, blessed with a divine revelation or mission. "A greater good never came, nor ever will come to humankind," wrote Iamblichus, "than that which was imparted by the Gods through this Pythagoras." What Iamblichus has in mind was not that Pythagoras inaugurated a new approach to nature or to mind. What he means is a little different. Just before making this statement he says that Pythagoras was associated by many with Apollo—Pythian and Hyperborean. Just after it he invokes Aristotle to the effect that one of the principal Arcana of Pythagorean philosophy was the division of beings into three kinds— gods, humans, and such as Pythagoras. In other words, Pythagoras was felt to augur a new kind of being, the possibility of a new kind of human being. Or rather, the claim implicit in Iamblichus is that consciousness manifested a new *redemptive* possibility in Pythagoras. It is this religious aspect, at once Orphic and Apollonian, that I want to consider first.

> A tree rose up. O pure over-rising!
> O Orpheus sings! O high tree in the ear!
> And all was quiet. Yet even in that quiet
> came forth a new beginning, sign, and transformation.
>
> Animals of stillness pushed from the clear,
> opened wood of lair and nest;
> and it happened that not from cunning
> and not from fear were they so quiet,
>
> but from listening. Bellow, cry, roar
> seemed small in their hearts. And where hardly
> even a hut had been to receive this,
>
> a shelter from darkest desire,
> with an entry, whose posts shake—
> there, in hearing, you made a temple for them.
> (Rilke, *The Sonnets to Orpheus,* I, 1)

Rilke clearly realized the mystery and the magic, the dream, the presence and the premonition that is Orpheus, sensing in him more than myth and history, something akin to consciousness itself. For Goethe, too, this was the case. Orpheus and the Orphic "Archetypal Words"—*Urworte*—came to stand for the archetypes of organic being. Before that, in the Renaissance, Orpheus was recognized as being of the *prisci theologi*—the Greek representative of "ancient theology," the peer of Moses, Zoroaster, and Hermes Trismegistus. This was the view of the Greeks themselves for whom, as Proclus said, all theology—whether taught by Homer, Hesiod, Pythagoras, or Plato— was the "child of Orphic mystagogy." Yet Orpheus is a mystery and has been so from the beginning, that is, from the time of Pythagoras and Plato, who, while tacitly proclaiming themselves Orphics, changed Orphism so much that what Gaston Bachelard would call "an epistemological rupture" was placed between them and their founder. We, as contemporary Pythagoreans and Platonists, have not yet succeeded in overcoming it. Therefore we know our task.

The problem behind this mystery is and was twofold. Firstly, the Orphic teaching, which is mythological, symbolic, connotative, concrete, and synthetic, was incompatible and increasingly incomprehensible to the rising analytic, denotative, and abstract self-conscious mentality which we know so well today. Secondly, his history was odd. From the beginning no one seemed to know where Orpheus had come from. As a "person" he was dated sometime between 1500 and 1200 B.C., for he had supposedly sailed, after a visit to Egypt, with Jason on the *Argo* in search of the Golden Fleece, eleven generations before the Trojan War. The search for the Fleece, of course, suggests an alchemical or Hermetic association. The visit to Egypt for its part, if occurring at that time, brings Orpheus and the Orphic impulse tantalizingly into association with Akhenaton (c. 1377). This pharaoh was the creator of a radical solar theism that rejected not only the subtle triadic theology of Amun-Ra-Ptah, but also the ancient canons of proportion and measure, substituting for them a kind of naturalism or humanism, in which Akhenaton and his family were portrayed in "androgynous" form. This is interesting because, esoterically, Akhenaton is considered to be a premonition of the coming Solar Age—a mixed, androgynous principle mediating between the passing Osirian and the rising Horian emphases. The relevance lies in the fact that Osiris and Horus, according to Plutarch, were Dionysus and Apollo of the Greeks, between whom, as we shall see, Orpheus is precisely the mediator.

The historical manifestation of Orphism, however, does not occur until about half a millennium after, when Orpheus appears as a prophet or priest of Dionysus, a reformer of the ancient Mysteries, who is at the same time paradoxically an initiate of Apollo and a proclaimer of a solar monotheism. This Orphism, while constituting a movement of religious renewal or reform, is actually more of a revolution. What Orphism proclaimed was the Orphic way of life, the possibility of any individual attaining by his or her own effort, together with the action of grace, a transcendent purity synonymous with divinity. The revolutionary aspect lay in the fact that the Orphic way was open to all and universalized the Mystery and hieratic initiations of the past epoch—releasing the Mystery religions from determination by sacred geography, and initiation from determination by caste and temple. It did so by teaching the possibility of resurrection—the idea of a transcendent, unfallen aspect of the soul, which we may call the *Daimon*.

Looking more closely at the myth, we discover that Orpheus was the son of the Muse Calliope—the Muse of Poetry, the Leader of the Muses—either by Apollo, their chief, or by Oeagrus, a Dionysian river-water-wine god. In either case his grandmother would have been Mnemosyne or Memory, the mother of the Muses, and Zeus himself would have been his grandfather. It was Apollo who gave him his lyre, which originally belonged to Hermes, who exchanged it for the *caduceus*. Apollo and Hermes and so also Orpheus are thereby brought into the closest connection, as are the caduceus and the lyre. Consequently, we may associate Orpheus with the *Hermetic* tradition, that is, with the science, cosmology (alchemy), and perfection of the intermediate or human realm, the realm mediating between Heaven and Earth.

Orpheus, taught to play his lyre by the Muses—and we imagine by Mnemosyne and Apollo—created the arts of song, dance, and, above all, prophetic poetry, including theology, mythology, and hymns. He so excelled at these that by the beauty of his harmonies all nature— trees, stones, and animals—united in peace and joy. His science was a magic that brought nature to a blessed consummation. In the same spirit, other sciences and inventions—medicine, agriculture, ritual, astrology, architecture, mathematics—were attributed to Orpheus.

This is the figure we see married to the fateful Eurydice, who, bitten by a snake, was taken down to Hades, where Orpheus descended to implore her return. This was granted him, on condition that he not look back and see her until she stood in the full sunlight. Later versions say that Orpheus failed; earlier versions have him completely successful. We may note that according to Heraclitus, Hades and Dionysus are one and the same. We may further note the similarity of this story—which the more timid medieval mind interpreted in terms of spirit and soul—and the Gnostic account of the Passion in terms of the drama of Christ and Sophia.

It is told of Orpheus, finally, that he rose daily to greet the Sun on Mount Pangaeum, calling Helios, whom he named Apollo, the greatest of the gods. For this, the Maenads, followers of Dionysus, dismembered him. They cast his head into the River Hebros, whence it floated out to sea, coming to land on the island of Lesbos, where it long continued to prophesy. Alternatively, it is said that Orpheus, having introduced the rites of Dionysus into Greece, had to suffer the death of his god. Rilke wrote:

> Finally they tore you, impelled by vengeance,
> while your sound still lingered in rock and lions,
> in trees and birds. You still sing there now.
>
> O you lost God! You endless trace!
> Only because in the end hate divided you
> are we now nature's mouth and listeners.
> (The Sonnets to Orpheus, I, 26)

We must consider something else, too. There is an echo in this Orphic story of something extremely archaic, of an almost primordial tradition and time. It comes at us from almost every aspect. If we had to give it a name we would call it "shamanic." As Mircea Eliade points out, Orpheus is a shaman not only in his descent into Hades, but in his healing, love of music, charms, and powers of divination. The key is music. Though Orpheus was the "divine musician" his music was primarily prophetic, divinely inspired *song*—that is, *poetry*. Orpheus harks back to an ancient time when words and things were not yet separated but were united in melodic chant. Naming, singing, was identical with creation, with making reality. Or rather, in naming, the gods spoke through the name. To sing was to invoke the gods, for only the god, the archetype, had a name. In this sense poetry was science; and language was knowledge and power. In the mouth of the prophet-poet-shaman, language was the language of the gods. As it says in the Vedas, "The gods created the hymns first, then the fire, then the burnt offering."

The essence of this view, which Owen Barfield has termed "original participation," is that something stands behind phenomena that is of the same nature as humanity. Music is the privileged model of this vision, as both cosmology and communication. Nora Chadwick writes of this primordial culture of poetry, prophecy, theology, and inspired knowledge: "Everywhere the gift of poetry is inseparable from divine inspiration. Everywhere this inspiration carries with it knowledge.... Always this knowledge is uttered in poetry, which is accompanied by music.... Music is everywhere the medium of communication with spirits." Behind every sensible phenomenon lies a reality of an animistic, supersensible order. Just as one can make an open string vibrate by sounding its own note on a nearby instrument, so one may conjure up and communicate with a spirit by providing it with a song or tone. The universe, which is body, is from this point of view song, and Orpheus is the child of what he teaches. "Song is being," says Rilke.

Marius Schneider in *The New Oxford History of Music* puts it this way: "To produce a sound, effort must be made. The bowstring has to be stretched, and the breath must impinge on a sharp resisting edge. The ground must be stamped down. All life arises solely from stamping, from the tension of two opposing factors, which have to sacrifice their strength, if need be their life, for the birth of new life." That in creation a sacrifice has been made and a debt must be paid is a fundamental Orphic notion, enacted, as we shall see, typically in the polarity of Aether and Chaos, Apollo and Dionysus. Life is a gift, imposing certain duties and obligations, behind which as cause and origin lies a cosmic, universal primordial sacrifice that must be atoned, harmonized. This is what Plato refers to when he says that we are prisoners of the gods—an idea which, seen in Orphic perspective and with Christian hindsight, is not primitive at all.

To explain all this, we begin with an ineffable First Principle or Principle of Principles, *Chronos*, conceived under the aspect of *Infinite Time*. Proclus describes it as "Once-Beyond." It is in fact irreducible, indescribable, and incomprehensible. Why under the aspect of Time?

First, this is a dynamic cosmogony of action in which action is anterior to time-space-movement-matter in any form. Second, the primacy of Infinite Time suggests the possibility of conceiving of the Orphic gods as rhythms, which become the Pythagorean numbers. In any event, Chronos, the Ineffable First, polarizes, that is, adds itself to itself, presents itself to itself, doubles itself, rhythmicizes itself, giving rise to two principles: *Aether,* that is Heaven or Fire, a male principle, and *Chaos,* which etymologically is that which is poured, "Water," a female principle. Demythologizing the two principles, the Platonic Pythagoreans will call them *Peras,* a principle of limitation or distinction, and *Apeiron,* a principle of unlimitedness or lack of distinction or indefinitude. As an Islamic source has it: "When from the Cause emanates One, there emanates from it Not-One," that is: Two. Thus, it is between One and Two that creation occurs. Plato therefore calls the Principle of Intelligible Matter, the *Apeiron,* the Indefinite Dyad.

It is important not to confuse the principle of the unlimited with anything related to matter as we know it. One of the first things to be overcome is, as Coleridge says, the obsession with matter, the need for a matter as a datum. "As soon as this gross prejudice," he writes, "is cured by the appropriate discipline, and the Mind is familiarized to the contemplation of Matter as a product in time, the resulting Phenomenon of the equilibrium of two antagonist Forces, Attraction and Repulsion ... the idea of *Creation* alone remains." Coleridge is very good on these things. Speaking as a "transcendental philosopher" he says not, "Give me matter and motion and I will construct you the universe," as Descartes does, but rather, "Grant me a nature having two contrary forces, the one of which tends to expand infinitely, while the other strives to apprehend or *find* itself in this infinity, and I will cause the world of intelligences with the whole system of their representations to rise up before you." In other words, "Every power in nature and in spirit must evolve an opposite as the sole means and conditions of its manifestation: and all opposition is a tendency to re-union." This is true universally. Even God, the Unknowable Cause without Cause, must evolve an opposite by internal necessity, and that opposite can only be himself, so that the principle of polarity becomes the principle of identity. To manifest himself to himself, to know himself, to take form, Chronos must place himself as Aether before himself as Chaos, or, rather, must "flow forth" from himself as Chaos to return to himself as Aether. Even the Nothing before itself becomes Something—as we shall see, becomes Seed, Light, Power, Vision, which we might call with Schwaller de Lubicz the "Cosmic or Divine I," the Divine "I Am."

This is the teaching from the beginning. As Philolaus, the first Pythagorean to write anything down, said: "Nature in the Universe was fitted together [i.e., harmonized] from the Limiting and the Unlimited, both the Universe as a whole and everything in it." Just so Plato, in his unwritten doctrines, affirmed that the One and the Indefinite Dyad were the principles of all things, even of the *Eide,* the Forms themselves. In the *Philebus* he calls it a gift from the gods, a gift passed on in the form of a saying: "All things that are ever said to be consist of a one and a many, and have in their nature a conjunction of limit and unlimitedness." Note the language: everything is formed, fitted together, by a conjunction, a marriage. "Great is the mystery of marriage," says the Gospel of Philip, "for without it the world would not have existed."

This is the Orphic version as well. Chronos, polarized by addition into Aether and Chaos, forms an Ellipse, an Egg. It is silver, bright, and shining. It is the golden germ, seed, womb, and embryo of all things, in Sanskrit the *Hiranyagharba,* which is but another name for *Prajapati,* the Creator, the Lord of Produced Beings. So, too, in Orphism the Egg cracks, revealing the perfected manifestation of the conjunction of the two principles, called *Phanes.* While Chronos must contain these two natures, it does so in utter darkness of potentiality, while Phanes manifests them—for Phanes, Protogonos, firstborn of beings, is threefold. He-she is Phanes, first of all, who first shone forth and appeared in a blaze of light, illuminating, lighting, creating. This name was said to derive from *pheinein,* to shine, from which we derive *phenomenon* or what is illuminated. But to begin with, Phanes only illuminates himself, that is, Chronos, giving him an ineffable body of light. He is thus the knower-known, the Creator-created, *Fiat Lux* and Logos: the primordial cosmic divine *Anthropos.* As threefold First Adam, he is also Erikapaius, power, which is masculine, and Metis, intelligence, which is feminine. In other words, the first form or alchemical salt, the conjunction of Aether and Chaos, Fire and Water, is Light-Intelligence-Power, a triple being also called in the cosmogony Eros, Pan, and Dionysus, the first of three.

Phanes-Dionysus is symbolized as a god without a body—he is entirely spiritual—with golden wings on his side, bulls' heads about him, and a monstrous serpent encircling his head, with every form of creature engraved upon it. He is, as Proclus has shown, the model or paradigm of the universe, the Seed of all. As Plato teaches in the *Timaeus,* the universe is one single, visible living being made by the Demiurge after the model of the most perfect intelligible living being. What difference is there, Proclus asks, thinking of the Orphic Egg, between calling it an Egg or Seed or that which is unfolded from it, namely Phanes, a being or animal? As the Pythagoreans knew, the difference is most important, for between Egg and animal, between Seed and fruit, the stages or logic of development unfold. Hence Phanes, unfolding from the Egg, as Proclus says, "antecedently comprehends or unfolds in himself the Causes of the secondary orders." The process of the coming into mediated identity of unspeakable Chronos as Phanes contains the idea of logical development. In Phanes, as Unity, all numbers—relations or phases of development—are contained. However, since at this stage there is not yet any space-time-movement-matter, these numbers or activities are identical with what undergoes them. They are what they know and govern. At this point we must recall that Phanes is both the Divine Self-Identity and Cosmic "I Am." "Keep these things in thy mind, dear son, and in thy heart," says Orpheus in a fragment to his student Musaeus, "well knowing all the things of long ago, even from Phanes." Here is the basis of a Pythagorean theory of knowledge. The innate consciousness of humanity is total.

Continuing this cosmogony, at once anthropogeny and epistemology, Phanes, having his own daughter-consort aspect Nyx, or Night, produces Ouranos and Gaia. Ouranos, according to Plato, means "looking upward" and signifies the pure intelligible world of Nous or mind, the level of contemplation according to Olympiodorus. In the *Cratylus,* Plato gives "looking upward" as the meaning of *anthropos,* or the human being. This reminds us that each level of the cosmogony is also "human"—a human capacity. As Olympiodorus says of these four reigns of Orpheus—Ouranos, Chronos, Zeus, and Dionysus—

they are "not sometimes existent, sometimes non-existent, but they are always there and represent in mystical language the several degrees of virtue that our soul can practice."

The level of Ouranos and Gaia in turn produces, by contemplation, as Plotinus will say, besides the Fates and Karmic Powers, the Titans—Chronos (Time/Saturn), Rhea (Earth), Okeanos (Space), and Tethys (Disposer). Chronos takes over from Ouranos, castrating him and marrying his own sister, Rhea. The age of Chronos begins, paradoxically at once, the Golden Age of Saturn or "the urn of Being"—Chronos is said to mean sated "intelligence" and purification—and also the beginning of time. It marks a fall, a fall into the body of both reason (soul) and birth and death. It is the realm of *dianoia* and marks the moment when, as Plotinus so beautifully puts it, the soul, through self-will, temporalizes herself. The Orphic *Hymn to Chronos* says:

> Unbreakable is the hold you have on the boundless cosmos,
> O Chronos, begetter of time, Chronos of contrasting discourse,
> Child of Earth and Starry Heaven,
> In you there is birth and decline, august and prudent Lord of Rhea
> Who, as progenitor, dwell in every part of the world.

Although with Chronos time and death arose, to begin with—one imagines, for the duration of the Golden Age or Earthly Paradise—Chronos ate his children, kept them within himself, until Rhea, giving him a stone instead, concealed Zeus from him. Zeus, in turn, on attaining sovereignty, overthrew his father, casting the Titans into Tartarus. Thus, the Age of Zeus began. However, we must not forget that each contains the whole. Zeus, for instance, is said to swallow Phanes, making himself the beginning, middle, and end of the universe. That is, the whole is still wholly present. Zeus then conjoins with his syzygy to produce Dionysus, Bakchos, also called Zagreus.

The story goes that Hera, another aspect of the consort Rhea-Demeter-Persephone, jealous of the child Dionysus, releases the Titans from Tartarus. These Titans, whitening their faces, lure the child, engrossed in his own image in a mirror, away from his guardians, tear him to pieces, roast him, and eat him. Zeus, arriving on the scene too late, strikes the Titans with his lightning bolt. From the ashes, or the smoke, Zeus then creates humankind, a mixed creature of Dionysian and Titanic elements. That is one ending. In the other, Apollo comes and gathers up the pieces.

We are faced with the relation between Dionysus and Apollo, than which, as Jane Harrison says, "mythology has left us no tangle more intricate and assuredly no problem half so interesting." Orpheus himself is clearly an Apollonian figure, yet his god, the god of Orphism, is equally clearly Dionysus. Orpheus, and Orphism, then, lead from one to the other. Yet we must not imagine any opposition between these, rather a kind of complementarity. The universe is of one piece. It is a "one only"—one humanity, one nature, one universe, one God. An opposition no more exists between Apollo and Dionysus than between the Sun and the Moon, or between principles of transcendence and immanence. Plutarch, in his essay on the meaning of *Ei* engraved over the gate of Apollo's temple at Delphi, at one point speaks of the "E" as representing the five or quinary, the primordial marriage of even and odd, two and three. At the same time, he says, five represents nature. Just as nature, taking a grain of wheat for seed, will produce many forms and species of growth, to return once again to a seed, which will contain the same potentiality, so the number five will always return to itself—when multiplied will produce either itself or ten.

And this as far as all number can extend, this number imitating the beginning or First Cause which governs the universe. For as that First Cause, preserving the world by itself, does reciprocally perfect itself by the world, as Heraclitus says of fire ... so the congress of five with itself is framed by Nature to produce nothing imperfect or strange, but has limited changes.... Now if anyone shall say, What is all this to Apollo? we will answer that it concerns not Apollo only, but Bacchus also, who has no less to do with Delphi than Apollo himself. For we have heard the divines ... saying and singing that God is of his own nature incorruptible and eternal, but yet, through a certain decree and reason, suffers changes of himself, having sometimes his nature kindled into a fire, and making all things alike, and otherwhiles becoming various, in different shapes, passions and powers, like unto the World, and is named by this best known of names. But the wiser, concealing from the vulgar the change … call him both Apollo from his unity, and Phoebus from his purity and unpollutedness. But as for the passion and change of his conversion into winds, water, earth and stars … plants and animals … this they obscurely represent as a certain distraction and dismembering; and they now call him Dionysus, Zagreus … exhibiting and chanting forth certain corruptions, disparitions, deaths and resurrections.

Dionysus is the Divine Principle in its genesis or becoming; torn to pieces, sacrificed by the Titans, it must be reassembled, remembered. Apollo is the transcendent principle, that aspect of the Divine whereby this reassembling is made possible and nature or becoming is made supernatural once again. As transcendent presence, Apollo is the directing wisdom of becoming, simultaneously present and ineffable in all natural processes as the other principle of wisdom.

From another point of view, Dionysus stands for the descent of the Soul, Apollo for its ascent or return—the Dionysus suggesting immanence or reincarnation, the Apollo transcendence and resurrection, which from the Apollonian point of view is reality. "The souls of men, seeing their images in the mirror of Dionysus, as it were have entered that realm in a downward leap from the Supreme; yet even they are not cut off from their origin, from the Divine Intellect," writes Plotinus. The Dionysian fallen soul may have forgotten its Apollonian, Daimonic nature, but it is not cut off from it. There is a part that remains forever unfallen, out of time. In this sense, Apollo is the savior of Dionysus. Damascius writes: "When Dionysus had projected his reflection in the mirror, he followed it and thus was scattered over the universe. Apollo gathers him and brings him back to heaven, for he is the purifying god and truly the Savior of Dionysus, and therefore he is celebrated as the 'Dionysus-giver'. Like Kore, the soul descends into generation, like Prometheus and the Titans she is chained to the body. She frees herself by acquiring the strength of Hercules, gathers herself through the help of Apollo and Athena … that is, by truly purifying philosophy."

With this, we return to Pythagoras, who "invented" the notion of philosophy that Damascius teaches, and whose god, as we said, was

Apollo. First it must be stressed that these notions that Orphism introduced, whether derived primarily from Egypt, Crete, Thrace, or even Babylon, were new to Greece. Apollo is always remembered as a "latecomer" into the company of gods, and the idea of a transcendent self was not known in Homeric times. More than a latecomer, however, I think we should think of Apollo as one who was "still arriving." Where from? He was called Hyperborean. Though the idea may have come from the north through Thrace and Crete, as Anne Macaulay suggests, we should not necessarily consider him as arriving only from the geographic north, but rather also from the Cosmic North, the sacred peak of the Cosmic Mountain, the pole of true orientation. Another similar interpretation makes him a "Shepherd God," another a messenger or mediator, like the Archangel Michael. These bespeak his transcendent origin, from which we may take his bow and lyre to symbolize projection, emanation into immanence.

Against this base, Pythagoras carries out his mission. He moves very fast and institutes radical changes. Let us pick him up as he arrives in Crotona, having passed years of wandering and apprenticeship. He has visited teachers in Phoenicia, on Mount Carmel, in Egypt, Babylon, and Crete. Finally, he arrives in Italy, as C. J. de Vogel says, with certain definite views: on the structure of the universe, the nature of human beings and their place in it, and on his own calling. The ancient sources are unanimous. "All show us Pythagoras as a man who, because of his views on cosmic order, felt called upon to form and lead a human community to teach people to take their appropriate place in the cosmos."

We have had philosophy as a Pythagorean innovation, and now we have *cosmos*, a word we must rethink to understand it as he meant it. Cosmos is much more than just the universe. It includes the idea of beauty, order, or goodness, and structural perfection that we might call truth. All are held together by the prior principle of unity. This unity manifests as cosmos—one mass of Life and Consciousness as the *Corpus Hermeticum* will say. It becomes the harmony, sympathy, and kinship of all things, a universal interrelationship and interdependence. But this harmony is also the void of God, the *a priori* law and divine order, incomprehensible in itself and presiding over all things. As Phanes was the model of the cosmos, so the process of unfoldment that he resumed and contained within himself—all the numbers, gods, archetypes—was Harmony, the relationship between the phases.

In his public speeches Pythagoras affirmed as cosmic law the primary principle of universal amity or friendship, whose embodiment could be achieved by temperance, responsibility, affection, honesty, respect, and spontaneity. And at the center he placed a religious emphasis: for the young, philosophy; for the Elders, the Temple of the Muses; and for the women, leadership in devotion.

As for the Pythagorean School, at its heart were the *Mathematici*, those who practiced disciplines, *mathesis*. First, there was an oral interview; next, a probationary period of observation; then, a period of neglect, a three-year residency on the periphery of the community; then, finally, entrance into the community, which began with a five-year silence. During this period one could listen, but not question; one began to practice the various disciplines of recollection, temperance, and memory. Memory was of great importance, and stressed as a daily practice. Music and chanting were likewise daily employed, both as purification (hence recollection) and as worship—these would be the "Orphic hymns"—and there was dancing. Goods were held in common, in a cenobitic life. This was the first stage. Next came the real mathematics or practices: arithmetic, geometry, theory of music, stereometry, astronomy, and music. These were still a means and not an end. Proclus says that the Pythagoreans recognized that everything we call learning is remembering, and that through awakened sense perception, learning has its source within, in understanding's attending to itself. The explanation is, he says, that what remembers is the understanding—*dianoia*, the level of Chronos in the cosmology—that part of the soul having its source and essence in the divine spirit, Ouranos, where the archetypes or numbers have their being. The soul has prior knowledge of these. Possessing them in a latent fashion, it can bring them to light when set free of hindrances, all of which stem from objectification by the senses. Every divisible thing, everything divided from us, is an obstacle to our returning upon ourselves. "Consequently," Proclus writes, "when we remove these hindrances we are able to know by understanding itself the ideas that it has, and then we become knowers in actuality, that is, producers of genuine knowledge."

There is one end of Pythagorean philosophy—to become a pro-ducer of genuine knowledge. The implication is that the forms of thought are the laws of form, and that thought which the mind under-stands is one with that through which the world is created. Knowl-edge of mind is knowledge of creation. "You see, then, my friend," writes Plato in the *Republic*, "that this branch of study really seems indispensable to us, since it plainly compels the soul to employ pure thought with a view to truth itself." The soul's self-knowledge in pure thought becomes its knowledge of the universe. The intention pro-posed to students entering the Pythagorean school was to become one—A-pollo, not many—by various disciplines, and by becoming one to enter into relation with all, or Dionysus.

That was the intention. However, as Proclus's description shows only too well, there was a tendency to isolate the knowing and the knower from what was known, a tendency which contained its shadow, namely the isolation and separation of the known. By the known, I mean the sense world. Though Pythagoras himself seems to have taken great care not to separate numbers from things, this was a vision that the consciousness of the time could not hold. By the time of Plato, who is a Pythagorean, the numbers, which he calls forms or ideas, are already separated from the sense world. They are no longer things. Nor are things, as they were for Thales, hiero-glyphs, and full of gods. They are and they are not. Plato is suspi-cious both of the senses and of the sense world. Consequently *epistimei*/knowledge/the world of ideas becomes separated from the sense-perceptible world—not that the senses do not mislead, but the idea that the senses can be transformed begins to be doubted. The ethical, moral nature of the sense-perceptible world begins to be lost. Though Philolaus says that "everything that can be known has a number, for without number nothing can be thought or known," and that "number fits all things into the soul through sense percep-tion, making them recognizable and comparable with one another, in that number gives them body," the emphasis in later Pythagorean-ism is increasingly one-sidedly turned upon the soul or mind and its laws. There is little suggestion of friendly congress—*philo-sophia*—with the wisdom of "nature" or the so-called sense world. There is no give-and-take, or rather there is nothing given in turn for what the "senses" have provided. The form of Pythagoras's school makes clear why this occurred.

Original Orphism harked back to and held the promise of something different. Orphic meaning and experience are one in the sense-object. What a thing is, its meaning, is revealed in the perception of it. Through sense-images, which are names, words, songs, the gods are spoken. Knowledge is concrete—something seen, witnessed, lived. By the time of Pythagoras, meaning and object were coming apart, the gods were growing silent. Meaning seemed to be moving to another dimension. As it did, the senses were more and more seen to betray and mislead.

It is the story of Orpheus again—the *Urgesang aller Wesen,* the "Archetypal Story of All Beings," as Herder called it. Orpheus lost the world, the beautiful soul of manifestation, and descended after it into Hades, which Heraclitus tells us is one with Dionysus, the granulated world of birth and death. He failed, in the version taught in Greece, to raise her up, but he forever holds the promise of so doing, of reuniting mind and nature, being and becoming, humanity and the universe. He presents the possibility of a non-objectifying perception, an imaginal thinking.

Pythagoras stands for the transformation, the development of pure thinking, of a thinking in some ways free of the senses. Thereby he opens the door to the docetism of the world as appearance only, and to idealism, to the kind of rational mysticism, mystical rationality that culminates perhaps in Hegel. This is only one side of Pythagoras's dream; the other is purely Orphic and has to do with the redemption and transfiguration of the cosmos. It is time, I think, to return to that, to the world of the senses, to respiritualize it. This is to return to art— the speaking, disclosing, embodying of truth—as the origin of culture. We are just at the beginning. Heidegger says,

> We are too late for the gods and too early
> for Being. Being's poem,
> just begun, is the human being.

Such non-duality is not easily attained, as Goethe explains in this characteristic piece:

In observing the cosmic structure from its broadest expanse down to its minutest parts, we cannot escape the impression that underlying the whole is the idea that God is operative in Nature and Nature in God, from eternity to eternity. Intuition, observation, and contemplation lead us closer to these mysteries. We are presumptuous and venture ideas of our own; turning more modest, we merely form concepts that might be analogous to those primordial beginnings.

At this point we encounter a characteristic difficulty—one of which we are not always conscious—namely, that a definite chasm appears to be fixed between idea and experience. Our efforts to overbridge the chasm are forever in vain, but nevertheless we strive eternally to overcome this hiatus with reason, intellect, imagination, faith, emotion, illusion, or—if we are capable of nothing better—with folly.

By honest persistent effort we finally discover that the philosopher might probably be right who asserts that no idea can completely coincide with experience, nevertheless admitting that idea and experience are analogous, indeed must be so.

In all scientific research the difficulty of uniting idea and experience appears to be a great obstacle, for an idea is independent of time and place but research must be restricted within them. Therefore, in an idea, the simultaneous and successive are intimately bound up together, whereas in an experience they are always separated. Our attempt to imagine an operation of Nature as both simultaneous and successive, as we must in an idea, seems to drive us to the verge of insanity. The intellect cannot picture united what the senses present to it separately, and thus the duel between the perceived and the ideated remains forever unsolved.

From the primordial beginnings until now the whole cosmic process has been moving toward a point where it is turned inside out. We are at that turning, the same turn that situated Pythagoras. We are doing what he did, only a little further on. It is clearer to us, perhaps, that having arisen out of the cosmic process it is time to return it, to give back what we have received. Heidegger speaks of art as creation, as the bringing forth of the unconcealedness of what is—a letting be and letting speak, the setting-into-work of truth, bestowing, grounding, and beginning. This is a new birth of the Orphic word, a return of Pythagoreanism into Orphism, a new directive from Apollo. It is a return to "language" as that which brings what is into the open.

Rilke points the way in the last of the *Sonnets to Orpheus*:

> In this night—out of superabundance—
> be the magic power at your senses' intersection,
> the meaning of their strange encounter.
>
> And if the earthly forgot you,
> say to the still earth: I run.
> To the rushing water speak: I am.

5

The New Song:
The Christian Mystery

*I*T IS THE DARKEST NIGHT OF THE YEAR, the dead of winter. Cut off from the Sun's light, Earth has breathed in her soul. She lies silent and closed. Human beings, left to their own resources, are at their lowest ebb. Tempted by matter, deprived of the gods, they yearn for warmth and consolation. Then, suddenly, the New Creation breaks forth and the Sun of Righteousness rises, sounding in the ears of the universe, once and for always.

Light returns, the air grows warm with love. The days grow longer. The heavenly hosts, the angels of nations, the first to know, say to themselves (in Origen's words), "If he has put on mortal flesh, how can we remain doing nothing? Come, angels, let us descend from heaven." They come down to the shepherds and, praising God, announce the coming of the true Shepherd. On Earth, too, in the stable, all creation rejoices in the moment of redemption, the turn so long awaited and so ardently desired.

"Behold the might of the New Song!" cries Clement of Alexandria. "It has made human beings out of stones, human beings out of beasts. Those, moreover, that were as dead, not being partakers of the true life, have come to life again, simply by listening to this Song." For Clement, the ineffable virtue of the Incarnation is that it is the universal medicine and elixir of life. By its healing power, matter and spirit are made one. For all things first sounded into form in the Word; and now the Word, that melodious, holy instrument of God, made flesh in time, sounds out again, recalling all things to their wholeness and their home ground.

The mystery, the absurd premise of this proclamation, is that universal creation turns upon certain apparently very human, material, and even shabby, but in fact most divine, events, occurring for a brief moment in an obscure corner of the Middle East. This is the true apocalypse or revelation: that for this simple world-creating deed, as preparation or by default, millions of years and untold metamorphoses of evolution were required. Millions of years—so much pain, hope, and suffering, so many evolutionary leaps and bounds—seem likewise to lie ahead. What is important is that only humanity stands between, unites, and gives meaning to these two unthinkable extents.

Truly, in the history of the universe, regarded as the meaningful speech of human beings and gods, the Incarnation of God's Word marks the turning point. Speech having become flesh, flesh can become speech. Full, living meaning is restored. What God spoke outside time—in eternity—is now spoken, lives, and may be heard in time. No wonder that human beings who felt so destitute can suddenly feel joy and certitude. Clement's emotion is not hard to understand. The savior of creation, the creator, has come. The king of the world, the teacher of humanity—God's Word—has given himself. The cause of being has become the cause of well-being. The supernatural, having become natural, can become supernatural once more and God, according to the primordial desire never deviated from, can become all in all. This is the meaning of resurrection, the meaning of meaning. What a task for human beings! What a prospect! God has spoken and it is for humanity to listen and respond, to hear God's word and return God's speech.

Yet the Word is always with us—even to the end of the world—continuously begotten in an everlasting begetting, as brightness is begotten of light. As the life and truth of all things, this New Song warms and lights creation through a continuous act of love. To know this is to come to inhabit the limitless field of creativity outside time and nature but ever forming and creating it. It is to die to oneself and to find one's true other, one's true place and origin in the cause, essence, and source of all. It is to meet the bridegroom secretly and dwell in Paradise by the Tree of Life planted in every soul.

Realizing this, Rosenstock-Huessy wrote, "A Christian is a person to whom Christ speaks. The body of Christ are those who listen to

Him." More than that—through us, through cognition and consciousness, everyone and everything can and must listen, for all of creation groaned and travailed in pain for this, and all speech, like all love, is a single unity. Therefore, Rosenstock-Huessy continues, "As speakers as well as lovers, we need assurance that we move in a continuum, that our discovery of real life and our words make sense for ever and ever. Otherwise we go mad and all spirit leaves us. It is impossible to assume that when we speak we do something different from the peoples of all times. Our speech would be up in the air, a meaningless stammering, unless we have the right to believe that all speech is legitimate and authorized as one and the same life process from the first day on which man has spoken to the last."

It is this tradition of those who listen before they speak that we must try to recover and make our own. The Word was spoken in the beginning and made all things; then, at the turning point of time, the Word was made flesh and dwelt among us. Now it is our turn. At the turn of the ages, when Christendom has all but disappeared and Christian teaching has practically been forgotten, we must connect with this tradition and set down for our time and way whatever we can find to know and tell.

6

The Mystery of Celtic Christianity

The Maker of all things,
The Lord God worship we:
Heaven white with angels' wings
Earth and the white-waved sea.

IMAGINE A VERY SPECIAL PLACE, in the midst of the sea, wild with craggy mountains, gloomy glens, brilliant green meadows, and sheer rock faces rising precipitously like bare knuckles from the churning tide. Imagine desolate moors and steep cliffs, intermingled with gentle rolling fields and fuschia-filled hedgerows. Imagine it dotted with ancient solar crosses and beehive huts, overspread with liquid golden light, and lashed from time to time (more frequently than comfortable) by unbelievable storms and rains. Imagine always and everywhere the waves of the limitless ocean steadily breaking on the rocks, patiently rolling up pale yellow sands.

Walk down by the sea or up a mountainside on this island and you will find yourself entering a state outside ordinary space-time. Inner and outer worlds effortlessly interpenetrate. Wind and water, sunlight and cloud, dream and vision, bird and animal, thought and silence ebb and flow like veils before the Face of God. This is Ireland—a place where the wall between the worlds is transparent and permeable. The presence of the invisible worlds of soul and spirit are so close, so insistent in their reality and unthreatening in their love, that one sets aside one's defenses and enters into heart-to-heart communion with the cosmos and oneself.

This poetic island poses a riddle: the riddle of continuity. We are so used to discontinuity, disjunction, opposition—between East and

West, inside and outside, prehistory and history, Christianity and so-called paganism, modernity and tradition—that, faced with the sense of seamless wholeness (despite present conflicts) that Ireland presents, we do not quite know what to do with it. There is a sense of continuity, of inclusiveness—a solidarity with creation, cosmos, human history, even evolution—that connects us at once with the most ancient and primordial times, the very beginning of things, and the future into which we are growing and which is ever calling us into being.

This enigma of continuity is clearest in the miracle of "Celtic Christianity." The Celtic Church stands for a purity, power, and innocence that, at least in Christian history, have never been surpassed—a time when Heaven and Earth, God and nature, humanity and the cosmos seemed more interdependent and interpenetrated than in other Christian ages. "If the British Church had survived," wrote H. J. Massingham, "it is possible that the fissure between Christianity and nature, widening through the centuries, would not have cracked the unity of western man's attitude to the universe." Everywhere in Celtic Christian Ireland—in the monasteries and hermitages, on the rocky promontories and steep hillsides, in the protected valleys like St. Kevin's Glendalough—we find a unique "holy intimacy" of the human, the natural, and the divine, as the following paradigmatic story shows:

An angel appeared to Kevin and commanded him to enter an order of monks for instruction, and he submitted to ordination and became a priest. The angel then told him to go into the desert glen that had been foretold him—to the slope of the lakes of Glendalough. Great was Kevin's courage in separating himself from the glory and beauty of the present life, and remaining in solitude listening to the converse of the angel who ministered unto him. He would lie by night on bare stones on the border of the lake; skins of wild beasts were his clothing. He would cross the lake without any boat to say Mass every day.... Seven years was he without food but nettles and sorrel; and for a long period of years he never saw a human being; and he would stand up to his waist in the lake saying his hours.

Once when Kevin was reciting his hours, he dropped his psalter into the lake. Great grief and vexation seized him. Afterward an otter came to him, bringing his psalter from the bottom of the lake. Not a line or letter was blotted!

Kevin was accustomed … to spend every Lent in a wattle pen, with a gray flagstone under him as a bed. His only food was the music of angels. One Lent, when he was acting this way, a blackbird came from the wood to his pen, and hopped on his palm as he lay on the flagstone with his hand stretched out. Thus Kevin kept his hand in that position so that the blackbird built its nest in his hand, and hatched her brood. The angel came to Kevin and bade him let the bird go, but Kevin said that the pain of his hand being under the blackbird till she hatched her brood was little compared to what his Lord suffered for his sake.

Kevin's story embodies the traditions of holiness, learning, and stewardship that lie at the heart of Celtic Christianity. The mystery is that we cannot say precisely what in it is Christian and what is pre-Christian. Celtic Christianity is a wonder. Among all the attempts to embody the Christian message it is unique; and yet it arises so naturally and spontaneously out of what came before that one cannot tell where it begins and where what came before, which was presumably pagan, ends. This is true of the material culture of the beehive huts and solar crosses. It is also true of the living being of Celtic Christianity itself, whose monks, saints, and scholars were able to integrate and incarnate, in a new individualized human form and a new form of community, the ancient sacred paths not only of priests and kings, but also of prophets, poets, healers, and shamans.

More astonishing still is the fact that all those layers of peoples who dwelled in old Hibernia seemed to have known this and sensed it as a mission. In the apocryphal phrase attributed to the preeminent shaman and bard of Celtic Wales, Taliessin, "Christ, the Word from the Beginning, was from the beginning our teacher, and we never lost his teaching. Christianity was in Asia a new thing, but there was never a time when the Druids of Britain held not its doctrines." In other words, the Celtic tradition experienced a continuity of cosmic process, a solidarity with all creation.

There is the myth, for instance, that Ireland existed before the Fall of Adam, as the image of Paradise on Earth. When the rest of the Earth fell with humanity and received fallen humanity as its partner and fellow pilgrim, Ireland remained unfallen, a place apart, still an image of Paradise on Earth. Perhaps this explains, in picture form, how and why such high wisdom concerning humanity, the cosmos, and the divine—reaching back to Paradise and forward to the future evolution of the Earth—could be preserved and transmitted in Ireland. No wonder that Paradise or original nature is more clearly discernible in Ireland.

The story also illuminates why later Irish Christian chronographers—the *fili* or historian-bards who had become the *fer comgne* or "synchronizers"—traced the lineage of the Irish back to Noah and, before that, back even to Eve and Adam. Just as Eusebius in early Christian times had composed his great *Chronicle,* showing in columns how the great world kingdoms of Assyria, Egypt, Palestine, and Greece had prepared the way for Christ, so now the *fer comge* prepared *their* columns. They showed how all of Irish history from the creation to the present fitted the same pattern and was continuous with it. At the pattern's center, these synchronizers, emphasizing continuity and solidarity, placed the story of the mutual self-discovery of Jahweh and his people Israel. The Irish knew that "salvation is of the Jews" and even saw themselves as Jewish before the fact—as they saw themselves as Christians before the fact. For the early Irish, these two, Jewish and Christian, were almost one, not two. They calculated the date of Easter by the Jewish lunar calendar, celebrating it on the Passover, until forced by the Synod of Whitby to integrate their views within those of the Roman Church.

Then there is the legend, reported by Keating, that the first visitors to Ireland *before the flood* were Seth and the three daughters of Cain. Behind this lies the legendary division of humanity (or human service to the divine) into two types. There are those whose task is to empty themselves and become pure vessels to receive the grace of the wisdom and knowledge of God. This is the so-called Abel stream. Then there are those who chose to create knowledge out of their own natures, to become wise out of their own efforts. These make up the so-called Cain stream. According to the Apocryphal accounts, Abel was born of

Adam and Eve and blessed by Jahweh for his service. Officially, he was the firstborn. Secretly, however, Cain was born first, as if by virgin birth before even Adam was created—born like Abel of Eve, not by Adam but by Semael, one of the Elohim. Thus, from the beginning, there was a great struggle between Cain and Abel, which culminated in Cain's slaying Abel, in whose place Jahweh gave Adam and Eve another son, Seth.

The children of Cain, such as Jubal Cain and Hiram of Tyre, architect of Solomon's Temple, gave humanity the arts and sciences, the crafts and the trades, and all the inventions that humanity wins for itself, even if it then offers them to God. The children of Abel-Seth, on the other hand, were the priests, turned toward the spirit, selflessly serving and receiving from God. These two streams may be seen as representing the Brahmans and the Kshatriyas of Vedic tradition, the priests and the warriors, the royal and sacerdotal paths. In the beginning, in the Golden Age, on the cusp of Paradise, the two coexisted in harmony like the two hands of God, but as evolution began, enmity and a struggle for primacy and dominance arose between the two— except perhaps in Ireland. For Keating's story of Seth and the daughters of Cain suggests a deep awareness of the necessary union of all aspects of the human-divine relation for the healthy sustenance of the whole. In this sense, Ireland foreshadows the Christian Mystery, insofar as Christianity initiates a new union of God, humanity, and cosmos through a mystical marriage of "own power" and "other power," sameness and otherness, male and female, Jew and gentile, warrior and priest, action and contemplation, science and religion.

The ancient Irish traced their intuition of the future union of the two powers back before the flood. After it, *The Book of Invasions* (the *Lebor Gabala*) tells of five waves of peoples washing across Ireland: the people of Portholon (agriculturists); the race of the Nemed (perhaps Scythians); the Tuatha de Danaan (the civilizers); the Fir Bolg; and, finally, the Miles or Gaels. It was as a result of the last migration of Indo-European people and wisdom from the Black Sea region, people bearing with them the culture of the Vedas from the East, that the bardic, tribal, aristocratic people we know as the Celts arose.

Theirs was a country and a people of individual, autonomous units. Placing great emphasis on freedom, they constituted no state or nation but rather a free federation of tribes. There were tribal chiefs served by warriors and, of equal status with the warriors, the *aes dana,* "the people of special gifts"—Druids, bards, prophets and visionaries, healers and historians, often in one. Believing in reincarnation, without fear of death, the Celts lived a life, as one modern authority puts it, "of spiritual freedom verging on anarchy." Jean Markale writes: "The essence of Celtic philosophy would appear to be a search for individual freedom, not based in any egoism, but founded in the belief that each person is special and therefore different from others, that behavior cannot be modeled on a pattern created by others."

Within this loose federation, the Druids were the sacred scientists—practitioners of astronomy, music, geometry, medicine, history, and theology. They were the friends and companions of the spirit beings who lived in the elements, worked in the kingdoms of nature, and ruled in the circling stars. They were the ultimate authorities, the readers of omens, the conductors of rituals and sacrifices. Beside them stood the prophets—the historians of past and future; and beside the prophets stood the "guardians of community," the bards or poets, who lived in close companionship with the ancestors, the dead.

This is not the place to describe the Druidic Mysteries. For our purposes, we need only recognize that these Mysteries, as in all traditional cultures, divide into two initiations—the Lesser Mysteries and the Greater Mysteries. The Lesser Mysteries were the mysteries of nature and human nature, of sunlight and shadow, of water, wind, and rock, of mist, cloud, and birdsong, of the elements—water, earth, air, and fire—and of the manifold life of mineral, plant, and animal. These Mysteries were integrated into the cosmos, and interacted with and interpenetrated the realm of the Sun, the fixed stars, and the zodiac.

The Greater Mysteries concerned the secret of God's life as perpetually coming into being and evolving in the cosmos itself. There was an understanding of creation, of God's sadness and yearning— exemplified in the saying of the Prophet, "I was a hidden treasure and I desired to be known." There was an understanding, too, of the struggles through which God's original intention to know and to be all in all, in and through creation, would be realized. The wise in Ireland knew in advance that God's Son, whom they knew in Heaven, and in the elements and in the sunlight, would die to Heaven and come to Earth and aid the Earth in its going forth to Heaven. The figure of Christ, the Christ that was to come, the Christ of the Future, was present to the Druids of Ireland who awaited only his coming. They watched the whole cosmic process, which is still taking place and will continue to the end of time. Long before the fact, they knew it would turn upon what passed upon the lonely hill of Golgotha.

The result of such "pre-Golgotha" Christianity was that, at that very moment that event occurred—Christ's death, descent into Hell, and resurrection—solemn ceremonies were performed in Ireland. Golgotha was witnessed spiritually as it occurred, as a direct revelation of meaning and image from the spiritual world. The spirituality present in Ireland was of such purity and vision that it was embedded in the nature of the cosmos itself and did not depend upon physical proofs or historical reasoning.

This is the origin of the legend, told by Yeats and others, of how King Conchubar saw the changes in creation at the time of Golgotha and asked Buchrach, the Leinster Druid, what was happening—to which Buchrach responded, "Jesus Christ, the Son of God, is even now being crucified." The story is that Conchubar had been wounded almost fatally in the head by the calcified brain of the Leinsterman Mes Gegra, hurled at him in battle. He is told that he will die if it is removed from his skull where it is embedded, but if allowed to remain embedded, he will survive—provided that he avoids all excitement. Conchubar does so, and all is well until the cataclysmic changes in the Earth, accompanying the Mystery of Golgotha, unfolded. Hearing of the cause of these changes, either by Buchrach or by the visiting Roman consul Altus, the calcified brain of Mes Gegra jumped out of Conchubar's head. As the earliest version says, "Conchubar is the first who went to Heaven in Ireland, because the blood that sprang from his head was a baptism for him." Others, too, were claimed as Christians "before the fact"—pre-Patrician Christians. There is Cormac, son of Art, son of Conn of the Hundred Battles, who "would not worship stones or trees, but would worship the one who had made them and was lord behind every creature, namely the one mighty Lord God who had fashioned creation." And Morann, who "went to Paul the Apostle and brought an epistle from him and it used to be around his neck."

Such stories bespeak a profound awareness of the momentousness, joy, and tragedy of what was occurring. Blathmac, a wonderful poet of the eighth century, describes it strikingly: "A fierce stream of blood boiled until the bark of every tree was red; there was blood throughout the world on the top of every great wood. It would have been fitting for God's elements—the fair Sun, the blue sky, the Earth—to have changed their appearance, lamenting their calamity."

Before Patrick came, then, the early Irish knew that Christ was the cosmic Christ. They knew that, before Golgotha, the spirit of the Sun had weaved and worked in nature—played in the mysteries of sunlight and shadow, danced on the waters and among the leaves, plants, and animals. They allowed this reality to penetrate their souls and hearts. They saw Christ had died—cosmically—to the Sun and knew that the Father had given him to be born on Earth. They witnessed the Son's dying and descending to the ends of the Earth where the Father could not reach. They saw his rising and understood that his life and the Father's and the Holy Spirit's would become one with the Earth itself and all it contained. For this reason, "there was blood throughout the world on the top of every great wood."

No wonder that we can find no beginning for Christianity in Ireland. It was always there. From the moment of Golgotha, the new dispensation was growing and the sacrificial task of the Celtic Church was laid down. It was to develop a true, whole Christianity and carry it eastward into Europe to seed the culture of the future. As we follow the stream of Celtic Christianity from the Hibernian Mysteries, through the historical saints and sages of Ireland—Brigid, Patrick, Columba, Columbanus, Scotus Eriugena, and countless others—we see the Celtic spirit metamorphosing, inspiring, and infusing our spiritual history.

Out of this Church, deeply involved in transmuting the ancient Mysteries out of the wisdom of evolution and history, arose a veritable army of holy men and women, mystics and magicians, scholars and true philosophers. They were at first only in Ireland but then, as the sense of mission ripened, they began to go *peregrinatio pro Christi*— "wandering for Christ," seeking "white martyrdom"—across the waters into Europe, where they laid down the material, social, and spiritual conditions for the metamorphosis of the human soul.

Volumes have been written about the richness of the Celtic Church and its deep spirituality, its selfless compassion, and perfectly modulated asceticism. Christians of all persuasions have found inspiration in its devotion to Christ (as well as to the Father, the Spirit, and to Mary) and its sense of the cosmic dimension of the divine—of the whole of nature being a spiritual kingdom. Scholars and mystics alike have praised its perfect understanding of the human social sphere, of the subtle interplay between individual, community and God: in a word, the intuition of the divine vocation of freedom as this was put into action by the communion of Celtic saints.

Of these, we shall consider here only the "great triad"—Brigid, Patrick, and Columba. To these, countless others can be added: Columbanus, Findian, Senan, Kevin, Brendan, Maedox and Molaise, MoChuch, Ciaran, Aidan, Cuthbert, Gall. All are exemplary.

St. Brigid or Bride asserts the primacy of the feminine divine in Celtic tradition and exemplifies better than any the mythological transformations that bind pagan and Christian together "in Christ." Called the Mary of the Gael, the Foster Mother of Christ, Bride the Calm, Bride of the Mantle, Bride of the Kine, St. Brigid manifests in different forms. Mythologically, she shines forth as the ancient Goddess of Song and of the threefold Wisdom of poetry, medicine, and smithcraft. Historically, she illumines history as the historical saint of Kildare, Abbess, founder of monasteries. Finally, we encounter her as the legendary Fostermother of Christ.

As a child, this Brigid prophesied:

> I am only a little child,
> … But my garment shall be laid
> Upon the Lord of the World.
> … The King of the Elements Himself
> Shall lean on my bosom
> And I shall give him Peace.
> Peace will I give to all who ask
> Because of the mighty Prince
> And because of his Mother that is the Daughter of Peace.

When this Brigid grew up, brought up by Druids, the story goes, she was led one day by a white dove through a grove of rowan trees to a desert place. This was the Holy Land. Here, in a stable, she assisted as "aid woman" or midwife at the birth of the Christ Child. It was she who placed on the Christ Child's brow three drops of water to unite him with the Earth; and because there was a drought in that desert land, it was she who sang the "runes of Paradise" to the cows, so that they could give their milk. Bride took the milk and gave the Child to drink of it, thus joining the Christ in a still deeper way with the Earth and all her children. As the Holy Child drank of the Earth's produce, Bride wrapped it in her blue mantle. Thus the ancient Goddess of Magic and Song helped give birth to the one the Celtic tradition often calls "the King of the World" or "the King of the Elements":

> Son of the Rising Mist, Son of the Clouds, Son of the Stars
> Son of the Elements, of the Waters, of the Dew
> Son of Worlds, Heaven's Son!
> Son of Distant Cosmic Space, of the Flame
> Son of Light, Son of the Spheres, of the Plants
> Son of the Moon, Son of the Sun.

Even more striking than this is Brigid's prophetic role as the once and future Divine Wisdom or Sophia. It is said of her: "She will wash Christ's feet and hair; She will be his Bride." Celtic tradition was always aware of the divine feminine as the holy Fourth at the heart of the Trinity.

The historic St. Brigid was born on the first day of spring in about 453 C.E. and died in 523, thirty years after Patrick died and forty years before Columba was driven to Iona. She was a great saint, and an exceptional human being. An accomplished administrator, she was also a cheerful, loving, holy, practical woman. Prophecies told of the greatness of the child who was to be born. "A flame and a fiery pillar" were hovered over the hut where she entered earthly life. Angels baptized her; light surrounded her cradle. Her childhood was not easy. She was a slave, daughter of a bondmaid and her owner, and her earliest childhood was one of hard work in the house, in the fields, with the animals. She did her work well, but continually broke the rules, always giving whatever she had, or could find, to the poor.

One day, at his wits' end, her father determined to sell her to the king of Leinster. Arriving at the king's fortress, he went to make arrangements, leaving Brigid in his chariot with his ceremonial jewel-embossed sword. As Brigid was sitting there, a leper came by begging for alms. Having nothing else to give him, Brigid handed him the jeweled sword. When her father returned to bring her to the king, he saw immediately that the sword was missing. He raged about the weapon's value. Brigid only replied, "Well, yes, and that was why I gave it to the leper." Arguing, they went to see the king. When he saw what was at stake, he said to Brigid's father, "Leave her alone, for her merit before God is greater than ours."

After entering religious life—reputedly on the Hill of Uisnech, where Mide the chief Druid of the Nemed lit the first sacred fire—Brigid established monasteries all over Ireland. Like Teresa of Avila, she was a great mystic and a great organizer, traveler, and politician—the bishops loved her. Most famously, she founded the great monastery of Kildare under a huge oak, and made it a great religious settlement where a perpetual flame burnt, a double monastery of both sexes, from whose workshops bells, crosiers, chalices, and above all the most beautiful illuminated manuscripts poured out over Ireland.

We may note briefly how extraordinary this idea of a double monastery is. While the rest of Christendom seemed to flee the reality of the sexes in terror and rage, the Celtic tradition upheld the idea of men and women—of human beings—working together as the most natural thing. Besides the double monasteries, two other Celtic institutions speak to the transgenderal unity of male and female. One is the institution of *conhospitae,* of women taking an active part in monastic worship, helping celebrate the mass, carrying the wine. The other is the tradition of "soul friends," *anamchara,* wherein two pilgrims of the way act as spiritual friends or counselors to each other in a relation of mutuality, intimacy, confidence, and love. Already in Druid times, it was said in Ireland that "anyone without a soul friend is like a soul without a body." Later, in Christian times, this tradition—which often joined the sexes, so that a man and a woman, a monk and a nun, would be soul friends to each other—gave rise to a deep practice of intimate, private confession, of repeated forgiveness of sins. This spread across Europe, where the tradition of confession was at that time still public.

Implicit in the *anamchara* or soul friend tradition is the belief that a complete human being is constituted of the mystical marriage of male and female, a union and a friendship that is both psychological and actual, inner and outer. The essence is "hospitality"—compassion in action, openness to the beings of Heaven, Earth, and the middle realms. It is the path of making a safe place, a transforming hearth, for the divine, the cosmic, the elemental, and the human—above all, the human. Wherever the Celtic saints went, their first act was to provide shelter, hospice, medicine, and fellowship—the only solid foundation for true culture or spirituality.

As for Patrick, Brigid's coworker, one cannot say that he converted the Irish for, as we have seen, the Irish were already Christian. The best we can say is that Rome sent him to Ireland. Rome, already heading toward materialism, was concerned that the fierce spiritual individualism rampant in Ireland smacked of the newly condemned heresy of Pelagianism—which laid too much emphasis on human choice and effort and too little on God's grace. But these two, nature and grace, are like the two hands of the Spirit, the two wings—as Scotus Eriugena puts it—that bear God into us and us into God. One cannot separate them. We can go only as far as God comes to us, and God can come to us only as far as we go to meet him. Patrick must have disappointed those who sent him, for he entered fully into the Celtic spirit, alchemically transmuting it into a bliss-bestowing, world-transforming, universal medicine that healed the split between nature and grace.

Patrick was born in Wales or Scotland about the year 387. At the age of sixteen, not yet knowing "the true God"—"an adolescent, indeed an almost speechless boy"—he was carried off with thousands of others by Irish raiders to Ireland. He was bound as a slave to Milliuc, a petty king ruling some hills in Antrim. Thus it was as a slave, tending sheep in the cold, damp solitude of lonely glens and mountainsides, that Patrick first experienced his "littleness" and "lowliness."

Patrick depicts his path to God through a series of remarkable dreams. All his dreams are astonishing, but two above all deserve mention. The first is both a spiritual encounter and a dream of rebirth. Patrick writes in his *Confession*:

> The same night, as I was sleeping, Satan greatly tempted me in a way that I shall remember as long as I am in the body. He fell upon me like a huge rock, and I was powerless in my limbs. But it came to me, into my mind, that I should call out, *"Helias."* And in that moment I saw the Sun rise in the heaven; and while I was crying out *"Helias"* with all my might, behold the splendor of that Sun fell upon me and at once removed the weight from me. And I believe that I was aided by Christ my Lord, and that his Spirit was then crying out for me, and I hope it will be thus in the days of my oppression, as the Lord says in the Gospel, "It is not you that speak, but the Spirit of your Father which speaketh in you."

The "double" invocation of *"Helias"* or *Helios* is remarkable. It brings together the prophet Elijah (*Helias*) with the threefold spiritual Sun (*Helios*). Invoking these, Christ, now linked to the solar Logos of the ancient Mysteries, appears with a new, universal all-healing face. Christ for Patrick is the "true Sun"—the Sun of Righteousness. Mary de Paor writes: "Patrick's vision involves a wordplay on *Helias,* Elijah, *Eli,* 'My God,' and *Helios,* Sun, and it seems implied that Patrick had a real experience of the dark desolation of Christ on the Cross when he cried out, 'My God, my God, why have you forsaken me?'"

Note that it was not the ordinary Patrick, but the Spirit of God speaking in Patrick who called out the magic name. The sense of being spoken, rather than speaking, is pervasive. "On another night," he writes, "God knows, I know not, whether in me, or near me, with the most eloquent words which I heard and could not understand, except at the end of the speech one spoke as follows, 'He who gave his life for thee is he who speaks in thee,' and so I awoke full of joy."

The sense of "not I but God in me" is continuous. On another occasion, he writes, "Again I saw him praying in me, and he was as it were within my body, and I heard him above me, that is, above the inner man, and there he was praying mightily with groanings. And I was stupefied and astonished, and pondered who it could be that was praying in me. But at the end of prayer he spoke as he were the Spirit."

It was a dream that finally led Patrick to escape from captivity. He was looking after the sheep, but now the Spirit stirred in him, and was fervent, and the love and fear of God increased daily, so that he prayed continually day and night, rising before dawn to pray through snow and frost and rain. In this state, one night while sleeping he heard a voice saying, "Thou farest well. Thou shalt go home to thy country." And then again, "Thy ship is ready." And, as Patrick says, "It was not near, but perhaps two hundred miles away, and I never had been there, nor was I acquainted with any of the men there. But I took flight, and left the man with whom I had been six years; and I came in the strength of the Lord, who directed my way for the good; and I feared nothing till I arrived at that ship."

Where the ship took him, we don't know. Probably to Gaul, for there is a legend that he was at Honoratus's monastery of Lerins in the Mediterranean, perched, like so many Irish monasteries, on a small island in the sea. From there, in the mystical year 432, Patrick returned to Ireland.

These free people Patrick, the slave—born of the Father, dead in Christ, reborn in the Spirit—met as equals out of his littleness. Respecting the truth of their native traditions and recognizing their great mission, he taught the truth and reality of the Christ's Incarnation, not as something new and alien, but as the fulfillment of their destiny. For he knew the Celts in Ireland had already known Christ, as the King of the Sun, the King of the Elements, before he descended through humanity into the earthly sphere. Therefore Patrick could speak of Christ and the Trinity to the High Kings and Druids with great honesty, and in words the Irish understood and recognized.

The famous example is his answer when the daughters of the High King of Connaught asked who the new God was:

Our God is the God of all people, of Heaven and Earth, of sea and river, of Sun, Moon, and stars, of the high mountain and the deep valley, the God above Heaven, the God in Heaven, and the God below Heaven; He has his dwelling place round Heaven and Earth and sea and all that is in them. He inspires all, quickens all, rules all, and sustains all. He lights the light of the Sun; he furnishes the light of the light; he has put springs in the dry land, and has set stars to minister to the greater lights....

This philosophy of God as in, through, and beneath all things was familiar to his auditors. They understood the closeness of God in all phenomena. They recognized that through the Incarnation there was nothing that the Trinity had not penetrated. From this moment, Celtic monasticism began, everywhere seeking the dynamic unity of the human, the natural, and the divine. Everywhere in Celtic Christian Ireland, we find a tremendous proximity of the human and the divine in nature. We find an abandonment to spiritual work and at the same time an intimate passion for the things and beings of the Earth—a unique passion for the sacramentality of the wild and elemental, coupled with a gentle human love for all creation, for all fellow creatures with God.

Thus arose a great new impulse based on a search for God in nature, Scripture, community, and self-knowledge, not as separate paths but as interwoven strands unfolding in a single pattern. This is the endless knot at the heart of Celtic Christianity. From it arose the great monasteries and hermitages, perpetual springs of living, mystical theology. Within a century of Patrick's coming to Ireland the Golden Age of Celtic spirituality flowered, sending forth its saints and scholars—wanderers in Christ, white martyrs—into the furthest reaches of Europe, whither they took the deepest, purest spirit of Christianity and sowed seeds so that it flowered.

There were numberless such saints. Of those numbered, perhaps the most legendary is Columcille, St. Columba, who went in exile to the holy island of Iona, off the northwest coast of Scotland. Columba was born of royal blood in 521, probably on December 7. Patrick had already prophesied his coming, for when baptizing a chieftain of his tribe, he had said:

> A manchild shall be born of this family
> He will be a wise man, a prophet, a poet,
> A loveable lamp, pure, clear—
> There will not be a word of falsehood in him....

Signs and wonders accompanied his birth. While his mother, Eithne, was pregnant, an angel came to her and showed her a mantle of exquisite beauty in which all the flowers of creation were woven in extraordinary colors. The angel gave it to her, but after a while asked for it back. Eithne returned it with sadness in her heart. Then the angel raised it up, spread it out, and allowed it to fly through the air. As it dispersed over creation, Eithne protested its loss. The angel replied: "Do not grieve, for you shall bring forth a son, so beautiful in character that he shall be reckoned one of the prophets of God, predestined to lead innumerable souls to Heaven now and always."

Wonders followed Columba as a child. One day the priest who took care of him was returning home from church when he saw a blazing light emanating from the house where the boy slept. Entering, he was amazed to see a great ball of fire hovering over the child's sleeping face. The priest fell to his knees, recognizing that the Holy Spirit was infusing his charge, that here was an elect of God.

As a youth, Columba studied with Finian, one of the masters of Scripture, at Moville. When Finian saw him coming, he saw that he was accompanied by an angel and said to those around him: "Behold, look now to Columba as he draweth near; he hath been deemed worthy of having an angelic inhabitant to be his companion in his wonderings." Columba also studied with Gemman, the Bard of Leinster, who was a master of the old ways. A magical story is told of his stay there. Gemman and Columba were outdoors, reading on the plain of Meath. A wild man appeared chasing a young girl, who ran to them for protection. They threw their cloaks about her, but the wild man penetrated with his spear and killed her. The girl died at their feet. Gemman was about to call upon God to avenge her death, but Columba stopped him. "In the same hour this girl's soul goes to Heaven that man there will go to Hell," he prophesied. With that, the murderer fell dead. Thus Columba's fame spread across the Irish land.

Columba was as much a poet as a monk. But he had dreams of founding a holy place, a monastery. As soon as he was ordained, he went into the wilds of Donegal, where he founded a settlement based on prayer, fasting, charity, and agriculture. Meanwhile he traveled, preaching and healing as he went—a person of great power (he never forgot the importance of bardic power)—and founding churches. Almost three hundred are ascribed to him.

What happened then is not known exactly. A squabble arose. Rumor has it that it was over a book. Finian had the book and Columba took it. Whatever the truth of this, there was a great battle and the men of Ulster slew three thousand of the men of Meath at the Battle of Cooldrevny. Columba was mortified, heart-struck. In penance, he swore never to set foot in Ireland again and set sail from Derry with twelve companions.

He came to Iona, a tiny island about three miles long, one of the holiest places on Earth. This "Mecca of the Gael," the ancient burial site of the Scottish kings, lies about one hundred miles in a direct line from Derry. Columba arrived there with his twelve companions on the eve of Whitsun, 563. Living in the Spirit, he irradiated an immaterial light. When he prayed, his fellow monks saw the space around him illuminated with a blinding presence.

The most typical story of Columba is the story of his death. Columba knew he was to die and when. On the day of his passing, he told his brothers. Then he went out in the fields. As he walked slowly onto the road to return to the monastery, his faithful white horse, which used to carry the pails of milk, came up to him, put its head in his bosom, and began to moan gently and weep and froth. Diormit, the saint's attendant, tried to drive the horse away, but Columba said: "Let him alone, he loves me." He blessed the horse, and then went on his way across the island.

Returning to the monastery, Columba blessed the granary, blessed all the animals, blessed the monks, and lay down as if to rest. In the middle of the night, he rose and went to the church, to the altar, and fell down on his knees before it. Diormit followed behind. Arriving, he saw the whole church filled for a long moment with angelic light. Darkness followed. "Where art thou, Father?" he called. Feeling his way forward, he found the saint by the altar, his eyes opened upward, looking about him with a wonderful cheeriness and joy. Columba then weakly raised his hand to bless them all once more and died.

By this time, the Celtic Church in its outward form was facing incorporation into Rome. But the seeds had been sown. Colombanus and an untold multitude of other saints were inseminating Europe with the spirit of true Christianity, "the light from the West," establishing monasteries, schools, hospices, not to mention herb and vegetable gardens, wherever they went. In the process they met and transformed both the historical stream of inward Christ-experience emanating from Palestine and the evolving consciousness that would become the dominant culture of the West. The Celtic task amid these stormy waters was to be the guiding light of esoteric Christianity. As we follow the stream of Celtic Christianity through European history, we see it creating a new culture. It is like an undying spirit that impregnates everything of value—the cathedral schools, the monastic revivals, the Grail romances, the women mystics, the new spirituality of the Beguines and the Brethren of the Common Life, as well as the more esoteric movements. Everywhere, we see this same Celtic spirit, metamorphosing, inspiring, and entering into all that is valuable in our spiritual history. The Celtic traditions of individuality, holiness, and learning became part of the European inheritance.

After many years of meditation and reflection on the mystery of "Celtic Christianity," it now seems to me that the heart of it falls into a sevenfold gift:

First, there is everywhere and always a deep sense of the *wholeness* of the human being—male *and* female, male *or* female—and of the human being as a child of God. In the words of the Orphic Tablet, everyone could say, "I am the child of Earth and starry Heaven, but my race is of Heaven." Celtic Christianity has its feet on the Earth, but its heart wide open to the heavens, to the "future," drawing it down— so much so that the Earth already seems in Heaven, and the future seems now.

As for "wholeness," traditionally and universally a human being was considered to be a whole of *three* parts, "body, soul, and spirit." In the West, however, at the Eighth Ecumenical Council of Constantinople (869 C.E.), the human being was reduced to two parts: body and soul only. Anyone who claimed that human beings had two souls (a soul and a spirit) was declared anathema, a heretic. This act crippled the metaphysical definition of the human being in the West. With the reduction to two parts, either the *spirit* was banned, in which case there was no organ of spiritual cognition, reducing knowledge to what was obtainable through the senses. Or else the *soul* was banned, in which case there was no interworld linking spirit and body, no imaginal realm, no realm of the dead or place of encounter with spiritual beings. One can look at it either way. No matter which one chooses, the consequences remain the same: literalism and abstraction.

There is none of this in the Celtic vision. A human being is whole—a single unique being of body, soul, and spirit. Nor do these distinctions imply any separation or division, and certainly no opposition. As human beings, we are each and every one of us unique, whole beings, the paradoxical union of male and female, Heaven and Earth—potentially one with all there is (and, Eriugena would add, all there is not)—manifesting in different states, enjoying a "simple unity, free of all compound," everywhere present to God and present in all things.

Second, there is a deep love of and identity with the Earth, understood in the largest sense as coextensive with the cosmos. We may think here of the modern Celt, Teilhard de Chardin, whose love of geology and the rockstuff of the Earth led him to a profoundly "en-Christed" understanding of evolution. Such is the "Celtic" Earth into which Christ incarnated and with whose destiny he united himself when, from his broken body on the Cross, blood and water flowed forth into the broken body of the Earth, making him forever its Spirit and the Earth his body. It follows that nature and the sensuous world are *sacramental,* and that the Celtic Church stands for the ability to apprehend all phenomena as symbolic—things, beings, and events as *theophanies,* manifestations of the divine. *Everything in God, God in everything.*

Third, there is a whole complex of myths and legends that call human beings to become ever more fully, freely, and individually themselves—to become children of Heaven and coworkers with God in the transformation of the Earth. We might call these "Grail" legends. Celtic mythology is filled with cauldrons, cups, chalices, and initiatory vessels of all kinds, providing everything from inspiration to rebirth. The stories that animate these vessels sanctify the soul of Ireland and make its sacred geography a living thing in which history and prophecy, nature and revelation magically intermingle. What all have in common, the Grail, is the identity between human beings and the Earth. For the Celtic tradition, the Grail seems to partake of two realities that are difficult to separate. First, the Grail is always the human being as a whole of body, soul, and spirit, but approached through the *soul*. In John Scotus Eriugena's interpretation of the woman of Samaria at the well, for instance, it is the woman, the *anima* or soul, who must call her husband. Then both *animus* and *anima* together may drink of the well of living water that springs up into eternal life. The soul, the vessel, must be empty, waiting, purified, and ready before the spirit, the "I" can drink of Christ's water and the body be filled with new life. All depends on the soul whose virtue, says Eriugena, is faith, while that of the spirit is knowledge. The teaching of this "Grail" is thus clearly feminine. "I must become Mary and give birth to Christ," or put another way, "I must become Sophia, Christ's bride." But what is true of the human being is also true of the Earth. For the Celtic tradition, the Earth too is feminine. She is the vessel that received Christ through the shedding of his blood on the Cross, so that "the top of every wood" was red. The Earth is body of Christ, bearer of Christ, and Christ is the spirit of the Earth present in every dewdrop, the "King of the Elements."

Fourth, there is a sophisticated understanding of the soul or imaginal realm as the interworld, the world of the dead, the place of living images, spiritual events, sacred histories, and encounters with spiritual beings—saints, risen human beings, gods, and divine beings, including Jesus and Mary.

Fifth, there is a profound ecumenical cosmopolitanism. To be "a Celt" is to be at home everywhere; it is to have the gift of languages, the ability to empathize and be at one with everyone and everything; it is to be dialogue incarnate, living conversation, to know the Word in the word.

Sixth, there is deep love of learning and study, study as a curriculum of the soul. Too often, learning and study are discounted, if not abused and reviled, as synonymous with intellectualism, abstraction, and literalism or conceptual bigotry. When study and learning are for the transformation of the student, and not for the mere accumulation of information, what is learned becomes who one is. It is difficult for us to understand this today when the disciplines of learning have become so "technologized" and dominated by utilitarianism that we can no longer understand the purpose of "useless" knowledge—useless because it does not lead to the transformation of the physical world. What good is it, we ask, if it changes only us? We want something that will make us more comfortable. The Celtic Christians were not interested in comfort; they were interested in becoming fuller, more realized human beings. Their learning was not something other than who they were. Theology and philosophy—the Seven Liberal Arts (grammar, rhetoric, logic, arithmetic, geometry, astronomy, and music)—were the marrow of their lives. They studied, they learned, in order to love. Their theology, their religion, was always practical, vibrant with life, mystical.

Finally, there is an implacable, impeccable ability to tolerate not only contradiction and paradox, but also sheer chaos and confusion. Therefore none of the above may be separated, and none should be thought without a smile!

This final gift amounts, when all is said and done, to the ability to accept and live a fully human life. It is what gives the Irish their lyricism and their sense of humor—which, in fact, may be said to constitute an *eighth* gift of the spirit, one that contains all the others.

7

What Ails Thee?

THE POEMS, TALES, AND CYCLES praising the unspeakable holiness veiled and unveiled by the Holy Grail represent the central initiation drama, or inner heart, of the Western mystical tradition. The Grail is the supreme expression of the gift the West has to give to our evolving universe. Just as all roads are said to lead to Rome, so all currents of Western wisdom and practice from the most ancient times are poured into the Grail's sacred cup. We find there the confluence and mixing of many traditions and ways. All mingle to be transformed by the miraculous transmutation wrought in the Earth and the human soul by the Incarnation of the Divine Logos—the birth, death, resurrection, and ascension of Jesus Christ—in Palestine nearly two thousand years ago.

A vast literature lovingly traces the themes. There will always be more studies, and more esoteric schools focusing on this material, for what is contained in the images and stories makes present a reality of infinite depth and wisdom. In the Grail, we have living evidence that, though it may not always seem like it, Providence guides our evolution. It appears that Providence fostered understanding of the hidden treasure brought to humanity by God's dying to Heaven for the sake of the Earth. The understanding of Earth becoming Heaven, of Heaven becoming available to Earth for the redemption of the universe, grew in human hearts. Providence gradually softened these hearts, washed them, and opened them to the possibility of the Universal Heart. Providence then allowed this maturing heart to be infused with all that humanity had been taught and had learned from primordial times.

Reading between the lines, we find portrayed in the literature of the Grail the encounter of the human heart with the great hidden traditions: Manichean, Alchemical, Celtic, Druidic, Kabbalistic, Sufi. Interpretations and readings based on these approaches are all appropriate. There are Celtic Grails, Cistercian Grails, Alchemical Grails, Templar Grails, Zoroastrian and Sufi Grails, Rosicrucian Grails, and so on.

I want to read the story of the Grail with "beginner's mind" for its simplest, most obvious teaching—one that I have been taught by my own life.

A few years ago, I was given the grace of accompanying my wife across the threshold. No matter how great the pain and the abyss of the loss endured, the gift that came with the physical loss, that of experiencing the abundance of life—the great life that includes and far surpasses birth and death—is something for which I shall always be grateful.

That great life was brought home to me one Sunday at church. I understood that in this one life that includes physical death, as it includes many little deaths and resurrections, all human beings, those in Heaven and those on Earth, are present at every moment with the great angelic hierarchy of beings. I understood that all of us are a single being, a single body, and are connected in such a way that each is responsible for all. That Sunday, celebrating the Eucharist, I recognized that just as all humanity (and also the Earth herself) was present in the sacrificial breaking of the bread, so too all the dead (and all the angels and spirits) were also present. I understood that humanity, embodied in Heaven or on Earth, was a single being, united with all beings. The sense of interconnection, kinship, and dynamic unity was overwhelming. I sensed what it meant to be members of one body, speakers in a single continuous conversation. In that instance, I knew that life was without end, our stories were endlessly interwoven, and every human was connected to, and in a sense part of and responsible for, every other. I realized that there was nothing to which I was not called to respond, for which I was not responsible. There was nothing of which I could say, "That's not my responsibility." I understood that we are all implicated in each other—and that only egoism cut us asunder. I understood that it was only a kind of egoism that allowed me to think of my feelings, thoughts, and actions as my own personal possessions—as existing for my sake. I knew that whenever I felt pain or joy—and did not hold onto and lay claim to my experience in a self-oriented way, but received it as a gift given for the sake of the world—then that pain or joy was the world's. I realized that whenever any one of us experiences pain or joy, that is an aspect of a larger and more important process than whatever it was I or another was going through—call it the pain or the joy or the learning of the world. Specifically, I recognized that another's suffering is all our suffering, as much mine as his or hers or yours, that I was somehow implicated in both its cause and its healing. I understood, too, that this one body that we are includes the whole world, the Earth itself and all its beings—mineral, vegetable, and animal—and that these are in conversation with Heaven and participate in this responsibility of each for all.

This experience is both a "Grail" and a "Sophia" experience.

By "Sophia" I mean a complex reality, a spiritual being, intimately related to both God and the human soul. We first hear of Sophia—Hebrew *Hochma*—in the Hebrew Scriptures, our Old Testament. The classic description is in Proverbs 8, where we learn that "wisdom" calls us, "on the height, beside the way, at the crossroads." She cries out to us to acquire her qualities of prudence, intelligence, and truth. She is originary, for she says: "The Lord created me at the beginning of his work, the first of his acts of long ago. I was set up at the first, before the beginning of the earth. When there were no depths I was brought forth, when there were no springs.... Before the mountains were shaped ... I was brought forth.... When he established the heavens, I was there.... I was beside him like a master worker; and I was his daily delight."

The figure of Wisdom, the divine feminine, Sophia, the first created thing—the creator's right hand and helpmeet—became in the first Christian centuries a central figure in the Gnostic interpretation of Christ's passion and resurrection. For the Gnostics, there were three Sophias—three who were one yet three. There was a fallen Sophia—Sophia *prunikos,* Sophia the whore, closely akin to the fallen human soul—who was the bride of Christ; and to rescue her Christ descended from the Sun to die and resurrect on Earth in order to return her to Heaven. Then there was a heavenly, unfallen Sophia *Ouranos,* one with the Divinity itself. Finally, there was an intermediate Sophia, Sophia as the Soul of the World, our Mother the Beauty of the World, who together with Christ would work to raise fallen Sophia from the depths of matter.

At the same time, during the early Christian centuries, a profound understanding grew of Mary, the Mother of Jesus, as Sophia, as the incarnation of Sophia—an understanding that culminated in the declaration of the Council of Ephesus in 431 of Mary as *Theotokos*, God-bearer, the Mother of God.

The Grail period, the moment in the evolution of consciousness in which the Grail Mystery was unveiled, was the time when Sophia or the divine feminine came suddenly into human consciousness in a new way. This occurred in many forms. We can find Sophia everywhere. She is present in the Troubadour culture of Love and in the recovery of the Goddess *Natura* at the Platonic School of Chartres. She presides over the new Marian mysticism that gave rise to the great cathedrals. She inspires the profound spirituality of figures like St. Bernard, as well as the new understanding of the Sacred Heart among the women mystics such as Hildegard of Bingen and the deep understanding of spiritual love lived and made explicit by the Beguines. In all of these manifestations we find three revolutionary virtues: a new sense of inwardness, a new embodied understanding of love, and a new understanding of the primacy of the human soul. These are the three Sophianic markers under whose sign the Grail Mystery unfolds.

With this as background, let us look at the Grail story as told by Wolfram von Eschenbach in his *Parzival*.

Wolfram begins his *Parzival* (in Jessie Weston's translation):

When the human heart awakens from dullness into doubt, the soul draws itself together within. The brave and manly soul then feels itself, at one and the same moment, both in dishonor and adorned with grace, like the enchanted bird the magpie which seems to be half dove, half raven; yet one thus bewitched may hope still to gain 'security of soul', if only in his heart Hell's darkness and the light of heaven alike have their lot and part.

This is simple enough. We are to start upon a journey by awakening from a kind of dullness or sleep—we might think of it as part self-absorption, part disconnection from the world, or oblivion of it—

into a split or divided state of uncertainty, guilt, or doubt. Wolfram speaks of Heaven and Hell, as if in this divided state we became simultaneously aware of our angelic nature and our "fallen" humanity. The doubt is not simply epistemological. It is not just a question of not knowing. It is more ontological—a kind of split in our beingness. We may expect that to be painful. But Wolfram says that if we are able to fully acknowledge the duality, making it transparent and integrating it—not disowning it or selecting one pole and allowing the other to escape, but holding the whole together—then by some circulatory alchemical process, *saelde* or wholeness will be ours.

The next clue he gives comes soon after the opening. He says that he "will renew a tale of great fidelity, of inborn womanhood, and manly virtue so straight as was never bent in any test of hardness." The three—great fidelity, inborn womanhood, and manly virtue— will provide the context within which the journey of transformation occurs.

Of the three, "manly virtue" seems the easiest to understand. In the first chapter, we learn that Parzival's father, Gahmuret, was heroic, daring yet restrained; was loyal, and kept honor and faith; practiced generosity (liberality), modesty, and courtesy; cultivated self-control and moderation; and in disposition was straight as straight could be.

Such are the knightly virtues of the chivalric world. They are essentially masculine, virile, outward, open, realistic, lusty. Affirming equality, tribalism, brotherhood, these virtues exalt courage, humor, daring, generosity, loyalty, marriage. Surely they are wonderful virtues. Many of us have dreamed romantic dreams in which we participated in such a world. Yet, if we examine them more deeply, we find something amiss that is deeply troubling, even fatally one-sided or wounded. As virtues, courage, generosity, and authenticity (or straightness) are wonderful soul qualities; and those who practiced them had set their hearts' sights on the heights, on the great realities of truth, beauty, and goodness. But at the same time there is something fundamentally egoistic about this world, which is founded in *violence*. The knightly world is riven with violence. It is washed in blood, violent through and through. Listen to this description of Gahmuret as he lay dreaming of his love Belacane: "He was on fire for love and battle. Now pray his wish be granted! His heart pounded till it echoed, it was near to bursting with battle lust, so that it arched the warrior's breast as sinew does the crossbow—so keen was his desire!"

In being violent, the chivalric world is part of the human condition as such. Violence is originary. It is the mark of Cain. We need only look at the twentieth century with its numberless anonymous dead. The hermit Trevrizent, Amfortas's brother and Parzival's uncle, who renounced the world of knighthood, says as much in chapter 9. He speaks of one son of Adam who was incestuously "driven by his discontent and his vainglorious greed to deflower his grandmother." When Parzival expostulates, "I doubt that it ever happened," Trevrizent replies: "The earth was Adam's mother, and by her fruits Adam was nourished. The earth was still a virgin then. It remains for me to tell you, then, who took her maidenhead. Adam was father to Cain, who slew Abel for a trifle. When blood fell upon the pure earth, her virginity was gone, taken by Adam's son. This was the beginning of hatred among men, and thus it has endured ever since."

Wolfram in his *Parzival* was not the only one at that time who realized the primacy of violence and sought to temper, reframe, and transform the manly virtues. The Troubadours, as we shall see in the next chapter, took them and turned them upside down. The Troubadours praised inequality rather than equality, solitude rather than brotherhood, inferiority rather than superiority, humility rather than pride, submission rather than dominance, distance rather than closeness, discretion rather than openness, and secrecy and a hidden life rather than outwardness. On the basis of this "reversal of values," they created what we might call a "feminine" culture, based upon an initiatory, psycho-spiritual soul path of love—a path of the service of love.

A different but related kind of reframing was undertaken by the great spiritual revolutionaries of the time. Both St. Bernard and St. Francis (and a couple of centuries later, also St. Ignatius of Loyola), loving what was best in the chivalric world, sought to transform those virtues by turning them from this world toward God.

Though he appears to begin at the same place, the deep meaning of the Grail as Wolfram frames it is different. Consider, by looking at the women in *Parzival*, what Wolfram means by "inborn womanhood."

The first woman to appear is Belacane, who will become Gahmuret's first wife and the father of Fierefiz, Parzival's magpie-spotted black-and-white brother. Belacane is black and beautiful, queen of Zazamanc. Her name means "Pelican," which in the Middle Ages symbolized Christ, for the pelican was believed to feed its young with its heart's blood by wounding its breast with its beak. "Pelican" is also the name of the alchemical vessel shaped like a pelican, in that at the top its neck curls around completely to reenter below. Thus it is closed in on itself, a single circulating system—a kind of *Ouroboros,* the snake with its tail in its mouth. Whatever is heated in the vessel will rise as vapor, condense, and then return again, transformed. This fact is important for understanding the nature of Parzival's journey. It is a journey without "outside."

Belacane, it is said, is "pagan." She is a Muslim. But she had been brought to an "unnamed" Christianity (she was "Christian" without knowing it), by the innate modesty of her heart and by "her devotion to sorrow and grief's true doctrine"—because of the loss of her love, Isenhart. Grief and loss were her conditions and would continue to be the sign under which she lived, even after Gahmuret married her. The nuptials were splendid. The nights of love sweet but brief—for Gahmuret left. Then, as Wolfram says, "Grief had at her with hack and thrust. Her happiness found the withered branch, as turtledoves do. They keep such faith that when they lose their mates they never fail to seek the withered bough."

What is this mystery of grief and "inborn womanhood"? Grief touches all the women in Parzival. We are reminded of Simeon's words to Mary: "This child is destined for the falling and rising of many in Israel, and to be a sign that will be opposed so that the inner thoughts of many will be revealed—*and a sword will pierce your own soul too.*"

This is certainly true of Herzeleide, Parzival's mother. When we meet her, she is described as a maiden and a widow—her husband Kastis had died immediately after the marriage. She is the widowed "Queen of Waleis and Norgals" and organizes a tournament, offering herself and her lands as prize. So radiant is she, it is said, that had the candles expired she would have given enough light on her own. Gahmuret wins her hand, which torments him, briefly, with grief, for he loves Belacane. But, spring has come; the tender shoots of green raise his spirits. He tells Queen Herzeleide that, if they marry, he will have to leave. Adventure, tournaments, deeds of arms will always call him.

Herzeleide accepts his terms, as she has to, such is her fidelity, for she loves him. For one night, "grief was discomfited and zest in life renewed." Then Gahmuret is off. Herzeleide counts on his returning until, most dreadful to tell, she is informed that the worst has befallen her. Gahmuret has died in battle. Herzeleide, bearing Parzival within her, falls into a deathly sickness. She revives, and Parzival is born. While she rejoices in the birth of her son, "her gay spirit was drowned at sorrow's ford."

Her heart filled with grief, Herzeleide decides she will withhold knowledge of chivalry from her son until he can think for himself. She withdraws from the world into the wilds of Soltane where, like the first Cistercians, she has to clear the ground to make it arable. No one is ever permitted to mention the word "knight" before her son. He is to be brought up ignorant of that world. But he hears of knights and of the great Arthur, the God who makes them. Then the story of Parzival begins in earnest. Herzeleide, for her part, bids him farewell with a kiss, and runs after him. As he rides off, she falls to the ground—"where sorrow gave her such a cut that death did not hold off." "O happy woman for having been a mother," comments Wolfram. "Thus did a root of virtue, stem of humility, go the way that brings reward."

Leaving his mother, Parzival meets another woman, Jeschute. The Duke Orilus had left her sleeping peacefully in a pavilion. Parzival, who had been given the advice to win a lady's ring whenever he could, tore the ring rudely from her finger, and then rode off. Returning to the pavilion and finding his lady distraught, the Duke, his pride deeply wounded, was enraged. Jeschute must suffer the unforgiving tempest of his spite. She must ride behind him, in rags, on a miserable nag, as a penitent. (Later, leaving the Grail Castle for the first time, Parzival meets Jeschute again. The description is horrifying. Her horse is on its last legs. Jeschute herself has become a wraith, her waist a mere rope. Thorns have tattered her shift, the sun has burned her. As she rides, she weeps, her breasts naked and bedewed with tears. Yet, when her husband the Duke Orilus is defeated and forgives her in an almost offhand way, she does as she is commanded. "Come here and be kissed," he says. "My renown has suffered great loss because of you. What of it? It is forgiven.")

Following his first encounter with Jeschute, Parzival meets another female figure, Sigune. Riding down a slope, he hears a woman's voice. "Below a spur of a rock a lady was lamenting from heartfelt grief. Her whole happiness had snapped in two.... Mistress Sigune was sitting there tearing out her long brown tresses by the roots in despair." On her maiden's lap, dead, lies the Prince Schionatulander. The Duke Orilus has killed him, when he really wanted to kill Parzival. Schionatulander, who had been Gahmuret's comrade, has died for Parzival. Now he lies lifeless across Sigune's knees, for all the world the image of Pietà, Christ in Mary's lap. When we realize how young Sigune is, a maiden bride, one cannot but think of Michelangelo's *Pietà* in St. Peter's in Rome, where Mary is so young, so fresh, and so innocent. It is this Mary-Sigune who recognizes Parzival and tells him his name, his true name: "Your name means 'Pierce-through-the-heart.' Great love ploughed just such a furrow through your mother's heart."

Parzival meets Sigune again, later, when he is already on the way to wisdom, just before his meeting with the hermit Trevrizent. He comes upon a newly built cell. Within it, he finds an anchoress, Sigune. Schionatulander, her love, unconsummated on Earth, consummated in Heaven, now lies buried. Sigune's life, Wolfram says, is one long prayer. She has given herself wholly to God. She lives only on nourishment brought every Saturday evening by Cundrie la Surziere. The atmosphere is one of greatest sorrow. Sigune speaks to Parzival of the importance of the question he should have asked Amfortas. She blesses him: "May the hand of Him to Whom all suffering is known succor you!" And sends him on his way.

What is the meaning of all this grief in the service of love? Of these four female figures—Belacane, Herzeleide, Jeschute, Sigune—who accompany and surround Parzival on his journey and in whose suffering he is implicated as the tale progresses? One cannot but be struck by their Marian quality. It is as if at the deepest level, they are all figures of *Mary*. Mary is one of the greatest mysteries of Christianity. Without her, the Mystery of Christ cannot be understood. She is the "Co-Redemptrix." These Marian women are at the heart of the Grail Mystery and play a similarly coredemptive role.

The figures are Marian above all in their fidelity. Like Mary, their whole being is a great assent, a great Yes. They are the handmaids of the Grail. Wolfram focuses on their grief. They are, finally, figures of grief. We begin to understand that grief is one of the greatest gifts. All too often when grief comes to us, when a sword is placed in our hearts, we close off to the world, and hold our pain close to us. But for these figures, grief is an opening to the world. There is no sense that they suffer for themselves. It is difficult to say what or whom they suffer for. Words, in our present state of consciousness, fail when we try to put into words what they are suffering for. We still live in a subject-object world. But what they suffer for, that for whose sake they are, is not a thing, or even a being separate from them. It is as if they simply "suffer for" in a completely open, nondual way. As if, in them, the suffering, the pain of the world itself is made manifest. Like Mary, they suffer for the world—as if within the confines of the tale they are expiating some primordial, and even cosmic, pain, separation, or division. For this, they have to give themselves utterly. That is the first movement of their fidelity. Giving themselves utterly, they receive the gift of grief—which they then give and give and give back. Their suffering is their giving.

More concretely, they suffer for the world, as it is constituted. The world of *Parzival* is a world of violence—separation, selfishness, and division. This is a hard lesson to learn. The apparent nobility of the knightly world, of its "manly virtues," as Wolfram describes them, can lead us astray. Generosity, courtesy, straightness, moderation, loyalty, courage, and so forth are doubtless great virtues. But, we must ask, in whose service, for whose sake, are these virtues practiced? Even as we find they are unfolded in the service of "love," we discover that this "love" is deeply implicated in violence. Courtly love unfolds in a culture of aggression and competition—a culture in which, like Cain, we define our brothers and sisters very narrowly and say, "I am not my brother's/my sister's keeper."

These figures of grief are not the only examples of "inborn womanhood" Wolfram gives us. There is also Condwiramurs, Parzival's love and wife, the bride of his soul. Her physical beauty introduces her in the first place. She is given Marian overtones. She is, Wolfram says, "like a rose still moist, with the sweet dew revealing from its bud its pristine glory of white and red." She awakens Parzival from his sleep. Parzival is sleeping, fully robed, but without his shoes, on a couch, surrounded by candles. During the night, Condwiramurs comes to this bedchamber, and wakes him, coming to him in sorrow to tell her story. The sound of her weeping wakes him, and he finds her kneeling beside him. She tells him what sorrow Clamide has brought upon her and how she will never marry him. For she is Parzival's. Then, after a year of marriage to her, Parzival realizes he must see his mother. His conscience is awakening.

There is another important image involving Condwiramurs. Parzival leaves the Grail Castle, having failed to ask the question, What ails thee? It is Michaelmas. Unseasonably, it has snowed. Arthur's men have been out falconing and have lost their best falcon. He comes to rest near Parzival. That morning, when Parzival had ridden off, he had passed some geese. Suddenly, the falcon is among them. There is great cackling. Swooping down, the falcon catches a goose and wounds it. Three drops of blood, red tears of blood, fall on the snow from the goose's wound. When Parzival sees the bright red drops on the pure white snow, he is cut to the quick. He says, "Who has set his hand to these fresh colors? Condwiramurs, these tints may truly be likened to your complexion. It is God's will to give me untold happiness in finding your counterpart here. May the hand of God be praised, and all his creatures. Condwiramurs, here lies your bright image!" Wolfram comments: "Mighty love held him enthralled, so sharply did longing for his wife assail him."

At the simplest level, we see the power of love to break down the barrier between inside and outside, self and world. Parzival's heart is opened, he carries Condwiramurs in his heart, and finds "her counterpart" speaking to, in, and through him in "nature." He praises God and all creation. Through his love, his soul expands to include the Earth. For this to happen, his love must have become selfless, free, without coercion or otherness. His heart has become one with the heart of Condwiramurs and so, a unity, is one with the heart of the world. Parzival is transfixed. His bodily senses are closed, for he is no longer in the body, but is ensouled—in the soul—lost to the world of dualism and violence. But he is not yet conscious. He has connected with the world soul, but cannot yet bring his experience down and embody it in consciousness.

The power of yearning has opened the world of images to Parzival. Love opened imagination in his soul. His world of images is a reality that includes nature, which now speaks to him in a new way.

This new way of speaking is larger than any he can yet comprehend. For when he finds Condwiramurs' counterpart in the three drops of blood in the snow, it is not too much to see in these three drops a reflection of the blood of Abel, spilled by Cain, and despoiling the Earth. Is it too much to suspect that in awakening to love there is a hope of redemption of that deed?

Remember that the Grail Mystery emerged during the twelfth and thirteenth centuries, which were a turning point, marking a true renaissance or resurrection of consciousness. Three gifts characterize this moment: a new interiority; a new understanding of the soul; and new understanding of love. In a word, a rebirth of the Feminine. We see it taking place everywhere — in the School of Chartres, in devotion of the Virgin Mary, above all in the emergence of Sophia and the Troubadours' discovery of the "Lady," *la Madonna Intelligenza,* as a way of transformation. This is the context in which we must seek the Grail. But to understand it, we must expand our understanding of the soul until it is one with Mary/Sophia — the threefold Mary/Sophia who is at once the purified soul, the soul of the Earth, and the soul of the stars, the Starry Soul.

Parzival, through these feminine figures, or parts of himself, goes through a similarly Sophianic transformation in order to become able to ask the question and become the Grail King

There is no better teacher on the nature of the soul than the Grail philosopher John Scotus Eriugena, who has a marvelous commentary on the story of Jesus and the Samaritan woman at Jacob's well (John 4:7–26):

> The woman is the rational soul [*anima*], whose husband [literally, *vir,* man/male, with the connotation of "active power"] is understood to be the *animus,* which is variously named now *intellectus* [intellect], now *mens* [mind], now *animus,* or even *spiritus* [spirit].... The head of the *anima* is the *intellectus,* and the head of the *intellectus* is Christ. Such is the natural order of the human creature. The *anima* must be submitted to the rule of the *animus,* the *animus* to Christ, and thereby the whole being is submitted through Christ to God the Father.... The *animus* or *spiritus* revolves perpetually about God and is therefore well named the

husband and guide of the other parts of the soul, since between it and its creator no creature is interposed.... Since therefore the *anima* can receive nothing of the gifts from on high unless through her husband, the *animus* or *spiritus,* the *anima* is rightly asked to call her husband or *animus* with whom and by whom she may drink spiritual gifts.... For this reason, Jesus says, "Call your husband and come hither."

It is a wonderful story. But the point of Eriugena's commentary is that the woman is the soul—the *anima*—and that the true husband that she must call, before they can *both* drink of the well of living water, springing up into eternal life, is the spirit: *intellectus, animus, spiritus*—the "I."

In the alchemy of the human being, the soul is critical. Unless the soul be purified, the spirit, the "I," cannot drink of Christ's well of living water. All depends on the soul.

The virtue of the soul, Eriugena says, is faith, while that of the spirit is knowledge. And Wolfram says that his tale of the Grail is one of "great faithfulness, inborn womanhood, and manly virtue."

But what is faith? Surely it is not a belief in some thing. Faith is a radical *openness*—"Be it unto me according to thy word." Mary is the figure, the very being of faith. She demonstrates what it means to be radically receptive, able to say "Yes" no matter what. To simply say "Yes" without preconception or judgment, without barriers or boundaries, memory, desire, or understanding—even without sense perception. Just "Yes."

Faith bespeaks an unmediated openness to experience, whatever the great current of life in its perpetual abundance brings to us. This may be painful.

In *Parzival,* Wolfram von Eschenbach shows three paths to such faith. We have seen the path of grief or sorrow in Belacane, Herzeleide, and Jeschute and Sigune. We have seen Condwiramurs teaching Parzival the meaning of love.

Repanse de Schoye, the Grail Maiden, represents the third path. When Parzival arrives at the Grail Castle for the first time, he is given Repanse de Schoye's cloak to wear, the purple cloak of reverence. Repanse de Schoye carries the "Grail"—the *lapis exsilis,* the exiled or banished stone—but at this first visit, Parzival does not see it. Not only does he not yet understand the path of grief and the way of love, he does not yet possess in his soul the necessary reverence.

Reverence, like Repanse de Schoye, is "of perfect chastity and has renounced all things false." Reverence requires forgiveness. Trevrizent says the Grail is so heavy that "sinful mortals could not lift it from its place." Parzival must say to Trevrizent, his soul on its knees: "Sir, guide me now. I am a sinner." He must atone. He must seek forgiveness.

Preparatory to being able to receive the healing of the Grail—one of whose meanings derives from the Latin *gradalis,* meaning steps or stages—Parzival, or the human soul, must pass through these three stages of (1) grief, (2) love, and (3) reverence, forgiveness, praise.

Grief is an opening of the whole being. Anyone who has known grief knows how somatic it is, how the whole "body" feels the pain— pain that is not so much individual, though it is experienced individually, as it is cosmic. Grief is a kind of dismemberment—an opening of the whole being to the deep reality of the world as suffering, as being torn apart. In grief, the world's pain flows through one. It washes one clean. To live through grief and not push it aside is a process of soul purification, one that awakes the heart as the heart of the cosmos.

Love allows a different unity with the world through the heart. As all lovers know—as the Troubadours knew—love has to do with an opening of the senses in a new way, with a kind of "exteriorization of the sensibility" whereby the human heart opens to the Earth and nature begins to speak a new, human language.

Reverence, which is close to praise and gratitude, is the highest in this sequence. Praise is central because we become one with what we praise. The same is true of gratitude and reverence—for these three are really but one. Nothing can interpose between the one who praises, reverences, thanks and the one who is praised, reverenced, thanked. Parzival must acknowledge himself a sinner, one who interposes himself. He must atone and seek forgiveness. Then, praising, reverencing God in his creation, he can become one with not just earthly creation, but also with cosmic creation, the world of the stars.

Parzival's path is Marian, Sophianic. Grief begins the path of purification—the return of the individual soul to a Sophianic state.

Through grief, like the grief of Mary at the foot of the Cross, we learn mercy and compassion.

Love allows the soul, mercy and compassion, to expand to include the whole Earth—the Earth as Sophia.

Praise and reverence expand the soul further to include the heavens, Mary's cloak of stars, in which Flegetanis, the heathen astronomer, saw the Grail inscribed.

This is an alchemical journey, a work with philosophical mercury, sulfur, and precipitating salt. It is essentially soul work—*anima* work, mercury work, in Eriugena's sense. It has to do with the perfection of the human state, in the largest sense. From this perspective, the story is very simple.

Parzival cannot ask the question "What ails thee?" until he has become the question and knows that he is the question. He cannot ask the healing question until he knows that he and Amfortas, the suffering Grail King, are one: what ails Amfortas ails Parzival, ails all of us. There is no separation. Thereby Parzival overcomes the curse of Cain. He becomes his brother's keeper, the keeper of the Earth, the keeper of the stars. He can do so because he has come to know that he is all of these—one body, one substance, all responsible for all, all working for all.

Then the Dove, bearing the Wafer, can descend upon the Grail of the completed, purified soul. *Anima* and *animus* can drink of the well of living water. As Wolfram insists, it is a matter of grace, of *Kairos*—the right moment as God knows it. As a Sophianic or Marian Mystery, the message of the Grail is "I must become Mary and give birth to Christ. I must become Sophia and become the Bride of Christ."

8

The Troubadours
and the Cultivation of Eros

Whoever flees pain
will love no more.
To love is always
to feel the opening,
to hold the wound
always open.
— Novalis

*H*UMAN BEINGS BY NATURE DESIRE TO KNOW, wrote Aristotle, meaning not that we are empty vessels, *tabula rasa*, wanting only information to fill us up, but that our nature is to desire to be transformed by knowing.

Aristotle was not talking about the sophisticated modern knower of objects. He was affirming that, insofar as we are human, we are only potential beings whose actuality is realized from moment to moment, as desire leads us to know. Desire opens us to what we are not yet, becoming the medium through which we taste fullness or actuality. The work of desire or eros is transformation, even creation. For desire intimates an absence or lack at the very core of being itself. If being lacked nothing, there would be nothing—no creation, no images, nothing to say, and nothing to know. Because of eros, the world is, and becomes more and more as we know it. Drawn by eros, we move from one state of being, one world, to another. In Blake's formulation, states exist, and human beings pass through them. The more we love, the more we are and know. At issue here is heart knowledge, the thinking heart.

More specifically, as Plato explained in *Cratylus,* eros is an influx, a cosmic reality, that, flowing into us from without, through the senses—above all, the eyes—opens us to new experience. Lovers have always known, in the words of Aeschylus, that "in the absence of eyes, all Aphrodite is vacant, gone."

This was the teaching of Diotima, the priestess of Mantinea, who, as Socrates recounts in the *Symposium,* initiated him into the mysteries of love and the method of inquiry appropriate to it—question and answer, the tantra of dialog, dialectic, and relationship. "Candidates for this initiation," she began, "cannot, if their efforts are to be rewarded, begin too early to devote themselves to the beauties of the body." First, they fall in love with one individual body, and their passion gives birth to noble discourse; then they see how one body's beauty is related to the beauty of another, and another, until the insight dawns that beauty herself lives as supersensible form in the sense world. By this they are led to tame their consuming passion for any particular body. Thus purified, they enter the world of soul—"the open sea of beauty"—where generative knowing permeates and quickens all things.

Diotima's path is well known. Metaphysically, it gave birth to the fecund doctrine of the hierarchies of beauty, formulated by the theologians and philosophers of the early Christian era, from Plotinus to Dionysius the Areopagite, who taught that through sensible signs understood symbolically we come to contemplate the realities of cosmic and divine beauty. Anyone who has visited the great Gothic cathedrals knows the power of this doctrine from experience. But the practice underlying its truth has often been forgotten—perhaps because other, less respectable channels carried it.

There is, first, the channel of the Mysteries, like those of Demeter and Persephone celebrated at Eleusis. The Mysteries, whose origins lie in primordial times, unfolded in scenes, myths, and images the intimate, codependent origins of human nature and the cosmos. They taught how human beings and the gods together form a seamless web of divine life. The cosmic processes of nature, visible in the everyday mysteries of the seasons, birth and death, germination and fructification, were sacraments of consciousness, whose celebration formed the evolutionary path of human beings and gods alike. As the evolutionary path unfolded, a sense arose that the older gods were becoming less active, while other, younger powers, like Eros, were entering their prime and seeking to transform humanity's capacities. For Rudolf Steiner, Persephone invoked the ancient powers playing out of the cosmos into human souls, while Demeter, her mother, invoked still more ancient powers—the memory of a time when humanity and the cosmos were completely integrated and interpenetrated. At the time of the Mysteries of Eleusis, these ancient clairvoyances were disappearing. Demeter was distant, and Persephone was sinking deeper and deeper into the unconscious, carried off by Hades into the underworld. It was at this moment, according to Steiner, that Eros first arose, to take the place of Persephone in human consciousness and mediate the ancient clairvoyance. Standing in for Demeter and Persephone, Eros expands human awareness beyond the senses.

We know very little of the teaching of the ancient Mysteries. Its living reality could not be written down. From the tragedians, philosophers, and poets who refer to it obliquely, on the basis of overheard, half-remembered knowledge, we infer the outlines of what was taught, not the kernel. Yet the vital essence did not die. It was carried on underground in the vernacular by popular, folk traditions that, despite the decay and final closing of the Mysteries, carried their message through the European Middle Ages, and into the Renaissance, where we find its final flowering in that majestic, encrypted tale, *The Dream of Poliphilo.*

We can call this tradition "Romantic" in the sense that it used "the Romance languages." Romantics, in this sense, are those who live and work, not in a dead, cloistered, epic tongue, such as Latin, but in their mother tongue, the lyrical vernacular of experience. For Ezra Pound, the first Romantics were the Troubadours of southern France, and "Romance literature" began with a Provençal "alba" or "dawn song" of the tenth century. Dawn, let us not forget, is at once a precious symbol of spiritual awakening and the moment when the cosmic nature of the Earth is most apparent. The stanzas of the *alba* were written in Latin, but the refrain is in the mother tongue:

> Dawn appeareth upon the sea
> from behind the hill,

The watch passeth, it shineth
clear amid the shadows.

Before the Troubadours there was Sappho (c. 600 B.C.E.), the lyric genius who celebrated eros, the great opener of experience—the daimonic mediator between sensory and supersensory worlds—in a lived, human, existential context. Sappho was the first to catch the actual event of love with gut-wrenching accuracy:

Eros, limb-loosener, sweetbitter,
impossible to fight off, stealing up,
again whirls me off

Sappho's description of the experience is precise. The event, the moment of love, is closely observed, caught forever. Eros blows us away, knocks us down. In the instant of desire, love dismembers us. We fall apart, split open, as if by a great wind:

A mountain whirlwind
punishing oak trees
love broke open my heart

Sappho understood that love is a path. She knew that, in walking it, we are broken down, burnt up, and resurrected. Finally, no longer identified with and condemned to defend the illusory boundaries of our skin-bound selves, we become metaphors, creatures of transference—creators and actors in the imaginal space between form and emptiness, something and nothing, male and female. "Sweet wound," Sappho calls it, "bitter honey."

Sappho was an isolated figure. She did not create a culture. To find such a culture based on love and beauty—a feminine culture exalting eros and the soul—we must turn to the medieval Troubadours. For about two hundred years, from the eleventh to the thirteenth centuries, these poet-philosopher-musicians gave expression to a unique view of the world at once visionary, initiatory, and nondualistically grounded in the quintessentially human here-and-now. Much was going on around them—for these Middle Ages are incomparably richer spiritually than we usually imagine—and even if there is no question of influence, all the various manifestations of love during this time certainly drew on a single source in the *mundus imaginalis*. Nevertheless, the Troubadours were pristine, unique. Their actual historical origins are unknown, though many have been suggested.

Scholars mention the following: Arabic (Sufi) poetry, Neoplatonic (Eleusinian) metaphysics, and Manichean (Cathar) Christianity. To which we may add: women's songs and songs in women's voices (*Frauenlieder* or *cantigas de amigo*), as well as various folk traditions to greet winter's end and spring's beginning.

During May Day celebrations, young men and women wended their way in processions through the fields into the woods to gather green branches to decorate the churches. They danced round dances around the Maypole and, for one night, authority and decorum were unloosed. Boys and girls paired off freely, without constraint. Before nine months were over, there were many marriages.

> Under the lime tree
> on the open field
> where we two had our bed
> you still can see
> lovely broken
> flowers and grass.
> On the edge of the woods in a vale,
> tandaradei,
> sweetly sang the nightingale …
>   (Walther von der Vogelweide, tr. Frederick Goldin)

Women's songs were just that—love songs in women's voices, expressing fierce longing, intense inwardness, joy, and sorrow. As old as time, a new tradition of such soul poems arose in the ninth and tenth centuries. Already in 789 Charlemagne had issued an order that "no abbess should presume to leave her convent without our permission, nor allow those under her to do so … and on no account let them write *wineleodas* [songs for a friend], or send them from the convent." An Anglo-Saxon song, "Wulf and Eadwacer," gives a flavor of what these must have been like:

… Wulf is on one island, I on another,
the island a fastness, imprisoned by fens.
There are cruel men on that island—
how they'll welcome him if he comes in their midst!
Our fates are torn apart.

I longed for my Wulf in his long wanderings,
when the rains came, I sat here in tears;
when the branches of his body embraced me,
I felt the joy—but the harshness too.

Wulf, my Wulf, I am sick with longing
for you, with the rareness of your coming,
the grief of my heart, not the famine I live in …

Born of human love in a monastic setting, the songs of these unknown poets gave a transcendental meaning to the transformational power of eros. Discovering a new inwardness, they understood that human and divine love, which were the end of human nature, though not simply one, were not radically two. It was women who brought this to consciousness—as demonstrated by the discovery in 1948 of poems in women's voices composed in the Mozarabic-Andalusian variant of Spanish spoken by Christians and Jews in Moslem Spain. These *kharjas,* occurring at the end of Arabic or Hebrew *muwashshahs,* are the first lyrics in a Romance language. They are love songs put into the mouths of chanteuses:

Ah tell me little sisters,
how to hold my pain!
I'll not live without my beloved—
I'll fly to him again.…
                    *

Do not touch me, my beloved!
I don't want any trouble.
The bodice of my gown is frail—
be content with beauty!
                    *

My heart is going away from me—
Ah God, will he [it] return to me?
It grieves me so for my beloved,
he [it] is ill—when will he [it] be well?

        *

He is taking my soul from me—
my soul, what shall I long for?

To understand the Troubadours, their vision must be distinguished from that of the courtly or chivalric tradition. The latter rested not on the primacy of the soul—the feminine voice—but on more masculine virtues. It affirmed equality, tribalism, and brotherhood. It was heroic, virile, outward, open, realistic, and lustful. It exalted courage, daring, generosity, loyalty, and marriage. The Troubadours practiced differently. They praised inequality, solitude, inferiority, humility, submission, distance, discretion, secrecy, interiority, and, above all, joy. Out of these virtues, they created a culture of beauty and transformation—an initiatory, psycho-spiritual soul path of love unfolding in seven practices: falling in love; joy; true love; the perfect lover; the perfect Lady; the trial of love; and the exchange of hearts.

Love, as Sappho had ascertained, first enters through the senses, wounding through the eyes and the ears, and descending to the heart. "I thank God and my eyes for this / that through their knowing / joy came to me," writes Dante Arnaut. But the ears, too, can play their part; not only does the Lady's voice have a magic charm, simply hearing of her can wound as well. But wounding alone is insufficient. The psychic wound must be held always open. Jaufre Raudel, Prince of Blaye, for instance, was a Troubadour in the late twelfth century. This was when the Holy Land drew the mind and heart of Europe as the earth draws the plumb bob. Jaufre's court welcomed the streams of pilgrims as they paused at the various holy sites along their way. It was from one such noble traveler, returning from Antioch in Syria, that Jaufre first heard of the Countess of Tripoli's great beauty. Her soul was of an angelic purity and virtue and was said to shine through her bodily form so radiantly that she seemed to hold within her slender frame the beauty of the world itself. Though he had never seen her, Jaufre fell in love, cultivating in his heart a deep fidelity to her image.

When the days are long in May
it's good
soft bird song from afar,
and when the melody leaves me
I remember my love afar …

For years, dwelling in her image, Jaufre composed verses in her honor. All the time, he yearned to see her. Finally, he could withstand no longer, and, in the words of his Provençal biographer, "took the cross and put to sea." But, his dream about to be fulfilled, Jaufre fell ill before the ship was out of port. Reaching Tripoli, the lionhearted crusader was carried on a stretcher to an inn. There he lay dying. The Countess heard of his arrival and rushed to meet him. She came to the bed where he lay and took him in her arms. Hearing her voice and smelling her presence as a profusion of wildflowers and blossoms, Jaufre knew with all his senses that it was she. Birds sang around them. It was spring. Rejoicing, he praised God that life had finally brought him this greatest joy. Then, turning toward her, he died. Face to face. The Countess, too, felt something stupendous had been accomplished. She had Jaufre buried with full honors in the house of the Templars, and that very day, true to her grief, she took the habit of a nun.

Distance is necessary for desire to become joy. The wound, occurring at a distance, indicates that in falling in love, the soul or heart is opened. A mysterious, magic substance—a fiery ray moving in a look, a glance, contained in a word, an overheard name—descends into the poet's heart. Since only like can cause like and each thing has its own seed (only wheat springing from wheat), the magic substance can have originated only in another heart. In the two hearts, it lights a fire that, if tended with patience, obedience, care, and humility, can grow in intensity from day to day and heart to heart. If obeyed, this fire will make two hearts one. A single desire, it unites two hearts. "The flame, the fire, the conflagration of love are born in the heart," writes Peire Vidal. As the fire burns, it purifies the lover, who sees the Lady no longer with physical eyes but with imagination's eyes of fire. Falling in love is an imaginal alchemy, a magic work with images and a purification of the senses.

The aim is joy—holding the wound open, maintaining openness, seeing all things in openness. This is the play of pure love, of psyche as such. What one loves is love and that love is joy, improvisation, creation out of nothing. "I shall make a verse about nothing, downright nothing," sings Guillem of Aquitaine. Joy is as natural to the human heart as new leaves to a tree in spring, as birdsong to the birds. In a sense, it is to decipher nature's multicolored gown and learn the secret language of the birds and flowers. This is an opening of occult organs to the figures and words hidden in all natural phenomena, what Ezra Pound calls "an exteriorization of the sensibility," "an interpretation of the cosmos by feeling." Sensibility and interiority must be cultivated. Desire must be held in the heart. Love must be of the image alone, a purely psychic event in which one sees all things in the image, the heart of the other. "I would rather have desire of you than what a carnal lover has," writes one poet.

The image of such joy is spring, dawn, youth. Extended to infinity, it is the beginning and end of all virtue. Arnaut de Mareil says: "Whoever has joy is given great honor, for everything springs from joy— courtliness, pleasure, learning, candor, measure, a loving heart, the desire to serve, mercy, insight, and the capacity to speak well and reply pleasingly." Joy, essential interiority, nonattachment, and purity of the senses, are the preconditions of true love, which is the beginning and end of all.

True love—*fins amor*—which is the end of love, is also the path of love. It is the joyful practice of the experience of desire without an objective, of desire purified of all egoism and possessiveness. "I am the most perfect of lovers, because I neither say nor ask anything of my Lady," writes one Troubadour. "I am her friend, and I serve her occultly, discretely, silently. She does not know the good she gives me, nor how I receive joy and value from her. I rejoice in her spirit and smile. I ask for nothing more." Rene Nelli writes:

> The Troubadours' effort was not at all simply to celebrate continence for its own sake—after all, these ladies were married and the Troubadours themselves often had mistresses in the flesh—but to affirm and reaffirm that love, whence all virtues derive, presupposes spiritual bases that can only manifest in all their purity

separated from sensuality, even though they derive from it and must in the end return to it. The Troubadours' whole philosophy is solely concerned with unfolding the idea of love. Their sole preoccupation was to attain its reality in their hearts. That is why a relation exists between this erotic work and alchemy.

The path of love involves becoming a perfect lover. "Perfect lover" is the name of the path one walks to attain pure love. To love is to serve, praise, honor, and conceal. It is the painful practice, the real suffering (*sofrir*) that makes certain other virtues—obedience, patience, hope, faithfulness, sincerity, humility, timidity, discretion, vassalage—possible. The first and last victory is over male pride or egoism; as Nelli points out, for men to experience love—the soul's own power—which the functional misogyny of the male had thus far impeded, male power had to be symbolically humiliated. As Arnaut de Mareil realized painfully, love required nobility to bow down. For the Troubadours there was a reciprocal relation between bowing down and being raised up—between the practices of inferiority and the perfection and ennobling of the soul. The cardinal rule was to please, to affirm, to receive. A great "Yes!" To achieve such active receptivity, patience in the practice of humility, sincerity, and fidelity was required. The true lover dies every day. Every day, likewise, he rises in hope.

Praise, the inward identification with moral grace, is another practice. Praising the Lady, the Troubadour becomes ever more inwardly united with her. What does the Troubadour praise in his Lady? Her courtesy and inward cultivation, her amiability and awareness of others' needs expressed in thought, word, and deed, her inner and outer beauty, her gentleness, her pleasant company, her smile, her freshness, her presence of mind. None of these practices were ever to be revealed. Discretion, containment, inwardness went without saying. The hermetic vessel must remain sealed. It must never leak.

And the perfect Lady? She is Love incarnate, the supernatural source and ground of desire. Hers it is to practice the more masculine virtues: nobility, merit, glory, power. An active and equally aware participant in the path of love, she is joy, intelligence, perfect beauty, hospitality. She is also the Active Intellect, the Angel of Knowledge: Wisdom, Sophia, *Sapientia*. In the words of Solomon, in this sense the first Troubadour, "She is the brightness that streams from everlasting light, the flawless mirror of the active power of God and the image of his goodness. She is but one, yet can do everything; herself unchanging, she makes all things new; age after age she enters holy souls, and makes them God's friends and prophets, for nothing is acceptable to God except human beings who make their home with wisdom."

Finally, there is the test of love and the exchange of hearts. This begins with the contemplation of the Lady naked in unmediated, direct vision—in both image and reality. The Lady gives the contemplation, which is received by her servant, the Troubadour. "She will call me into her chamber where she undresses and, by her command, I shall be by her bed, on my knees, and humbly, if she offers me her foot, I shall pull off her slippers," writes Bernart de Ventadour. This act, reminiscent of Jesus' washing of his disciples' feet, led to the great test of love, imposed on the masculine by the feminine. It is a question of the inner perfection of the Troubadour's nature. "How much would I give to hold my Lord in my arms for one night, provided he thinks himself happy enough to receive what I would give him," writes the Countess of Dia. "I give him my heart, my love, my spirit, my eyes, my life," she continues. Then she adds, "O handsome friend, charming and kind … if only I could have you in my arms for an hour and embrace you lovingly. Know this, I would give anything to have you in my husband's place, but only if you do my bidding."

Here the test of love becomes enlightenment in the exchange or the fusion of two hearts—two hearts united in one love. The heart is the vessel of the practices. The mutuality of the lovers resides in their opening their hearts to each other, in their contemplating each other's heart. This is an imaginal act; the union is an imaginal union. For this to happen, the lovers must rest breast upon breast, as equals. The exchange of hearts makes absolute equals. I = not-I = Thou. This is the erotic ideal of the Middle Ages: *to live in the one heart that is love.* The Troubadour and his Lady rest without outwardness on each other's breasts, just as St. John rested on Christ's breast.

The "exchange of hearts" is the great mystery. In another modality, we find it underlying the heart-based mysticism of the women mystics such as Gertrude of Helfta and St. Lutgard who were the Troubadours' contemporaries. In their case, the exchange of hearts is with the heart of Christ himself, the sacred divine-human heart of Jesus that opened up to become a fountain of living water for the world. Above all, they sought to return to the heart its cognitive capacity. For a heart to become true, pure, and perfect, they believed, it must put aside all blindness and deafness. It must renew its eyes and ears and become open to Christ, who is the heart of Creation. "Stamp my heart with the seal of your heart," prayed Gertrude of Helfta. "Enter the penetralia of my heart." "Behold, now, the bedchamber of my heart is open to you."

Another example is St. Lutgard of Aywieres, who, as a child, had a vision of the humanity of Jesus, the wound in his side bleeding as if recently opened. By the encounter, she became intimate with the Lord. Later, when she was burdened by the crowds that followed her because of the grace of healing that had been given her, she turned to Jesus and cried out, "What use is this grace to me since it so hinders me from intercourse with you?" "What do you want?" asked Jesus. Lutgard thought she would like to understand the secrets of Scripture, so Jesus gave her this understanding. But then she felt her learning inadequate to make use of it, wondering, "What is it to me to know the secrets of Scripture, who know only one language and am an uncultivated, uneducated nun?" Jesus again asked her, "What do you want?" "I want your heart," Lutgard said. "No, rather it is your heart I want," said Jesus. "So be it," replied Lutgard, "but on condition that your heart's love is mingled with mine and I have and hold my heart in you."

As her biographer writes, "A correspondence, a communion, of hearts occurred from that time on…. From that day forth, just as a nurse watches over an infant in a cradle with a fan lest flies disquiet it, so Christ held close to the entrance of her heart like a watchman, so that no temptation of the flesh nor the smallest unclean thought might discompose her mind even for a moment."

As René Guénon has pointed out, the heart that contains the precious blood of human life is a vessel like the Holy Grail, that cup which held the holy blood and water flowing from Christ's side on the hill of Golgotha.

The story by no means concluded with the Troubadours. Subsequent chapters unfolded in Italy, with Dante, Guido Cavalcanti, and their friends. The Renaissance Platonists and magicians—Giordano Bruno and Pico della Mirandola—raise the stakes to a full-blown gnosticism of love. Before they have done so, another movement unfurls, focusing on Shakespeare, especially the Shakespeare of the Sonnets, as Joel Fineman recounts in his book *Shakespeare's Perjur'd Eye*. Finally, Romanticism—above all, Goethe, Novalis, Hölderlin, and Keats—prepares our present moment, the work we have to do.

What faculty entered through the Troubadours? What faculty began in the Mysteries of Eleusis and with Plato and Sappho, then passed on through the Troubadours and Dante to the Renaissance and Shakespeare, before passing to Goethe, Novalis, Freud, Jung, and countless others? Let us call it "the thinking heart."

9

The Meaning of the Rose Cross

THE ROSE CROSS CHALLENGED the early seventeenth century as a mystery, a question, and a promise. It perplexes us still today. Announcing itself as the hidden, symbolic center of a general reformation of science, art, and religion, the Rose Cross arose in a paradoxical, uncertain time marked by religious strife, spiritual renaissance, burgeoning nationalism, individualism, cloak-and-dagger politics, and imminent apocalypse. The compound of conditions and motives caused confusion, outrage, and fanatical enthusiasm in equal measure. Despite an enormous bibliography on the subject, it still does so today. The historical wounds are by no means healed, nor do human beings seem any wiser than they were.

One must tread lightly when entering this territory. Conspiracy theories abound. Religious and political ideologies still polarize into oppositional stances, making the spiritual communion of humanity seem utopian. Materialism is more rampant than ever. Worshipers of Moloch rule the roost, while atheist humanists flee in terror from anything suggesting the occult. Nevertheless, the promise was and is clear. New possibilities still dawn for human consciousness. Now, no less than then, a brave new age awaits its realization by those who heed the call proclaimed by that emblem of immaculate purity, the Rose Cross.

As a symbol, the meaning of the Rose Cross is necessarily inexpressible in words and hence unbetrayable. I can give no secrets away. Yet, the symbol itself is an open secret. Inexplicable though it is, it makes possible its own understanding. If enacted as a rite and allowed to act, it does the inner and the outer work that is its teaching. It does so because a symbol is not a thing but a synthesis of complements, a paradoxical process, a *way*, something that one must do. It embodies an injunction. Do this—conjoin the Cross and the Rose—and you will understand; you will attain what I am, what I *do*. The traditional derivation of the Greek *rhodon*, "rose," from *rheein*, "to flow," makes the active aspect very clear. Able to evoke what it stands for, the symbol is available to all. Erudition is not required, only openness of heart. For this reason, the framers of the *Fama* hoped that "it would be set forth in every-one's Mother Tongue, because those should not be defrauded of the knowledge of it, who (although they are unlearned) God hath not excluded."

With the hindsight of four hundred years, the original context in which we encounter the Rose Cross seems clear. The Christianization of the perennial wisdom and cosmology of the ancient theologians by the early Renaissance humanists and magi (and the plethora of secret and semisecret societies it spawned) had made possible a marvelous rebirth of embodied beauty, truth, and goodness in a new sacred science and art. By the seventeenth century, this possibility was in danger of falling apart under the pressures, at once reactionary and progressive, of a rationalist and dogmatic Counter-Renaissance. The Counter-Renaissance, seeking refuge from the bloodshed and instability of the times, would in turn give birth—out of the ruins of Renaissance dream—to the need for "intellectual certainty" and what we call, without a trace of irony, *modern* science and philosophy—not to mention modern religion. From this point of view, the Rose Cross stands for a last attempt, before going completely underground, to recapture the high ground. As it were for the "last time," it sought to realize, in the form of a universal cultural transformation, what the creators of the Renaissance—people like Gemistos Plethon, Marsilio Ficino, Leon Battista Alberti, Nicholas of Cusa, Francesco Colonna, Pico della Mirandola, and others—had only dreamed of.

There is a certain truth in this. The "Rosicrucian Enlightenment" did arise as a kind of second, northern, Renaissance, stopped in its tracks by historical and intellectual counterforces. But this explanation is deceptive for two reasons. The first is that, while building upon the "renewal of wisdom" associated with the sages of the *Quatrocento*, the Rosicrucian Enlightenment did not share all the assumptions of the Platonists and sought to bring something new into human consciousness. The "new" thing, although it can to some extent be explained by invoking the names of Paracelsus and Luther, has deeper roots. The initiatory center of the first Renaissance is undoubtedly in the various Italian academies that arose suddenly and mysteriously, as if brought into being intentionally. But other initiatory wisdom streams, currents, and traditions exist, going back into the Middle Ages, to the "twelfth-century Renaissance." When we try to understand the meaning of the Rose Cross, we are faced with the mystery of the historical process as it is woven from vertical and horizontal, spiritual and historical, modes of transmission. To unravel some of these, we shall have to cast a wide net.

> Seeing the only Wise and Merciful God in these latter days hath poured out so richly his mercy and goodness to Humankind, whereby we do attain more and more to the perfect knowledge of his Son Jesus Christ and of Nature, that justly we may boast of the happy time wherein there is not only discovered unto us the half part of the world, which was hitherto unknown and hidden, but He hath also made manifest unto us many wonderful and never-before seen works and creatures of Nature, and, moreover, hath raised human beings, endued with great wisdom, which might partly renew and reduce all arts (in this our spotted and imperfect age) to perfection, so that we might thereby understand our own nobleness and worth, and why we are called microcosmos, and how far our knowledge extendeth in Nature.

So begins the *Fama* or announcement "of Christian intent" of the Fraternity of the Rose Cross (R.C). The founding assumption is the reality of "these latter days" when "the only Wise and Merciful God ... has poured out so richly his mercy and goodness."

The assumption is neither new nor unique. The visionary mystic Marie des Vallées, for example, who, with Margaret-Mary Alacoque, was the means by which the sacrament of the Sacred Heart was received as a universal consecration in the seventeenth century, was asked by Jesus in a vision to repeat one thing three times. "Whose is it? Where shall I find it?" she asked. Jesus replied, *"Spiritus Domini replevit orbem terrarum"* (The Spirit of the Lord will be poured over the orb of the Earth), adding,

This refers to the times when the Holy Spirit will spread the fire of divine love over all the earth and so create his floods. For there are three floods.... The first was the eternal Father's and was a flood of water; the second was the Son's and was a flood of blood; but the third belongs to the Holy Spirit, and will be a flood of fire. It will cause as much unhappiness as the others, for it will find much resistance and much green wood that will be difficult to burn.

Thus, in Catholic France (and there are other examples, as we shall see) we hear a precise echo of the announcement that began to circulate in Lutheran Germany some forty years earlier.

This was not new, being as old as Christianity, or older.

Historically, the apocalyptic side of Christianity is closely linked to Judaism, whose sages and prophets, awaiting the messianic age in fear and hope, endlessly meditated the unfolding reality of God's activity in time and in relation to his people as a unified, divinely predetermined whole. Starting with Lactantius, this same contemplation of the end also gradually filled the Christian West until, by the Middle Ages, the expectation of supernatural, radical change was almost universal. Christ's advent, it was believed, marked a new historical dispensation. More than that, it instituted a new era of creation: a second creation in which the Creator entered creation, utterly transforming it. No longer outside, beyond, and above creation, the divine was now in creation, overturning what had seemed from time immemorial the hierarchic cosmic norms of above and below, inside and out, beginning and end. The Lord of the World had become the King of the Elements. But this would not become fully evident until the Second Coming. Then history would close. Just before the curtain of the Last Judgment finally fell, a millennial Golden Age would ensue. The signs of this could be read on every side. As the Rosicrucian *Confessio* says: "God hath most certainly and most assuredly concluded to send and grant to the World before her end, which presently shall ensue, such a Truth, Light, Life, and Glory, as the first Man Adam had."

Medieval Christians felt themselves to be living in an interim period, an endless pause between revelations, in which the Church, as an institution, functioned as antechamber. It was a difficult role, fraught with tension and paradox. In an attempt to defuse these, the

Church sought to de-emphasize history and discourage apocalypticism, but to little lasting effect, since these were inherent in its teaching. This was clear by the twelfth century. We need instance only two important figures. First, Hildegard of Bingen (whose most popular writings were her prophecies, later collected in a text entitled *The Mirror of Future Times* and much studied by Paracelsus's teacher, the legendary Trithemius of Spondheim) and, second, Joachim of Fiore, the influence of whose prophetic understanding permeated the entire Rosicrucian ambiance.

Joachim was born in southern Italy, in Calabria, ancient Magna Graeca, about 1135. Many stories are told of his prophetic gift. As a youth, he is said to have gone on a pilgrimage to the Holy Land where, as he lay thirsting in the desert, he was told in a dream to drink from a river of oil. Awakening, he found the meaning of the Scriptures revealed. Another tale has a vision of the Scriptures with the numerical scheme of their interpretation coming upon him on the Mount of the Transfiguration, Mount Tabor. Yet another has him walking in the gardens at Sambucina, in the early days of his monastic life, and receiving a miraculous draft of inspiration from angelic hands. In these tales, the illumination was immediate; but behind the immediacy lay much "laboring on the way," as he struggled to understand the Psalms, the concordance of the Old and New Testaments, and their fulfillment in the Apocalypse of St. John.

The parallels with Luther are unmistakable. Like Luther, Joachim struggled to break through the hard surface of the dead letter to the living Spirit within, seeking the spiritual fruit beneath the skin. But his mind seemed to meet immovable obstacles. The ways of reason availed nothing; prayer, repentance, repetition of the Psalms seemed the only path this pilgrim could take. Sometimes, after arduous labor, he would lay his task aside; then, if he was lucky, grace would intervene, the stone would roll away, the light of spiritual intelligence would flood his heart, and he would return to the Scriptures and read them with new eyes.

Joachim did not regard his experience of illumination as exceptional, but he did regard it as prophetic. He saw it as a foretaste of the spiritual intelligence that would be poured out on humanity before the end of history. It had been given to him to understand that just as one spiritual Intelligence united into a single comprehension the Old and New Testaments, so, in history, the work of God the Father and God the Son must be followed by the work of God the Holy Spirit. The Trinity was built into the time process itself. There was an Age (or *Status*) of the Father, then an Age of the Son, and, proceeding from these, the Age of the Spirit—the Spirit of Truth, the Comforter or Paraclete, who testifies of the Word and guides human beings into all truth.

> The first age was that of knowledge, the second that of understanding, and the third will be the period of complete intelligence. The first was servile obedience, the second filial servitude, and the third will be freedom. The first was affliction, the second action, and the third will be contemplation. The first was fear, the second faith, and the third will be love. The first was the age of slaves, the second the age of sons, and the third will be the age of friends.

Although each age was present and active in the other and Joachim's scheme was not straightforwardly linear, his conclusion was nevertheless inevitable. No matter how complex the wheels, or *Rotae,* of twos, threes, sevens, and twelves were, history would culminate in the pouring out of the spiritual intelligence of the Holy Spirit. The Incarnation of Christ had no other purpose. St. Augustine had equated the seven ages of the world with the seven days of creation: five before the Incarnation, the sixth from the Incarnation to his own time; and the seventh, the Sabbath age of rest. When this would begin was the great question. For the authors of the *Confessio,* assiduous students of Joachim's *Rotae,* their own time bore the unmistakable sign that "the Lord Jehovah ... doth turn about the course of nature." For Joachim, the Sabbath age coincided with the third state—that of spiritual humanity. That he, who was no prophet, magician, or mere speculator, had been able to clearly understand the meaning of the Scriptures, and of history, merely by the *donum spiritualis intellectus,* the gift of spiritual intelligence, meant that this moment could not be far off. It meant, too, that the Antichrist likewise stood in the wings, and beside him Elijah, or Elias, the type of the Holy Spirit, who "will come and restore all things" in the great *renovatio.*

There were many signs of its approach. This was the time of the
great Grail cycles, the *Tale of Flor and Blanchflor,* and the *Romant de la
Rose.* It was also, and not unrelatedly, the time of "the discovery of the
individual," from Abelard's discovery of the inner voice of moral
responsibility to Aquinas's unfolding of the personality in pure thinking. It marked the dawn of the divine feminine Isis-Sophia-Mary and
a new devotion to the Blessed Virgin and the humanity of Jesus—
which, as we shall see, are not two, but one. At the School of Chartres,
hermetic Platonists, renewing the microcosm-macrocosm analogy,
sought to reopen the Book of Nature and create a new sacred science
of the Goddess Natura—the *Anima Mundi*—while St. Bernard, the
spiritual director of the Templars (guardians, like the Grail knights, of
the "Holy Land") gave evidence in music and architecture of profound Pythagorean understanding. This was the time of the first
translations of alchemical texts from Arabic into Latin, beginning
with Morienus around 1182, and of the compilation by Moses de
Leon of the *Zohar.* Among the Beguines and in the new Cistercian
monasteries, or "schools of love"—and what is love but to "profess no
other thing than to cure the sick, and that *gratis*"?—women mystics
were initiating a nondualistic path of love, penetrating the mysteries
of the Sacred Heart, and creating a vernacular devotion to the
Eucharist—the sacred blood and body available to all. Meanwhile, in
the south of France, Troubadours and Cathars were drawing together
Christian, Ismaili, Manichaean, and Sufi traditions to create a lived,
vernacular culture for the transformation of the world in the human
soul—the rescue of the sparks of light scattered and mixed with darkness in every perception.

Underlying the different manifestations is a new understanding of
the centrality of the heart, the purified soul, and the feminine "I"
(three aspects of a single reality).

Let us begin with the heart, never forgetting that "Rosicrucian"
alchemists like van Helmont, sickened by the verbiage and prattle of
the *ratio* and seeking the divine "kiss" that would bring illumination
to the unmediated perception of things as they are, spoke of the necessity of cutting off the head. *"Summa scientia nihil scire,"* ends *The
Chemical Wedding,* affirming that the height of knowledge is to know
nothing. The aim was to become a virgin and give birth to Christ—in

Meister Eckhart's language, to a human being devoid of all foreign images and as void as when he or she was not yet. This is the territory not only of purity of heart but also of poverty of spirit. These interdependent virtues marked the twelfth century. Its saints and mystics called for the purification of the soul—the creation of a new, spiritualized heart.

This heart is neither a biological pump nor, metaphorically, the personal seat of affective emotion. It is not even personal. To attain it, detachment from all desires is necessary. We may call it "transpersonal," if we understand transpersonal as extending to the cosmos. "Cosmic" would be a better designation. It is the center of that "globe" whose circumference is nowhere and whose *centrum,* or heart, is everywhere. Remember that the *Fama* and the *Confessio* speak of *axiomata* that lead "like a Globe or Circle to the only middle Point and *Centrum*" and of "the concurrence of all things to make Sphere or Globe, whose total parts are equidistant from the center." The center is the heart—indeed, the Sacred Heart, the heart of the world. To understand it, several "hearts" must be superimposed.

First, there is the heart of Jesus. Before invoking the "Sphere or Globe, whose parts are equidistant from the center," the *Fama* had spoken of the truth—that given to Adam—as "peaceable, brief, and like herself in all things" and "accorded with by Jesus in all parts." This is a tradition going back to the prophet Ezekiel, to whom the Lord said: "And I will give them one heart, and I will put a new spirit within you; and I will take the stony heart out of their flesh, and give them a heart of flesh." Now, in the last days, at the end of time, this was becoming known. "I and Jesus have one heart," said St. Bernard. Whether or not this was a new revelation, it was received as such by the saints of that time. "I was charged to announce to the Church now being born," wrote St. Mechtild of Magdeburg, "the uncreated Word of God and, as for the Sacred Heart, God left it to be known for the end of times when the world would begin to fall into decrepitude to reanimate the flood of his love."

Everywhere—among Troubadours and knights, Platonists and Franciscans, hermetists, Cathars, and lay brethren, and above all in monasteries, those laboratories of the soul—St. Benedict's ideal was taken to new heights. "To move down the ways of the commandments of the Lord to the heart and with the unutterable sweetness of love." The task was to become one with the heart of the world, the divine-human heart of Christ Jesus opened up by the spear of Longinus to become a fountain of living water for the world's transformation into the divine body of God. From the opened heart, water and blood poured over and into the Earth, permeating it, filling it with the spirit of creative love, ennobling it as the growing heart of creation.

In the monastery of Helfta, Gertrude the Great began her *Spiritual Exercises,* presented in seven books or seven stages—we may call them the seven roses—with the fundamental gesture of the heart's wisdom: affirmation. "Let my heart bless," she begins. By the practice of affirmation, the heart becomes true, perfect, whole. Wide open, innocent, it enters the "penetralia" of Jesus' heart, living in that "cavern" or "bedchamber"—empty of memory, desire, and understanding—living in dying, void, capable of being made anew, stamped, fashioned, modeled on the heart of Jesus. One becomes an organ of creative, loving perception—no longer blind, deaf, and dumb but "converted into a paradise of all virtues and a red berry bush of total perfection." This is the heart as the whole person, the person as an organ of perception.

Gerhard Dorn, commenting on Trithemius's alchemical treatise writes:

> First, transmute the earth of your body into water. This means that your heart, which is as hard as stone, material, and lazy must become supple and vigilant.... Then spiritual images and visions impress themselves on your heart, as a seal is impressed on wax. But now this liquefaction must transform itself into air. That is to say, the heart must become contrite and humble, rising toward its Creator as air rises toward heaven.... Then, for this air to become fire, desire, now sublimated, must be converted into love—love of God and neighbor—and this flame must never be extinguished. At this point, to receive the power of things above and things below, you must begin the descent.

This is what it is to transform oneself "from dead stones into living philosophical stones."

A more graphic explanation is revealed in the phenomenon of "the exchange of hearts" that also arose at this time among the Troubadours, where the exchange of hearts was with the *Madonna Intelligenza*, the Active Intelligence. Among the monastics, St. Gertrude experienced such an exchange of hearts with Jesus. Striving to pay complete attention to each note, word, and thing in the liturgy, and failing, hindered by human frailty, she asked, "What profit can there be in a labor in which I am so inconsistent?" Christ, hearing her, gave her "his divine heart in the form of a lighted lamp," saying: "Here is my heart.... I hold it before the eyes of your heart; it will supply what you lack." Then Gertrude asked, "How is it that I am aware of your divine heart within me in the form of a lamp in the midst of my heart and yet, when I approach you, I find it within you...?" To which the Lord replied: "Just as you stretch out your hand when you take hold of something and, when you have taken it, you draw it back toward you; so, languishing for love of you, when you are distracted, I stretch out my heart and draw you to me; but when your inmost thoughts are in harmony with mine, and you are recollected and attend to me, then I draw back my heart again, and you with it, into myself, and from it I offer you the pleasure of all virtues."

To understand the significance of the Rose Cross, one must realize that what is at issue is not only a personal mysticism of union with the divine, but a cosmic transformation, regeneration. For Christians, the incarnation is a cosmic event. God entered creation itself, became flesh, penetrated the very entrails of matter, so that he might be all in all and the hidden treasure known. God entered creation for the sake of creation itself—not just for the comfort of fallen, skin-bound, human beings, but so that these beings might again assume their cosmological function as cosmic beings. Human beings are called to be participant coworkers with God, capable of raising up the world and God himself, who was now one with it. This is the meaning of St. Paul's great lines in Romans 8 when he writes:

> For I reckon that the sufferings of the present time are not worthy to be compared with the glory that shall be revealed in us. For creation herself waits with eager longing for the revealing of God's children; for creation was subject to futility, not of its own will, but

of the will of the one who subjected it. Creation herself will be set free from the bondage of corruption into glorious freedom of the children of God. For we know that the whole of creation has been groaning in pain and labor until now.

The "dulcet heart of Jesus"—rosy-fleshed Jesus—as invoked by the mystics, is not a thing to be located anywhere. It is the activity that is the center of all things, the potential center of every perception, the magical fulcrum of every marvel. This is one meaning of Christ in all things.

A further clue is given if we consider the recovery of Sophia, the divine feminine, as taught by Hildegard of Bingen (b. 1098), of whom the monk Guibert wrote that no woman since Mary had received so great a gift. Hers was the gift of being able to see in the reflection of the living light and in the living light itself. Like Mary, Hildegard was a "poor little figure of a woman," and it was this that allowed her to recognize that the humility—"littleness" St. Thérèse of Lisieux would call it—of the feminine exalted it over every creature.

For Hildegard, Sophia, whom she calls either *Sapientia* (Wisdom) or *Caritas* (Love) is the complex reality—the cosmic glue—articulating many things we usually keep separate. Primarily, she is the living bond between Creator and creation, God and cosmos. It is by her perpetual mediation that the divine can manifest and be known. Sophia lives in the encounter of God and creation, where God stoops to humanity and humanity aspires to God. Sophia makes possible not only creation—she is the cosmogenic, playful companion of the creator, "set up from everlasting," but also the incarnation of creation in time, namely, redemption or new creation. For Hildegard the new creation was the cause of all, the event for which the world had been made. For Hildegard, the event of Christ's Incarnation was the world. The process of the Incarnation would not be complete until the entirety of creation had been subsumed in the body of Christ.

A woman, Mary accomplished the new creation—the union of divinity and humanity and the Earth. For Hildegard, woman, the feminine, is the means of God's becoming all in all. But the feminine—Sophia: Wisdom and Love—is not limited just to Mary. It extends, firstly, to Jesus, the Humanity of Christ—"Jesus, our mother"—and then, by extension, to the "Church," humanity, the Earth—which is, in turn, one with the cosmos itself. Jesus, the crucified Christophore, humanity, matter, the Earth, the cosmos, is feminized as Sophia, the place where the heart of Christ must come to dwell.

The hearts of Jesus and Mary are therefore one—they are the heart of Sophia—and are also the heart or center of the cosmos itself. The dawning realization among twelfth- and thirteenth-century adepts was that creating a heart by the process of radical purification of the soul—occultists would later call it the "astral body"—made possible the indwelling of Christ and the gift of the Holy Spirit. At its highest level, it was understood that this inner work renewed a cosmogenic or Adamic function for humanity. Once the soul was so purified that it was one with Sophia, the being in whom it was purified was perfected in the three realms that are traditionally the perfection of the human state. Perfected in these, one becomes "Trismegistus"—master of the three realms. Hildegard has a marvelous antiphon that describes the realms—realms that, through the presence of Christ, become four and one:

> O energy of Wisdom,
> encompassing all
> you circled circling
> in the path of life
> with three wings:
> one flies on high
> one distills from the earth,
> and the third flies everywhere.

Thus St. Dominic's institution of the Rosary (encouraged, it is said, by an apparition of the Virgin) and Arnold of Villanova's alchemical *Rosarium Philosophorum* have more in common than one might suspect. For the symbol of Sophia—the purified soul with access in the three realms—has always been the Rose. Sixteenth century alchemists called it the *flos sapientium,* the flower of wisdom. For them, to accomplish the Great Work was to have "attained the Rose." Throughout the Middle Ages, the figure of the Rose—*Rosa Mystica,* that rose planted beside the waters—is used indifferently of Jesus and Mary, always referring to the purified heart of humanity in which the Christ—the center of the world, the immanent transcendent principle—can dwell. In Dante's words, it is "the Rose wherein the divine Word made itself flesh."

Mention must be made of the Grail, which, as Guénon pointed out, following Charbonnneau-Lassay, echoes the symbolism we have been following. The Grail, too, is a heart or flower and belongs to the prehistory of the Sacred Heart. Guénon was led to this insight by the Egyptian hieroglyph for the heart: a vase or vessel containing the blood of life. In several versions, the Grail is the vessel in which Joseph of Arimathia gathered the first drops of blood from the wound in Christ's side. In Guénon's words, "this cup stands for the Heart of Christ as receptacle of his blood." The "Heart" is the new, incarnated archetype of the "sacrificial Cup" that everywhere represents the center of the world, "the abode of immortality." As for the Rose, does not this flower too, like all flowers, contain a chalice in its calyx and evoke the idea of a "receptacle?" No wonder, then, that we find twelfth-century molds for altar breads that show blood falling in little drops in the form of roses, and altar canons where a rose is placed at the foot of the lance down which the sacred blood flows. Nor should we forget that whether it is a cup or dish borne by women, a celestial stone or stone of light (or simply immaterial), the primary virtue of the Grail is a unique, nourishing, healing light—a brightness as of six thousand candles—the light of the Holy Spirit, the Dove, whose coming age Joachim of Fiore first foresaw.

It is difficult to trace the vernacular language of the heart buried beneath the mud of dead tongues. The earliest intimations, as we saw in the previous chapter, are to be found in the *cantigas de amigo* or *Frauenlieder*—love songs in women's voices—that dawned almost simultaneously in the monasteries of the north and in Mozarabic Spain in the ninth and tenth centuries. The flowering comes with the Troubadours and the *fedeli d'amore,* whose master, Dante, would write a spirited defense of "vulgar eloquence"—"our first true speech." In this, he shows that each person's mother tongue represents a development of the primordial language with which Adam discoursed with God and named the things of his experience. In this spirit, the vernacular shaped the great courtly epics and poems and, above all, the movements of lay spirituality such as the Beguines, Beghards, Lollards, and Waldenses.

These "little women" and "little brothers without domicile," practicing an apostolic life of poverty, prayer, preaching, healing, and mendicancy—free spirits, called together by the Holy Spirit—were "noble travelers," Rosicrucians before the fact. Translating the Bible and reading commentaries in the vernacular in the public square, they created a new mood in Christian piety, becoming not just Christlike but one with Christ in nature—taught by him, acting in him, speaking from him. They were condemned in the fourteenth century, but what they had started could no longer be stopped. Penetrating ever deeper into the human souls, the movement was impelled by such mysterious figures as the "Friend of God from the Highlands" (an incarnation of the Master Jesus, according to Rosicrucian tradition). It was absorbed and transmitted by mystics like Meister Eckhart, Johannes Tauler, Heinrich Suso, and Thomas à Kempis, and became known as the "modern devotion" (*devotio moderna*). As such, it permeated communities like the Brotherhood of the Common Life, the Community of the Green Isle, and, later still, the Hussites and the Bohemian Brethren. These revolutionary vernacular and visionary spiritualities of common experience embody a new interiority, a new sense of the inwardness of the letter, whether of Scripture or of nature—and, as Henry Corbin points out, a new spiritual hermeneutics based upon the heart as the organ and realm of transformative meaning.

The same period saw the rise of medieval alchemy or hermetism, which is the distinguishing mark of the Rose Cross and whose innermost teaching parallels the paths of experience opened up by these vernacular spiritual movements. Morienus tells Khalid: "No one will be able to perform or accomplish this thing which you have so long sought, nor attain it by means of any knowledge, unless it be through affection and gentle humility, a perfect and true love." Only a purified heart, according to alchemical teaching, can receive the gift of God—a *donum dei,* according to the *Summa Perfectionis*—for God alone gives "direct, unerring access to the methods of this science." He "in his mercy has created this extraordinary thing in yourself." But God and nature, the human soul and the world soul, are one, not two. The alchemist is a coworker with God; prayer must accompany manipulation.

We see this implied in the first major Western alchemical treatise, the *Summa Perfectionis,* attributed to Geber, but probably written by the Franciscan Paul of Taranto in the fourteenth century. The *Summa* begins by telling the aspirant: "Know, dearest son, that whoever does not know the natural principles in himself, is already far removed from our art, since he does not have the true root upon which he should found his goal." To find this root a person must have "natural ingenuity" and "a soul subtly searching the natural principles and foundations of nature." Alchemy depends upon a purified heart— knowing the natural principles in oneself that are one with the root of all things—and the ability to observe the processes of nature directly, precisely, and closely. The *Summa* calls such observation "the highest scrutiny," a scrutiny dependent upon a profound purification of the soul and senses. As Gertrude of Helfta in her monastic enclosure realized, it is the transformed heart that must acquire eyes and ears. Neither nature nor God are to be naturalistically analyzed but are rather revealed, received by one with the eyes to see and the ears to hear what will be given.

Alchemy, which entered the West from Arabic sources—as in Morienus and Geber—underwent a profound sea change in the transmission. It was spiritualized. This is not to say that alchemy had not had a spiritual and mystical component in Hellenic times, but to suggest that in Islam it had assumed primarily a practical, quantitative form. It worked almost exclusively with the four elements. The "fifth essence," or spiritual, Sophianic substance potentially uniting nature, God, and the human soul, played little part in the original Arabic Jabirian corpus. Yet in the West the quintessence came to found a new sacred—"eucharistic"—science for the transformation of the world. Precisely how this came about is as yet unknown. A primary influence, suggested by Dan Merkur, must have occurred in the transmission of the *Emerald Tablet* that became the Bible of Western hermetists. In the Latin translation, the text begins: "That which is above is like to that which is below and that which is below is like to that which is above, to accomplish the miracles of the one thing." In the Arabic version, however, it reads: "That which is above is from that which is below, and that which is below is from that which is above"—a straightforward reference to circulation. In the Latin, which became popular in Hortulanus's *Commentary,* not only is there the suggestion of parallel universes—supernal and inferior—but also of their ultimate identity.

All this would have been known by the one called Christian Rosenkreutz, who was born, according to legend, in Germany, in 1378. The tale told by the *Fama* and *Confessio* is well known and summarizes many of the elements already discussed. Raised in a cloister, Christian Rosenkreutz determined when still a youth of fifteen or sixteen to go to the Holy Land—Palestine in a literal sense, but symbolically the supreme center or heart of the world, the Sacred Heart or Holy Grail. Geographically, he never reached his goal of Jerusalem, visiting instead Damascus, or Damcar, Egypt, and Fez. He learned Arabic, and studied "mathematica, physic, and magic" with the hermetists and spiritual masters of Islam. Accepting this account, we may say that in Arabia he was fully initiated into the sacred sciences of the group of medieval Arab philosophers known as the *Ikhwan al-Safa* or Brethren of Purity and studied their fifty-two *Epistles*—fourteen of which deal with the mathematical sciences, seventeen with the natural sciences, ten with psychology, and eleven with theology. In Fez, through which the great Ibn 'Arabi had just passed, he would have met with the highest levels of Sufi intellectual realization. As a fifteenth-century historian wrote:

In Fez one finds masters of all branches of intellectuality, such as grammar, law, mathematics, chronometry, geometry, metaphysics, logic, rhetoric, and music, and these masters know all the relevant texts by heart. Whoever does not know by heart the basic text relating to the science about which he speaks is not taken seriously.

Although he believed that what he was taught was "defiled" by his teachers' religion, Christian Rosenkreutz "knew how to make good use of the same." He found his Christian faith strengthened and "altogether agreeable with the Harmony of the whole World" and its evolution through "periods of times." After two years in Fez, he decided to return to Europe, which was already "big with great commotions," and laboring to give birth to a new world. But no one in power would listen to his nonhierarchical, unified vision, and he was forced to return to Germany, where in solitude and secrecy he founded the Fraternity of the Rose Cross with its celebrated six-point rule:

First, to profess no other thing, than to cure the sick, and that *gratis*. We have already remarked that this rule is a rule of love. "Compassion," wrote Paracelsus, "is the true physician's teacher." "Compassion," of course, means "feeling with," and what is love (or healing) but to feel another's suffering as one's own and recognize that the disease is one in all. The primary orientation is toward the world, the *Liber Mundi*—toward other beings, for we can love only other living beings. The Rosicrucian works for the sake of the world, not the individual soul. Granted that from a nondualist perspective there is no difference between the healing of one's soul and the healing of the world, the Rosicrucian rule nevertheless affirms the primacy of service and of action. If one is a true Rosicrucian, one walks "the true thornstrewn way of the cross"—the renunciation of all selfhood—for the sake of the redemption of the world, "the building of the New Jerusalem." That is why the rule specifies that the service aims at "healing," understood to include nature herself. Nature, like humanity, fell with Adam and is sick and needs healing. Like humanity, nature is not the unity it ought to be. It groans and travails in pain; it is diseased. Paracelsus called this state of separation and disunity the *cagastrum*. Yet to heal this disease, to renew the unity of nature in and through humanity, Christ came. As Prince Lapoukhin writes, Christ not only "mystically sprinkled every soul with the virtue of his blood, which is the tincture proper to the renewal of the soul in God … but also regenerated the mass of immaterial elements of which he shall make a new heaven and a new earth." In other words: "The crown of all the mysteries of nature adorns the altar of the sanctuary, lit only by the light of the stainless Lamb … [whose] precious blood, sacrificed for the salvation of the world, is the sole tincture that renews all things." To conjoin the Rose and the Cross in nature as a whole, to heal and unite nature and human nature in its center or heart, is the Rosicrucian aim.

The second rule states: That no one should be obliged to wear distinctive dress but should adapt oneself to the customs of the country.

At its simplest, this is the injunction to live anonymously, unpretentiously, plying some ordinary trade, and draw no attention to oneself. At another level, since chief among the customs of a country is its language, the rule invokes the "gift of tongues," often mentioned as a Rosicrucian characteristic. This gift is of the Holy Spirit. One who possesses it addresses everyone in their own language, that is, in the way and at the level appropriate to their understanding. As Guénon points out, this implies that the person who has attained the Rose Cross is attached to no form, no name, not even his or her own. Some sources therefore add that the second rule includes the injunction to change one's name with each country one visits. Here is the true meaning of the designation "cosmopolitan" found throughout the literature— true Rosicrucians live at the center or heart of the world. They are at home everywhere and nowhere. This rule of nonattachment to phenomenal forms extends also to beliefs. Ibn 'Arabi notes, "The true sage is bound to no particular belief." The partisan Protestant context in which the announcement of the Rose Cross is embedded is strangely antithetical—indeed, diametrically opposed—to its spirit.

The third rule enjoins thus: That every year on Christmas Day they meet together at the house *Sancti Spiritus* or write the cause of their absence. *Sancti Spiritus* or Holy Spirit is the name Rosenkreutz gave to his "building," naming it after what it housed. The "mother house"—the Church or Temple—of the Rose Cross is invisible. It is the Temple of the Spirit, the Inner Church, which is the redeemed Sophia, the mystical body of Christ. It is the Church of the Fire of Love. Prince Lapoukhin, in *Characteristics of the Interior Church*, discounting faith, prayer, fasting, the seeing of visions, the gift of prophecy, miracles, and even humility as distinctive—for these can be deceptive—concludes that the only true sign is love. "Love is the manifestation of Christ's spirit, which can only exist in love, and can only work by love." Only what proceeds from the spirit, the fire, of love is good and true. We return again to the heart, this time as the Temple of the Rose Cross.

The last three rules seem simpler: first, each Brother must choose a successor. This means there is to be no Rosicrucian school or similar institution. The Rosicrucian, working alone, anonymously, for the sake of humanity and the world, seeks one intimate friend to continue the work. Second, the initials *C.R.* should be their seal, mark, and character. As their seal, the Rose Cross is stamped on their heart. It has become their heart, their work. As their mark, it radiates like the light of six thousand candles. As their character, it affirms that they will be known by their fruits of love. Finally, the last rule: they shall remain secret for one hundred years.

Christian Rosenkreutz was born in 1378 and lived one hundred and six years. He died in 1484—though his tomb was not discovered and opened for 120 years, in 1604. Much went on then between the putative founding of the Fraternity and the publication of the primary documents around 1614 and 1615. Indeed, the documents, written by Johann Valentin Andreae and his friends sometime between 1604 and 1614 acknowledge the revolutionary impact of the preceding century and a half.

First, there was the visit of the initiate George Gemistos, known as Plethon, to Italy for the last ecumenical council of Florence/Ferrara in 1438–1439. It was Plethon who fired Cosimo de Medici with the idea of a lineage of ancient theologians reaching back into primordial times. Cosimo "conceived in his noble mind a kind of Academy" and, about 1450, asked the son of his favorite doctor to organize it and start translating the texts of the ancient masters that Plethon had provided. Thus the Platonic Academy of Florence came into being, and Marsilio Ficino began his epoch-making translations, including those of Plato, Plotinus, Iamblichus, Porphyry, Proclus, the *Corpus Hermeticum,* and the Chaldean Oracles. But Plethon's influence outran even this. Besides Cosimo, Plethon met and equally inspired Leon Battista Alberti and Nicholas of Cusa whose association in the "other" Academy, that of Palestrina, was to have far-reaching effects.

It was Plethon who, while Christian Rosenkreutz was laying down the foundations of the Fraternity of the Rose Cross, publicly introduced the project of the Christianization of ancient wisdom. To what extent Plethon himself believed in the project, or whether he would have preferred a return of the most ancient solar cosmic religion, must remain a moot point. Some, like Jean Robin, have attributed to his offspring a sinister stream of counter-, or at least counter-Christian, initiation. Plethon's influence was enormous. He did much more than inspire Ficino's translations and Cusa's philosophy. It was he who brought the symbol of "fire" to the center of the tradition and pushed the idea of ecumenicism to the bounds of heresy, upholding the universality of all forms. His position was, to adapt a current slogan, "to think religion globally and embody it locally"—as good an explanation as one can find of the Fraternity's second rule. As for fire, drawing on the Chaldean Oracles and what he knew of Zoroastrianism and the Persian theosophers of light (of whom, Corbin proposes, he was a student), Plethon considered fire to be the all-luminous substance, the pure luminescence or Spirit, the nature and source of all created things. All things were filled with tongues of Sophianic flame, descended from a single fire. Fire was the quintessence and as such the medium of magic and of alchemy.

The consequences of this initiation (or counter-initiation) were far-reaching. Most important was the influence on Paracelsus of the ancient Gnostic and Platonic texts translated by Ficino (to which we must add Pico della Mirandola's initiating of Christian Kabbala, then carried on by Trithemius and Johannes Reuchlin). These provided the great precursor with a vocabulary of ideas he could oppose, transform, and play with in an individual, prophetic manner—but only with a vocabulary. Although the consequences of the Florentine and Roman Academies were great, and formed modern esotericism as we know it, their efforts were contingent, not essential. Even though Paracelsus used many of the Platonic, Gnostic, Kabbalistic, and Hermetic ideas flowing forth from the Academies, he was, like Luther, and the Fraternity of the Rose Cross itself, more a radical and innovative continuer of the medieval traditions we have been following than a "Renaissance Magus."

I realize that to say this is controversial. Nevertheless, the three primary documents of the Rose Cross are unarguably Christian in essence and are founded in Luther's return to the fundamental fact of the Incarnation, the Cross. Because of this, the central device of the Rose Cross is *Ex deo nascimur, in Jesu morimur, per Spiritum Sanctum reviviscimus*: From God we are born, in Jesus we die, through the Holy Spirit we are reborn. *Jesus mihi omnia*, "Jesus is all to me," they repeat. Behind the affirmation of the universal necessity of death and resurrection lies Luther's radical understanding that everything must be viewed in the light of, and pass through, the life-giving crucible of the

Cross. The experience of the Cross must everywhere be interiorized. The process of interiorization led Luther to his existential and epistemological breakthrough. Interiorizing the Cross, Luther realized that the meaning of God—God's justice, goodness, wrath, etc.—was to be understood nowhere else than in himself, in his own experience, his own heart. The meaning of God is what God works in us.

Luther was the first to take as his emblem the Rose and the Cross: a large five-petalled white rose, enclosed within the blue circle of the world which is bounded by gold, at whose center lies a heart, wherein sits a black cross.

> The first thing expressed in my seal is a cross, black, within the heart, to put me in mind that faith in Christ crucified saves us. "For with the heart man believeth unto righteousness." Now, although the cross is black, mortified, and intended to cause pain, yet it does not change the color of the heart, does not destroy nature, i.e., does not kill, but keeps alive.

The rose is white, writes Luther, because white is the color of all angels and blessed spirits. The fact that it is so, and not red, the color of incarnation or embodiment, and single, not sevenfold, shows that Luther was more a mystic than a hermetic sacred scientist. Yet Luther appreciated the hermetic science—not only for its many uses "but also for the sake of the allegory and secret signification … touching the resurrection of the dead at the Last Day." He understood that alchemy, too, in the final analysis, depended upon the Cross—Christ crucified—and that, in the Lutheran Khunrath's words, "The whole cosmos was a work of Supernal Alchemy, performed in the crucible of God," where the fundamental fact of existence, the "crucified God," becomes the key to the nature of God, humanity, and the cosmos.

For this tradition, the meaning of history, evolution, nature, resurrection—is to be sought in the Cross. Since Christ's Incarnation, this Cross—making possible the reality of resurrection—is everywhere, in the substance of things. It is the root fact of existence, closer to human beings than their jugular veins. One can easily understand why this reality makes a mockery of institutions or speculative philosophies that seek to "mediate" between the central fact of existence and human existence as such. God and nature, nature and grace, grace and gnosis, or revelation, are two sides of a single coin. Luther reaffirmed the possibility of each soul's having direct, unmediated access to God and to God's nature and processes. What had been separated before was now united in and through the Cross. To pass through the Cross, to enact it, was to participate in the new creation—the transubstantiation—that it alone made possible.

Yet Paracelsus was no friend of Luther. He felt Luther had dogmatized his revelation so that it had become a justification of privilege and election. Paracelsus took his stand on experience, against all authority, espousing the interdependence of radical religious and intellectual freedom, freedom of the will, pacifism, and the unity of humanity. He was on the side of the poor and the oppressed. Everything he did was motivated by love for the fallenness of creatures, and the goal of all his work was to hasten the great redemption or healing. Though disapproving of Luther, he shared the Reformer's insight into the Cross as the Rosetta Stone of the Great Work. But he did so while bringing to consummation and transforming the medieval traditions of vernacular spirituality we have followed. He took the practice of sticking close to experience out of the cloister, out of the hermetic order, and into the world. He sought teachers, experience, and wisdom wherever he could find them—in nature, in the mines, among peasants, herb gatherers, gypsies, in the schools of anatomy, at the feet of Kabbalists, magicians, scholars, and monks, in his father's alchemical laboratory. He took nothing on faith or on the basis of someone else's theory; he had to prove what was real by experiencing its truth in himself. He traveled, crossing and recrossing Europe and, according to legend, passing even into Turkey, Russia, and perhaps China.

In the process, Paracelsus discovered the truth of the Cross and the Rose in nature and in himself. As he studied the ancient authorities, though he found much that was of value in them, he found them deficient, because he realized that the world had changed since they had had their experiences. The world after the Incarnation was not the same as it was before. The world was a growing, changing organism. It was ever in the process of becoming more perfect. For the sake of this perfection, it had been turned inside out from its center, but in such a way that there was no longer any outside. Through the Incarnation, the Godhead, the Holy Trinity, had entered the world—or at least the *Mysterium Magnum*, "the one mother of all things," what Hildegard called *Sapientia* or *Sophia*—and was now in the world, actively participating in its drama, seeking its own redemption in the microcosm/macrocosm. Consider the magnificent opening of Hortulanus's prayer that begins his famous *Commentary on the Emerald Tablet:* "Laude, honor, power, and glory, be given to thee, O Almighty Lord God, with thy beloved son, our Lord Jesus Christ, and the Holy Ghost, the Comforter. *O holy Trinity, that art the only one God, perfect man,* I give thee thanks."

Here is why so much of Paracelsus's effort went into combating simple-minded reliance on the ancient doctrine of the elements. These four elements, like the diseases preying on humanity and nature, have been utterly transformed by the immanence in humanity and nature, microcosm and macrocosm alike, of the three principles he names Sulfur, Mercury, and Sal. These always represent in some degree the Trinity—*Ex deo nascimur, in Christo morimur, per Spiritum Sanctum reviviscimus*—but a Trinity that is now in the world, the principle of all.

Paracelsus's great accomplishment—for which he was forever invoked as the great precursor—was to unite the mystical and the alchemical, the religious and the cosmological, in a life completely given over to service of humanity and the world. What the medieval mystics saw as the promise of the mystical union of the three hearts—their own, that of Mary-Jesus, and that of Christ—Paracelsus realized more practically as the union of the human with nature and the divine. The image of the alchemist or Rosicrucian as a universal lay priest celebrating a healing Mass in which not just bread and wine were transformed, but nature and human nature in its entirety, derives from Paracelsus. It was he who fully respiritualized alchemy into a cosmic liturgy, a universal path of healing and worship in the largest sense. Paracelsus was the type of the new priest who realizes in himself—by means of the star in him, the Imagination—the identity of macrocosm and microcosm. On the basis of such knowledge—by identity or experience—the new priest understands the world from within as a complex field of signatures, seminal images, and analogies, and acts in it, healing and transforming it.

Paracelsus died in 1541, but not before prophesying the return of Elijah, *Elias Artista,* who would inaugurate an age of *renovatio,* "at which time there shall be nothing so occult that it shall not be revealed." As Christ had said, "There is nothing covered that shall not be revealed; and hid, that shall not be known" (Matt. 10:26). So far, God had allowed only the lesser to appear. The greater part still remained hidden, but, as Paracelsus prophesied, all would emerge with Elias who would usher in a new "golden age." "Humanity will arrive at true intellect, and live in human fashion, not in the way of beasts, the manner of pigs, nor in a den"—after the defeat of the Antichrist. In the course of the next half-century, this and other prophecies echoed, amplified, and resounded against the turbulence of social, religious, and political unrest. And not only prophecies—for it seemed on the basis of the new discoveries, imperial voyages of exploration, and the magical universes being opened up, that the new age had to be near. Dee had published the *Monas Hieroglyphas* (whose symbol adorns *The Chemical Wedding*) in 1564. "Cosmopolitans" like Alexander Seton and Michael Sendivogius began to circulate through Europe, producing wonders and disappearing. Lutherans like Libavius and Khunrath strove to usher in the new epoch. Some, like Simon Studion, announced it.

With hindsight, the Rosicrucian call comes as no surprise. In a sense, it is self-explanatory. The texts, in their emphases and their polemics, make the Lutheran origin of the documents very clear. Frances Yates has demonstrated the political ends to which the General Reformation was intended. What then is the mystery? It has to do with the distinction, contained in the documents themselves, between "Rosicrucian" and "Rose Cross." Rosicrucians are those who wish to usher in a new epoch of sacred science, art, and religion, and work for cultural transformation. Those who bear the "Rose Cross"—whose "seal, mark, and character" it is—have united inner and outer, spirit and matter, divine and created worlds, and bear that union and intimate congress of Heaven and Earth in their hearts. They move about in the world as servants of the Word, invisibly serving, healing, and creating for God's greater glory and the salvation of all creatures. They are something else. Only if you know them will you recognize them. Who is to say whether St. Vincent de Paul or St. Francis de Sales or

Berulle of the Oratory or St. John Eudes—all contemporaries of the Rosicrucian Enlightenment—are not true Rosicrucians, as Jean Robin has suggested? Who is to say? The legend is that following the Treaty of Westphalia in 1648—which marked the end of the Thirty Years' War—the true Rose Cross left Europe for the East. Yet the practice of the Rose in the Cross and the affiliation to the Invisible Temple or New Jerusalem continued. It continues still. We still await the out-pouring of spiritual intelligence that Joachim of Fiore foresaw.

10

The Love that Moves the Stars: Friendship and Walking

"*H*ow many pairs of shoes did Dante wear out writing the *Divine Comedy?*" asked the Russian poet Osip Mandelstam. For Mandelstam, poetry and walking were so closely connected that he could not imagine Dante composing his great work other than on foot, walking the streets of Florence and the Italian towns and countryside of his exile—Bologna, San Gemignano, Treviso, Padua, Lucca.

Mandelstam himself, like many poets and artists, knew that he had to move whenever he felt a poem or piece of prose "coming down." The experience would begin with a musical phrase, ringing insistently in his ear. At first, he would try to escape it, tossing his head, as though the phrase could be shaken out of his ear like a drop of water. Then, in a heightened state of excitement and anticipation, he would begin to move. He would start to walk, first inside his apartment, and then out into the streets, bending slightly forward, straining to catch this music from another source and translate it into words. Sometimes he would walk for twenty-four hours or more, crisscrossing Saint Petersburg, stopping rapt in thought when the occasion demanded, until the inner voice—the daimon—ceased.

What is walking? Rebecca Solnit, in her book *Wanderlust, A History of Walking,* says walking

> is the intentional act closest to the unwilled rhythms of the body, to breathing and the beating of the heart. It strikes a delicate balance between working and idling, being and doing. It is a bodily labor that produces nothing but thoughts, experiences, arrivals. The rhythm

of walking generates a kind of rhythm of thinking, and the passage through a landscape echoes or stimulates the passage through a series of thoughts.

No one knew it better than the greatest philosopher of walking, Henry David Thoreau, who, lamenting the loss of the art of walking in his day, wrote in his inimitable way:

> I have met but with one or two persons in the course of my life who understood the art of Walking, that is, of taking walks,—who had a genius so to speak for *sauntering;* which word is beautifully derived "from idle people who roved about the country in the Middle Ages, and asked for charity, under the pretence of going *à la Sainte Terre,*" to the Holy Land, till the children exclaimed, "There goes a Sainte-Terrer"—a Saunterer—a Holy-Lander. They who never go to the Holy Land in their walks, as they pretend, are indeed mere idlers and vagabonds; but they who do go there are saunterers, in the good sense, such as I mean. Some, however, would derive the word from *sans terre,* without land or home, which, therefore, in the good sense, will mean, having no particular home, but equally at home everywhere. ("Walking")

To walk is to move one's body, soul, and spirit rhythmically and harmoniously through the world, all one's senses engaged in its variety, its beauty, truth, and goodness. The walker, in the high sense Thoreau alludes to, is in the world but not of it. Like the Son of Man with nowhere to lay his head, the true walker wanders forever toward the Holy Land, sending, as the alchemist Morienus puts it, "large amounts of gold to Jerusalem every year." One can do this alone, in solitude, or better together with others, either with a best friend or in a group. One never really walks alone. In either case, walking initiates one into a quasi-esoteric order—the order of friends, for walking and friendship go together. A friend is the one with whom we walk the path. As Thoreau writes, "My companion and I, for sometimes I have a companion, take pleasure in fancying ourselves knights of a new, or rather an old, order—not equestrians or Chevaliers, not Ritters or riders, but Walkers, a still more ancient and honorable class I trust."

Walking does not sound very esoteric. Yet walking alone or with a friend, as Dante and Ficino did, is a hidden key to their spiritual lives. Imagine two or three friends gathered together to stroll through a garden, a city street, or the countryside. The conversation is warm and animated and bears upon what is of the highest importance to them—how they might embody the highest teaching and the highest reality in their everyday lives and selves and contribute to the creation of a new culture. They dream of a social and religious transformation that might affect everyone. Now and then they pause to discuss a most critical point. Standing in a grove of trees, beside a statue, or before a particularly inviting shopwindow, the talk becomes heated. Then they fall into silence and begin to walk once more, united in contemplation of the reality to which they aspire.

If walking suggests something more akin to "prayer," this is not unjustified. Prayer moves toward God, "the One Who Is"—who is Eternity, present now and always, a reality wholly accessible to us as whole human beings of body, soul, and spirit. "An unchanging unity," Ficino calls it; "a single stillness." Traditionally, it is said that the way to realize this is a path of knowledge and of love—Intellect and Will. Aquinas tells us that "our intellect is extended to infinity," also that "love resides in the will" and that "the movements of the free will are not successive [in time] but instantaneous." Walking and friendship (or love) invoke the will, while conversation (or thinking) bespeaks the intellect. Rama Coomaraswamy tells the story of a blind man and a lame man set out for "the Holy City." They could make no progress until they joined forces, the lame man climbing on the back of the blind one and directing his footsteps. Something of this kind is involved in walking and friendship, and in the conversation and thinking—the presence of the Holy Spirit, in Christian terms— which they engender.

Indissolubly linked with the concepts of thinking in the highest sense and with friendship, walking has always been central to the Western tradition—and to all traditions, since vertical bipedalism is a distinguishing feature of our shared humanity. In Japanese, for instance, the word for *walk* is the same word used for Buddhist practice. The practitioner is the walker, the path the walk walked. Everywhere walking is the principle metaphor of the spiritual journey.

Nevertheless, in the West, walking has always had a special significance. Walking, friendship, and insight are by no means closely linked only in Dante and Ficino, who with their friends—in the immense holding capacity of friendship "to draw boundaries and cross bridges"—created so much that changed the world. All the great turning-point moments in the Western tradition were gestated in a social womb marked by deep friendship and much walking.

The great Western thinkers have been great walkers. And the more spiritual they were, the greater their capacity was for friendship.

Hegel walked the *Philosophenweg* (the Philosopher's Way) named after him in Heidelberg, and Kant as an old man still shuffled down the *Philosophen-damm* (the Philosopher's Wall) in Königsberg. Kierkegaard endlessly paced and recorded his pacings through the streets of Copenhagen. Schwaller de Lubicz and Julien Champagne (the most likely candidate for Fulcanelli, the "master alchemist") walked up and down the Philosopher's Alley, a natural cathedral of plane trees outside Schwaller's home in Plan de Grasse, France, discussing alchemy in ways that would change the twentieth-century understanding of it. Goethe, frequently mentioned in those conversations, dictated all his works on the hoof, walking back and forth in his garden. He walked alone, his secretary a few paces behind him. Centuries before, the Troubadours, nomadic, sauntering composers, walked (or rode) through Provence, creating the first civilization based upon love. Dante walked with Guido Cavalcanti and the other poets of the *dolce stil nuovo;* Ficino walked with his friends, who made up the Academy. Closer to our own time, the Wordsworths and Coleridge walked in the Lake District—and English Romanticism was born. Meanwhile, in London, "little" John Keats had his greatest insights— "negative capability," for instance—walking with his friend Dilke. In America, Emerson, Thoreau, Bronson Alcott, Margaret Fuller, Melville, Hawthorne, and Whitman all walked, many of them together, to create Transcendentalism. Rousseau, another great walker, when writing his *Reveries of a Solitary Walker,* would leave his cottage at dawn and return at nightfall, having walked all day, to write out a complete meditation, never needing to alter a word. Much of twentieth-century physics, too, emerged in the ambulatory conversations of such as Nils Bohr and Werner Heisenberg (who wrote that physics was made in the conversations—read friendships—of physicists). Leon Rosenfeld tells of a visit with Bohr: "He began to walk around ... all the time explaining in a low voice his thoughts on 'complementarity.' He walked with bent head and knit brows; from time to time, he looked up at me and underlined some important point by a sober gesture.... It was one of the few solemn moments that count in an existence, *the revelation of a world of dazzling thought.*" Rousseau put it most succinctly: "I can only meditate when I am walking. When I stop I cease to think."

Rousseau, as always, was perhaps too extreme. Stopping, in fact, is as inherent to walking as absence is to friendship. Think of barefoot Socrates, fountainhead of Ficino's beloved Platonic tradition, cruising Athens and the quiet, sacred spots around it, in search of knowledge to be imparted and gained through conversation. From time to time he too, like Mandelstam, would be halted in his tracks by direct congress with the gods. Then he would stand, riveted to the ground, for hours on end, and those with him would simply have to wait. As Apollodorus puts it in the *Symposium,* "It's quite a habit of his, you know; off he goes and there he stands no matter where it is."

In this practice of walking, Socrates was following a pattern well established by his rivals, the Sophists, who were famous wanderers and roving lecturers. Plato, likewise, walked and talked with his Academy, stopping now and then, like Jesus, another famous teacher five hundred years later, to elicit geometric insights by drawing figures in the dirt. After Plato, Aristotle, when he set up his school, created a special colonnade or covered walk, called a *peripatos,* which gave the school its name: the Peripatetic (or walking) School. The *Peripatos* led to the temple of Apollo, or connected the temple with the shrine of the Muses. Here Aristotle lectured and walked about conversing with his students. When he was absent they met there to talk and meditate, just as Christian monks would do later in their *peripatos,* called "cloisters."

Jesus himself was a great—perhaps the greatest—walker, moving constantly from one place to the next with his disciples and the women closest to him. He would teach (talk) as he walked, conversing on the dusty road with those about him, stopping whenever a crowd gathered and addressing them before moving on again. He, too, often felt the need to stop and be alone. Then he would withdraw to pray.

Sometimes he did this alone; sometimes he would ask those around him to pray with him. When seen in this light, Jesus provides the hidden paradigm for Dante, Ficino, and the other masters of the Western tradition, for the essential metaphor of his teaching united walking in the deepest sense with friendship. Friendship—with one another and with God—is his central and final message to his disciples. "This is my commandment, That ye love one another as I have loved you. Greater love hath no man than this, that a man lay down his life for his friends. Ye are my friends, if ye do whatsoever I command you. Henceforth I call you not servants; for the servant knoweth not what his lord doeth: but I have called you friends."

Like walking—closely related as two sides of a single reality—*friendship* is another forgotten aspect of our spiritual lives: "the one silent space that remains open in our examined lives," as Ivan Illich put it. We have only the faintest memory left of what it was in earlier times. Scholars see the great divide as falling sometime between the fourteenth and the sixteenth centuries. After the turning point, it was thought individuals could be redeemed—or enlightened, or reach Heaven—*on their own;* and that once there (in Heaven or with God) they would remain on their own. Heaven became a place of great "solitude," a "desert"—essentially meaningless and empty. Before that time, in the classical world and throughout the Middle Ages, friendship and salvation were essentially interdependent, Heaven was densely populated, and everyone lived with the imagination of the "communion of saints." This loss is a great pity, because, as Ficino well knew, friendship is the engine of change, both its midwife and sustainer. Interestingly, the Nazis recognized this and therefore made sure that their SS units were frequently reconfigured—every three weeks or so. They recognized that friendship was one of the hardest things for those in power to control and that in a context of friendship people think different and new thoughts and dare to act upon them. Yet friendship has been virtually forgotten—or is rarely considered to be essential to our human and spiritual lives.

To begin to understand something of the subtlety, density, and depth with which the Florentines experienced friendship and its place in human life and human seeking, it will be helpful to look briefly at the forgotten tradition of friendship in the West. Friendship or "friendship-love"—for friendship is an aspect or modality of love—is, in Greek, *philia,* in Latin: *amicitia.* It is one of four Greek words for love. *Eros,* which was experienced as an influx, meant to direct one's whole feeling toward an object, person, or ideal; to surrender oneself to it; to unite with it; to feel and perceive for it. *Philia,* for its part, connoted, as Pavel Florensky, the great Russian Orthodox polymath, puts it, "an inner inclination toward a person induced by intimacy, closeness, common feeling." It is a natural, organic, tender, inward expression of love based on personal contact. It is person to person and implies closeness and deep soul insight. With the addition *toi stomati,* with the lips, it means, "to kiss." From this we can see why D. W. Winnicott has called friendship "the matrix of transference," while James Grotstein names it "the quintessence of shared experience ... deeper than love." Drawing on the same psychoanalytic tradition, Robert French, an organizational theorist, defines friendship as a capacity—the capacity to put aspects of the self into the other and to receive them; above all, the capacity to hold or contain. It is a vessel. For the Greeks, it also includes an element of satisfaction, for it is associated with the loved person, by an intimacy and a unity in many things. Ancient lexicographers defined *philein* as "being satisfied with something, desiring nothing more." Thirdly, for the Greeks, there was also *storge/stergein,* which was not a passionate or striving love, but "a calm and permanent feeling in the depths of the loving one." This is the love that a mother bears for her children, a husband his wife, or one has for one's country. *Agape,* lastly, was "rational (or conscious) love." It is what became Christian love or *caritas.* Difficult to define, it originally meant "a love in which one has joy or even amazement."

All these loves, though distinguishable, are obviously not divisible. Human perfection, the highest love that human beings can strive to embody, must contain all in a perfect harmony and balance, as indeed does God also, who creates, sustains, regulates, and draws all toward him by love—by yearning, friendship, mother love, and sacrificial love. It is difficult to say which is the class and which are the types. Nevertheless, for a time in the West, for those on the spiritual path, friendship became if not the highest, then the ground or *sine qua non* of the highest form of love—love of God, and love of God in every human being.

The ancient, classical texts they drew on—which they had to transform, digest, and turn into the flesh and blood of their own living relationships—were primarily Aristotle's two chapters on friendship in the *Nicomachean Ethics* and Cicero's *De Amacitia* (On Friendship). Aristotle laid the ground. He said there were three kinds of friendship, depending upon whether they were based on pleasure, utility, or goodness and virtue. The first two were transient, the latter enduring. "The perfect form of friendship is between those who are alike in virtue or excellence. For these friends wish alike for one another's good because they are good and because they seek the good. Those who wish for their friend's good for their friend's sake are friends in the truest sense, since their attitude is determined by what their friends are…. Hence their friendship will last a long time." Concealed within the definition lies the understanding that such friendships are really the condition of virtue. Since the good is something we go toward, we go toward it together, and our going toward it together, our relationship, is the vessel through which, going toward the good, we become good. The practice of virtue is relational. Friendship is the basic glue of community and even of government. Aristotle is pragmatic. He deals with the practicalities of friendship—betrayal, absence, and so on. He understands its ground in the one-to-one relationship of human beings, but sees nothing of a supernatural divine gift. For him, friendship is completely natural. There is nothing divine about it.

Cicero resumes much of Aristotle, but translates it into Latin, so that it becomes the basic text through which the monastic writers of the Middle Ages thought about friendship. For Cicero, friendship is the most important and attractive human bond, one that is good in itself. Friendship means living together and sharing everything. From such close friends, true "society" emerges. Though completely natural, such society has something divine in it. Friendship is the immanence of divinity's love among human beings. There is something delightful, sweet, and gentle about it—a human capacity that is also heavenly and available to all (not just to outstanding beings, as Montaigne was later to think). Cicero, finally, importantly connects friendship with *trust*, which he says is the foundation of true friendship.

After Aristotle and Cicero, the next milestone familiar to Ficino would have been Augustine. Throughout his life, Augustine wrestled with the concept of friendship. The paradox was that, though he sought only to find rest in God, he found he could not live without friends. He acknowledged that what he felt for his friends was love. "How well [Horace] put it when he called his friend the half of his soul," he wrote after a friend had died. "I felt that our two bodies had become as one, living in two bodies." He realized that to be eternal and not just transitory, such love must rest in the love of God, for only it makes other loves possible and enduring. This is Aristotle's unity of friends in pursuit of the good. But it is also something more: "He truly loves a friend who loves God in the friend, either because God is in him or so that God may be in him." This provides Augustine with his fundamental "law" of friendship. We desire to have friends, he writes, "so that together in harmony we can look into our souls and at God. And then it happens easily that the one who is the first to find truths brings them to the others without difficulty." These ideas will reemerge transformed in Ficino.

Augustine was not alone in writing about friendship. Many early Church Fathers such as Paulinus, Cassian, Benedict, and Gregory the Great developed further aspects. It was Gregory who coined the famous phrase that a friend is "the guardian of one's soul or spirit" (*custos animi*). Friendship was extolled as harmony, possibility, consolation, and the mother of the virtues. Aelred of Rievaux, in the twelfth century, sums it up in his little treatise *On Spiritual Friendship*:

> I think the word *amicus* [friend] comes from the word *amor* [love] and *amacitia* [friendship] from *amicus*. For love is a certain "affection" of the heart, whereby it seeks and eagerly strives after some object to possess it and enjoy it. Having attained its object through love, it enjoys it with a certain interior sweetness, embraces it, and preserves it....
>
> A friend is called a guardian of love or, as some would have it, a guardian of the spirit itself. Since it is fitting that my friend be a guardian of our mutual love or the guardian of my own spirit so as to preserve all its secrets in faithful silence, let him, as far as he can, cure and endure such defects as he may observe in it; let him rejoice with his friend in his joys, and weep with him in his sorrows, and feel as his own all that his friend experiences.

Friendship, therefore, is that sweet virtue by which spirits are bound by ties of love and sweetness, and out of many are made one. Even the philosophers of this world have ranked friendship with the things that are eternal. And Solomon agrees with them when he says, "He that is a friend loves at all times." Thereby, he manifestly declares that friendship is eternal if it is true friendship. If it ever should cease to be, then it was not true friendship.... Only those do we call friends to whom we can fearlessly entrust our heart and all its secrets; only those who, in their turn, are bound to us by the same law of trust and security.

Underlying the philosophy of friendship was the central reality, forcibly expressed by Aquinas, that *all* friendship rests in and depends upon *friendship with God,* an idea not thinkable by Aristotle. What God shares with us, we share with our friends. Such friendship, for Aquinas, as for Ficino, is true happiness. It is important to remember, as the great Renaissance scholar Paul Oskar Kristeller pointed out, that Ficino, while laboring to unite Platonism and the ancient tradition of pagan theology with Christianity, did so as a *Tuscan* and against the background of a deep devotion to Aristotle, Augustine, and Aquinas. We must never forget that Ficino was a patriotic Florentine who assiduously read the old Tuscan poets, to whose "conscious cult of love and friendship," in Kristeller's words, he gave great clarity and depth, and who translated Dante's *De Monarchia* into Italian.

Ficino is one of the great philosophers of friendship in the West and one of the great friends in the Western tradition. Just as Dante had *his* Cavalcanti—Guido—so Ficino had his unique friend, Giovanni Cavalcanti, with whom he was "united in divine love," as he was with Amerigo Corsini, Bernardo Bembi, and many others. The Platonic Academy in Careggi, at its heart and in its essence, was a community of friends who were united in love and in passionate pursuit of the One. We know a lot about the Academy now, thanks to many scholars, seekers, and researchers. Yet, despite the plethora of information we have about it, when we try to put it together, the resulting attempt seems fragmentary and full of contradictions. We have bits and pieces, but the whole, the essence, the guiding spirit, escapes us. Luckily, however, Ficino was a great letter writer—and, thanks to

Clem Salamon's fine work with his colleagues at the London School of Economics, we have *The Letters* in English.

    The Letters provide a guide to the heart of Ficino's world and his philosophy of friendship. All the letters are implicitly about friendship. They are about practical human friendships because Marsilio is a deep soul, melancholic and in touch with his feeling, and his letters are personal, passionate expressions of love; but they are also about friendship in a larger sense. As we read them, it becomes clear that friendship is the real glue that holds the universe together, not just the human universe, but the world of nature and the world of the stars. The friendship-love that we feel for each other draws us together in a commonality, a community. It does so by drawing us toward wisdom, where we discover ourselves in each other and in God. Thereby it draws us toward beauty, truth, and goodness, and into multiple relationships with these and other spiritual values and beings. Finally, friendship also moves nature and the stars. Proclus in his *On the Hieratic Art of the Egyptians* claimed that everything "prays"—everything in nature is united to its higher being and ultimately to God by the sympathetic magic that is prayer. He took the example of the heliotrope, which turns to follow the course of the Sun. He could have taken the Sun itself and the stars that walk the heavens. They, too, moving in their rounds, pray to the leaders of their choir.

    Instead of prayer, Proclus could have said friendship, as Plato did in the *Gorgias* when he wrote:

> Wise men, Callicles, say that the heavens and the earth, gods and man, are bound together by fellowship and friendship, and order and temperance and justice, and for this reason they call the sum of things the "ordered" universe, my friend, and not the world of disorder or riot. But it seems to me that you pay no attention to these things in spite of your wisdom.

Friendship binds the world together because all things are friends with each other and with God, the One. The natural magic of the universe sustains it in its unity.

    At first, much in Ficino's letters sounds familiar. The topic is introduced gradually. The first mention is in a letter to a fellow philosopher,

Gregorio Epifanio. Marsilio has just been given the Villa Careggi and seeks to retire there for a while into what he calls the "one unmoving watchtower of the mind." There, he hopes, "the unseen light" will shine on him unceasingly. Then he adds, "You have heard the proverb: 'For the good man, without his friend, joy in possession soon will end.' I know of no companion it would give me more joy to have with me than you." Even solitude is enhanced by the presence of a friend.

Marsilio's special, "unique" friend is Giovanni Cavalcanti, whom he had known and loved from the time when Giovanni was only seven years old. Giovanni is the one, best friend, "the other self, who does not fail," who stays faithful and never deceives. He is a doctor, as all friends are, and friendship is perfect medicine. Marsilio calls him "hero," since "in Plato's view, heroes are born from love of the gods … [and] philosophers are reborn from the love of heroes."

Though serious, and full of love, the relationship, as Ficino speaks of it, is light, and teasing. He often misses Giovanni and wonders whether he should call him back—but that might induce him to stay away! Perhaps he should give some news. Everyone in Florence is talking about Marsilio. They are asking why he is alone. Then he confesses he shouldn't be saying these things. "I do not require you to write, but to speak of them. If we speak together, my hero, we speak about the same things; if we write, we write about different things."

Giovanni, as friends often do, sometimes fails to write. Marsilio misses him. Has Giovanni forgotten him? With this question, Marsilio becomes playfully serious, invoking the doctrine of the friend as a second self; of friendship as involving the union and interpenetration of two souls wherein each becomes transparent to the other. "My friend," he writes, "has not forgotten me because he has not forgotten himself. Look, he has already granted my prayer. Here he comes. Yes, he comes! Run to meet him, lucky feet. Embrace him, fortunate arms." Such friendship, though not sexual, is a form of love.

In another letter, Marsilio, having complained of not receiving letters, feels Giovanni is now writing only because he promised to write. This is not right. Marsilio wants letters of love, not barter—for they are friends by love, not contract. The teasing and teaching go on. These are important letters because they convey the living reality of friendship. Marsilio writes to Lorenzo de Medici: "Get angry if you like, jealous man; provided you are passionate. The fire of anger and the fire of love are alike; for when I become angry with you, which I often do, then I burn with the fire of love."

We must remember that Ficino addressed his letters not just to their recipients, but also to posterity. The volumes of *The Letters* are not only profound teaching, but also a finely crafted, completely conscious work of art. Before speaking of the philosophy of friendship and love, Marsilio wants us to taste its reality and understand that the love of friends does not concern only spiritual things (philosophy, music, and religion) but life's reality. It is the *practice* of the union of souls in a higher reality, of the shared life in which everything is in common. "For nothing can be called personal where there is one common soul" is how he puts it.

How does one get there? "I have often looked for myself, Giovanni," he writes. Marsilio has looked in the mirror, gazed at his own face; he has touched his hands to his chest, his body. But that is not who he is. Who is he who does the seeking and whom is he seeking? Surely, he writes, he is seeking spirit alone, because he is spirit. Yet, when he has withdrawn in meditation, the spirit self has eluded him. He found neither rest nor peace. With Giovanni, with other human beings, he can look for himself in the other and find himself at the same time in himself. Friendship enables him to become himself, to enter the infinite realm of soul-spiritual sympathies and affinities. Friendship allows the many to become one, while remaining many and individual, to find themselves as individual unities within the unity that is the whole—individual rays within the one ray that is truth, splendor, beauty, goodness, love.

Many topics are discussed—indicating the profound metaphysical conversations at the Academy—but the chief topic is love, the right end of which, for Ficino, is union. The unity is akin to what Christian tradition calls the "mystical body." It is a metaphysical unity by which, becoming one with God, we become one with each other and vice versa. Becoming one with each other, we become one with One. In our unity, the One indwells us. Such "becoming one" is love, and love makes us human and divine—makes us whole, impels us to union, and unites us with our friends and ultimately with God—union and love being one and being the presence of the divine in and among us.

True friendship is founded in the search for God, however we may name that reality. As Ficino says, "The Platonic philosophers defined true friendship as the permanent union of the lives of two people. But I think that life is one only for those who work toward one end, as it were walking the same path toward a common goal. I believe their fellowship will be permanent only when the aim that they have set themselves as a common duty is not only single, but also permanent and sure." This goal, he says, must rest in the acquisition and exercise of a "single and permanent virtue of the soul." The virtue is wisdom, the understanding of the divine, which illumines us by grace, if only we cultivate our souls for its reception. If we do, God "reveals himself, delighting us by that revelation." "Therefore," he concludes, "God is for us the way, the truth and the life; the way because by his rays he turns us, leads us to him, and gathers us up; the truth, because when we have turned to him, he reveals himself to us; and lastly the life, since by that blessed vision he constantly nourishes and gives joy to our soul."

Such, for Ficino, is the way of friendship: "the supreme harmony of two souls in the cultivation of God." God, the One, is the third in every relationship. Friendship is union. Union is unity and there cannot be unity without one. What, he asks, "is that *one* to which two, aspiring with one accord, become friends, and are known as friends?" This "one" is not opinions; we argue about those; nor desires, for we fight about them. Perhaps it is some "infinite good" that we desire; but, writes Ficino, that doesn't really work, for, as he says, "By some natural instinct all of us desire good of this kind.... Yet we do not all love one another." What we desire cannot be good in general, but must be the good that is all Good—that is God. This is "the One without whose warmth nobody can love anything, without whose splendor nothing can be loved." "Without the friendship of that One, the more friendly things seems to be, the more harmful they are," he writes to Lotterio Neroni, adding, "O how wonderful is the bond of goodness, of beauty, and of love! For where the goodness of things shines, the beauty of the beautiful sheds its splendor, and there too the love of loves is aflame." To Girolamo Amazzi he writes: "Divine love, kindled by the flames of the virtues and growing stronger from celestial rays, seeks to return to the sublime heights of heaven.... Of such a kind is our mutual love, Amazzi."

As for our relationship to God, we can either desire to receive or to give. The wish to receive is common to all; but the desire to give—to return all that we have been given—is the path of the true friend.

> Most akin to the divine mind are minds that are dedicated to God before all else. And so, such minds are straightway drawn by ardor and sweetness of love beyond telling, toward both God and each other, as they first freely give themselves back to Him, as to a father, and then give themselves up in utter joy to each other, as to brothers. All other so-called friendships are nothing but acts of plunder. True charity, as the Apostle Paul says, "seeketh not its own" but the benefit of another.

Here Ficino is writing a general letter to "his fellow philosophers, especially Ermolao Barbaro," a distinguished Venetian humanist and diplomat. It is a powerful letter. Ficino makes it clear that true friendship-love loves the divine in other human beings and in all things. Loving the divine in others, he loves it in himself. He sees some as closer to the divine, more ardent lovers, than others. He chooses these for his friends. Thus Ficino concludes: "With these he leads a heavenly life on earth and in heaven a life that is beyond the heavens. Among these alone there is true friendship, that is, true union, from one and in one God. For a true and abiding union of many cannot be accomplished except through the eternal unity itself."

Friendship—the ability to be friends with others and the world—expands from and is the fruit of a single, deep, permanent, blood brother or sister bond. This is the friend who "sticketh closer than a brother," as, in the highest sense, David did to Jonathan and St. John did to Christ, leaning on his bosom. This is why, furthermore, as Florensky says, Jesus, having chosen twelve disciples, sends them out two by two, with the gift of healing and power over devils. "As for the fact that he sends them out two by two," writes Augustine, "this is the sacrament of love, either because two is the commandment of love or because no love can exist between fewer than two." It is why Jesus says, "If two of you shall agree on earth as touching anything that they shall ask, it shall be done for them of my Father which is in heaven. For where two or three are gathered together in my name, there I am in the midst of them." Giovanni Cavalcanti was such a friend to Ficino. From such friendships, friendship-love expands to include humanity and the world in all glory.

Another such friend was Naldo Naldi, a member of the Academy and Professor of Poetry and Rhetoric at Florence University. In a letter to Naldi, Marsilio explains the progression of such friendship from grace through love to faith—and finally to friendship. He puts it thus: "Grace moves through Love, Love begets Faith, Faith embraces her father Love, and through the heat of this embrace, by Love gives birth to Friendship. Then Faith feeds this infant Friendship, allowing her to grow daily, and completely protecting her from destruction."

Why does this happen? "Because when other things grow older, they become weaker, but Friendship as it grows older grows stronger." This does not have anything to do, in principle, with anything friends do, any "outer formalities," for "Friendship is obtained by free will and not at a price." It is *the act of faith,* made firm by time, that confirms friendship, the same faith by which "Goodwill becomes at the same time most ancient and most strong." Therefore Marsilio praises faith above all else. "For the learning of anyone belongs to one only, but Faith belongs to at least two; for what you know you know for yourself, but you are faithful both to yourself and to [your friend]."

Implicit is that faith and love are acts of free will. "No necessity is more freely chosen than a loving necessity; no free choice is more necessary than the free choice of love," he writes to Giovanni. "For what is more freely willed than love, which is the first, highest, and enduring quality of will and makes us utterly unwilling not to love? What again is more necessary than love, which, unseen, directly and indelibly burns in the unguarded heart by means of rays and flames of the celestial sprits? And the lover already experiences the full-grown flame before he perceives the ray and the radiating point. He needs must burn, if he burn by heavenly decree."

He asks: "Whence comes such a wonderful blend of freedom and necessity, except from God?" God is supreme necessity and supreme freedom: in love, in friendship, these become one. For Ficino, love is the highest manifestation of will, which is the inclination, the propensity, the desire, and the appetite even, for the good. It works in consort with the second aspect of the soul, which we may call intellect. "Good things move everything under the concept of goodness." "The soul knows all things under the concept of truth and desires all things under the concept of goodness." All human willing, as Kristeller says, is essentially a will toward God. Love, on the other hand, by definition "has the enjoyment of beauty as its end." It desires beauty. But beauty is an aspect of goodness. It is the splendor of the Good. It is its grace and favor, calling us to respond. "The Glory of the Lord," the great theologian Hans Urs von Balthasar would call it. Love and will are really one, and "only love of goodness transforms the soul into God."

Friendship is such love habitually practiced together, and Ficino's Academy was such a group of friends, brought together in "divine love."

Let us return to walking. When Ficino and his friends walked, talking, or talked, walking, in the gardens of the Villa Careggi or in the gentle hills surrounding his house, which he named *Due Fontane* or Two Fountains—one in Heaven, one on Earth—they united in their unity the unity of those two fountains of Heaven and Earth. The love that moves the stars truly moved them. The stars circle above, conversing in friendly congress with each other and with the One, whose radiant, spherical effulgence they are. So, too, the true friends on Earth, Ficino's Academy, sought to embody and radiate the wisdom (truth, beauty, and goodness) of the same One—the one and only One.

There is a verse by Rudolf Steiner:

> The stars once spoke to humanity
> But it is the fate of the world
> That the stars are silent now.
> To feel that silence
> Can be painful for human beings.

> But in the deepening silence
> The word that human beings can speak to the stars
> Is ripening:
> To become aware of that Word
> Can strengthen the human spirit.

"The silence of the stars" should not, I think, be taken literally, but as the ways in which we have become "cosmic hermits," cut off from the larger whole to which we belong. To return to the whole is what we seek. It was the goal and purpose of Ficino's work. If we read him carefully, we find clues about the way home, the word that we must speak. I suggest that it is friendship and love that Ficino proposes should guide us. Friendship, in the here and now, walking the path with those about us. As friends, anything is possible.

11

The Magus of the North

We LIVE IN AN UNPOETIC AGE, an age of prose, of the calculation of naked details. Hemmed in and cut off by dead words and things of our own making, we are captives of our intelligence. In Hölderlin's phrase, we come too late. True, the gods live, but they live elsewhere, in the other world that Hegel called the world of poetry. Hegel, the philosopher of Romanticism, distinguished two spheres of consciousness, the poetic and the prosaic. For him, the ancient, pre-Socratic world was essentially poetic. It was alive; poetry was lived, rather than written. Human consciousness and nature, nature and the divine, were a seamless unity. Word and thing were one transparent, organic whole. The world was not yet opaque. It was a living world of mind, and the gods were present in all things, active participants in human affairs.

Today's world, by contrast, is prosaic. Prose has become the ruling norm of perception. In Hegel's phrase, it "has appropriated to itself everything that is of the mind, and impressed the stamp of prose upon it." For Keats:

> Deep in the shady sadness of a vale
> Far sunken from the healthy breath of morn,
> Far from the fiery noon, and eve's one star,
> Sat gray-hair'd Saturn, quiet as a stone,
> Still as the silence round about his lair;
> Forest on forest hung about his head
> Like cloud on cloud. No stir of air was there
> Not so much life as on a summer's day
> Robs not one light seed from the feather'd grass,
> But where the dead leaf fell, there it did rest.

A stream went voiceless by, still deadened more
By reason of his fallen divinity
Spreading a shade.

(*Hyperion*)

Ours is a dead world, the world of the letter, of imageless abstraction on the one hand, and naked physicality on the other. The spirit has gone to sleep. It is a silent, voiceless world. Nothing speaks anymore; nothing has much meaning. Such literalism or nominalism—Owen Barfield calls it idolatry, for it assumes that the world consists of impenetrable things, not transparent images or words—is our condition. In our need to poeticize the world, to reanimate it and make it whole, we are Romantics.

Hugo von Hofmannsthal's "Lord Chandos Letter" makes this clear. In his fictional confession, Lord Chandos explains how, when young, he had moved brilliantly from inspiration to inspiration, writing marvelous pastorals and plumbing the living structure of Latin prose. In those days of continuous intoxication, the whole of existence seemed a great unity. Spiritual and physical worlds formed no contrast. In all things he felt the presence of "Nature." Life was that presence; it was fullness, meaning, continuous revelation: "Everywhere I was at the center of it, never suspecting mere appearance. At other times I divined that all was allegory and that each creature was a key to all the others; and I felt myself to be the one capable of seizing each by the handle and unlocking as many of the others as were ready to yield." From the state of grace—or hubris—Lord Chandos fell into its opposite. He disintegrated. He lost the ability to think or speak coherently. Words crumbled in his mouth. Disconnected from their larger, connotative meanings, they became mere denotative sounds. Above all, he lost the connective tissue, the sense of relationship that bound everything together. It became increasingly difficult for him to voice an opinion on the most trivial matter. Overwhelmed by the enormity of ideas, the inability to articulate anything caused him great anguish. Without words, his world died. It became sheer surface, without inside, only exterior. What had once been a living whole fell apart. "As once, through a magnifying glass, I had seen a piece of skin on my little finger look like a field full of holes and furrows," he wrote, "so now

I perceived human beings and their actions. I no longer succeeded in comprehending them with the simplifying eye of habit. For me everything disintegrated into parts; no longer would anything allow itself to be encompassed by one idea. Single words floated around me." Congealing into eyes, these words stared at Lord Chandos, who, returning their stare, found himself plunged into a void.

In a desolate spiritual state of isolation and loneliness, Chandos lived a life of numbed detachment broken only by moments of ineffable presentness or intensity that he could not put into words. The moments, occasioned by the humblest objects, opened in him a great presence of love. Then all was filled with life and meaning—but this he could as little present in sensible words as he "could say anything precise about the inner movements of his intestines or blood." He remained silent. As he confesses, "The language in which I might be able not only to write but also to think is neither Latin, nor English, neither Italian, nor Spanish, but a language none of whose words is known to me. It is a language in which inanimate things speak to me and in which I may one day have to justify myself before an unknown judge." This language we still seek in our inability to speak from and listen with the heart, open to its deep well of meaning. We no longer hear the speech of the world; we can no longer speak it. Nature, literature, and Scripture reveal their meanings only occasionally with great difficulty, while the writing of poetry, as well as poetic philosophy and poetic fiction—the imaginative life—becomes harder. "How then shall we raise from the dead and the dead language of nature," cries J. G. Hamann, the Magus of the North, but "by pilgrimages to blessed Araby, crusades to the Orient and a restoration of its magic reconquered for us by an old woman's ruse."

The impossible task was attempted by many great souls during the second Renaissance that we call Romanticism. Poets like Blake, Keats, Goethe, Novalis, Hölderlin; philosophers like Schelling and Hegel; theosophers like Swedenborg, Oettinger, Franz von Baader; prophetic theologians like Hamann—all tried to hasten the great restoration. I have chosen Hamann as guide because he most directly and conveniently maps the terrain of "the living Word." In what follows, the exposition will seem theological. But the true subject is not theology. It is the whole domain of the Logos, the world of the informing Word, in its aspect of communication, imagination, understanding, cognition—the world of speaking and hearing, dialogue, conversation, marriage; of human experience, human nature—which, for Hamann, is revelation, witness, prophecy, and above all, poetry.

Johann Georg Hamann (1730–1788) is an extraordinary, prophetic, solitary, heroic visionary. "I work alone," he wrote, "with no one to come to my aid with his understanding, judgment, or even taste." The close friend and critic of philosophers like Jacobi, Herder, and Kant, much admired by Goethe, Schelling, Hegel, and even Kierkegaard, Hamann could—and should—have been the intellectual and spiritual father of his age (as theologian Hans Urs von Balthasar says) had his literary gifts and style been different. Henry Corbin, too, felt this way, and it is to his prescient exposition of Hamann's thought that we owe the clearest vision of his importance for any hermeneutic or encounter with the Word.

Behind Hamann (and Corbin's reading of Hamann) lies the long shadow of Luther. Luther is critical, because it is he who, at the beginning of the age of prose, of the dead word and world—the two are synonymous—first broke through to renewed, existential understanding. Luther founded his life upon two radical premises, a twofold method: the path of *Verbum solum habemus* (we have only the Word) and the light of *significatio passiva* (passive meaning) as the illuminative way to be followed on that path. For Luther, as for Hamann and Corbin, Spirit comes first. My consciousness does not constitute itself. It opens to things. Luther's obedience, his "thorough listening," is the opening of the imagination to the I AM rather than an act of the will. The philosopher-poet-theologian is called and answers. To speak is to be a responsible, transparent, witness. The human being is the listener, one who awaits the call. "Spirit can only reveal; I can only listen." The meeting of caller and called is the only reality.

Rejecting the traditional fourfold interpretation of Scripture, Luther struggled with the meaning of the Holy Word, particularly, as he tells in his autobiography, with the phrase "the justice of God," whereby "the just shall live by faith." "I hated this word, *justitia dei*," Luther writes, "which by the use and consent of all I was taught to understand philosophically in terms of that formal or active justice, with which God is just and punishes the sinners and the unrighteous.

For, however irreproachably I lived as a monk, I felt myself to be before God a sinner." Luther grew to hate the God who punished sinners, laying the weight of his wrath over and above the damnation of human sin and suffering. But God was merciful. Luther slowly began to understand the justice of God "as that by which the righteous man lives by the gift of God, namely by faith." The work of God is what God works in us, through us, by faith. What we experience of God is who he is, what can be known of him; and we only know what we experience, what opens, in our souls, when we are open, waiting. We only truly understand when we understand with our whole being. Then we are what we understand. God's goodness makes us good, his wisdom makes us wise, and his power makes us strong. His being is what gives us being. All we must do is be open and not resist. "For God wills to save us," wrote Luther, "not by our own righteousness and wisdom, but from without, not one which comes and is born within ourselves, but which comes to us from without, not growing in our own soil, but which comes from heaven." In other words, "Human beings can receive nothing unless it be given them from heaven." All is given. Experience is revelation.

Luther's experience of the Word's capacity to transform his consciousness and values is paradigmatic. He realized that the Word of God is not general communication—an objectified recitation of events that once occurred in the past—but a living truth. This truth confronts an individual human being in his present particularity. It is a word uttered for and through him or her alone. For all traditions of the Book, the need to understand is a matter of life and death. This Book is the rule of life. Everything hangs on understanding it. To understand it is to live, not to understand it is to die. Understanding it is thus the key to all life. But herein lies a paradox. Our whole being depends upon understanding, but our understanding depends upon our being. We see, we hear, only as we are able. "When the Word of God Messiah is read," writes Swedenborg, "it penetrates into each according to his state." Again: "The Word of the Lord is itself dead, as it is bare letter, but in reading it becomes vivified by the Lord according to the faculty of intelligence and perception granted to each one by the Lord. Thus it lives according to the life of the person who reads, on which account it is marked by an endless variety."

For the believer, such understanding is not just a part of life. It is life itself—true life, the goal of human existence, in which being and understanding are one, a single meaning and action.

The obstacle is the letter, the stone that must be rolled from the tomb for the Spirit to rise. As Swedenborg says, "The interior sense of the Word can by no means be perceived, unless the sense of the letter is, as it were, obliterated." Or overcome, seen through, by the organ of faith that recognizes by grace the invisible in all things visible.

The Book, which is revelation, descends, comes "down" from Heaven to rest in the outwardness of outer meaning. Descent, revelation is externalization, an outering of more inward meaning. Ascent, conversely, is internalization, the progressive realization of ever more inward, more comprehensive, profounder meaning. There is an inside to this world. "The interiors of its word are of great beauty," writes Swedenborg. How central the metaphor of language is! From one point of view, to descend is to speak, and to ascend is to understand what has been spoken, to interpret or translate. For what are speech and understanding but a kind of translation? As Hamann puts it: "To speak is to translate…. From the language of words, objects become names, images become signs." These signs may be "kyriological [of the *Kyrios or* Lord]; historic, symbolic or hieroglyphical; or philosophical or characterological." Such translation is not the decipherment of something already existing. As Corbin says, it is "the very apparition of things, their revelation by their being named." Descent is progressive revelation.

In the same vein, Swedenborg speaks of three levels (celestial, spiritual, natural) of meaning, and invokes the idea of "translation" as the mode of correspondence of the worlds with each other. For Swedenborg above all, whose life was a continuous intercourse with spirits, the Lord is speech and word, cognition and understanding—in a word, *imagination*. In his *Spiritual Diary,* he notes: "The speech of spirits is a universal speech; from it spring and, as it were, are born all the languages. For it is spiritual ideas that constitute the speech of spirits and when these inflow into a person's memory they excite words corresponding to the ideas which the person has in his or her memory."

The speech of spirits is a speech of thoughts or images. More precisely: "Spirits speak with the primitive idea of words; for it must be known that every word has some idea therein, and every composition of words is a composite idea expressed by many thoughts. Such as are our thoughts without words, such is the speech of spirits with each other…. But angelic language is still more interior."

It is more primary, involving in a moment more things than can be unfolded in many pages.

It is important to remember that levels, worlds, or languages, though apparently discontinuous with each other, are not mutually exclusive. They cannot be so, for the divine Word is sacred, and whole, and speech too in God is sacred and holy, so that the letter is also potentially properly holy, for God seeks to be and is all in all and the universe is one. The arrangement is hierarchical, but not linear or successive. Life is presence and simultaneity, not succession, which is already dead, because involved with the past. Celestial and spiritual meanings—the speech of angels and spirits, both of whom have a human shape—are simultaneous with and interpenetrate the letter of natural meaning and natural speech, even if these do not obviously reveal them. It is in the nature of the letter that a person's body immediately reveals his or her soul to prosaic consciousness. The letter is in the same relation to God and the Spirit as the phenomenal world. Like the world of phenomena, it is a theophanic event that reveals or unveils the spirit, which becomes visible and audible, while remaining veiled and concealed. Like the text of the natural world itself, the letter both announces and conceals. It is an open secret. For those who have eyes to see and ears to hear, it contains them. It is only a question of reading.

This is traditional knowledge. For religions of the Book, God always speaks in two ways—through nature and through Scripture, "each revelation declaring and supporting the other," as Hamann says. Nature and Scripture are the two great commentaries upon each other that reveal the presence of the Living Word. In them God, who is hidden and unknowable by nature, appears while remaining hidden and may be known while remaining unknown. "He is hidden after his appearance or, to speak more divinely, even in his appearance," writes Dionysius. The appearance must be read. It must be named, interpreted, translated. It is only in being named that God appears. In the act of interpretation, which is human nature, Spirit reveals itself. God appears, theophany occurs.

Humanity is the place of the revelation of appearances; the space of manifestation is the act of interpretation that makes them possible. In Blake's phrase, "The imagination is not a state; it is human existence itself." It is the living place where the names of God do their work. "We are all capable of being prophets," writes Hamann. "All phenomena are dreams, riddles, and visions, which have significance and secret meaning. The book of nature and the book of history are nothing but ciphers, hidden signs, which need the same key as unlocks Holy Scripture, and is the point of its inspiration." But what is the key? Hamann's biography reveals it.

In February 1758, in despair and penury, having during the period of about a year changed his London lodgings almost monthly as he "rung the changes in debauchery and reflection, reading and knavery, industry and idleness," Hamann went out in search of yet another room. God was gracious. He found one with very good and honest people, the Collinses of Marlborough Street. Here he bought a Bible, and began to read it through, at first with imperfect understanding. What then occurred he describes in the simplest terms. Words that had lain upon the page dead took on life and meaning in his soul. They gave meaning to his life. Indeed, they became his life. Suddenly, he realized in his heart that "each Biblical history is a prophecy accomplishing itself in the life of each single human being"; that "all the miracles of Holy Scripture take place in our souls." God's acts, from Genesis to the coming of the Kingdom of Heaven, are acts God performs in the human soul. History and nature are God's deeds in the human soul. Nature is human nature and history is of the soul. The more Hamann read, the newer and more divine he perceived to be the content and effect of what he read. There was no question about it. In the history of the Jewish people he found himself confronted with his autobiography. Discovering himself, he found his God. For the Word was God. "I recognized my own crimes in the history of the Jewish people, I read the course of my own life and thanked God for his long-suffering.... Above all, I found in the books of the Law a remarkable disclosure—that the Israelites, however crude they appear to us, sought from God nothing but what he was willing to do for them." Hamann became a philologist, a lover of the Logos in its unity, divine and human words: "the living, impressive, two-edged, penetrating, marrow-dividing and discerning Word, before which no creature is invisible; but before whose eyes all things are naked and transparent."

Then, on the evening of March 31, reading the fifth chapter of Deuteronomy, Hamann fell into deep thought. "I thought of Abel," he writes, "of whom God said, The earth has opened her mouth to receive thy brother's blood. I felt my heart thump, I heard a voice sigh in its depths and wail like the voice of blood, like the voice of a slain brother who wanted to avenge his blood if I did not hear it.... All at once I felt my heart swell, and pour out in tears, and I could no longer—I could no longer conceal from my God that I was the fratricide, the murderer of his only-begotten Son." Following this, in spite of Hamann's great weakness and resistance, the Spirit of God went on to reveal more and more. In this way, "with sighs that were brought before God by an interpreter who is beloved and dear to him," Hamann continued his reading, enjoying "that very help with which it was written," until he brought it to an unbroken conclusion "with extraordinary rich consolation and quickening."

Hamann's encounter with the quick and the quickening Word, his sudden hearing of its call and the prophetic philosophy that was his witness to the call, can help us pass beyond the state so well described by Hofmannsthal's Lord Chandos. Hamann is Christian, but his Christianity is originary, for he sought what was fundamental. For Hamann the same Spirit brooded over the waters in the beginning, wrote the books of Scripture and Nature, spoke with the prophets and understanding, and inspired his speech and words. For the Spirit is the only one able to seek out and utter the infinite paths of divinity.

If it is the same Spirit, it is the same Word also. If the Spirit is primordial, ever present, ever one, then so also is the Word. The Word is the beginning, the first deed or principle, the possibility of speaking or creation, the reason why there is something rather than nothing. As Dionysius the Areopagite says, "All things, even those that are revealed to us, are known only by their communication. Their ultimate nature, which they possess in their own being, is beyond mind, and beyond all being and knowledge." Creation is but the communication, the appearance of God's hiddenness. It is his speech. The heavens declare his Glory in which, revealing himself, he remains hidden. Yet it is not so hidden. For the Father's Word, through whom all was made, is one with the Father and "in the bosom of the Father he alone has been the exegete of fullness of grace and truth." In the beginning, now, and forever are the Word and Spirit, in whom is neither outside nor inside, neither immanence nor transcendence, neither divine nor human— only relationship, communication, meaning, cognition, understanding. Being is revelation. "Being certainly is the sum and substance of every single thing," Hamann wrote. "But unfortunately the *to on* [Greek "being"] of ancient metaphysics was transformed into an ideal of pure reason, whose being or non-being it cannot explain. Primordial being is truth, something imparted, grace." Or, more radically, in a letter to the philosopher Jacobi, Hamann wrote: "What you call in your language being, I prefer to call Word."

In the world of meaning—of words—the primary act is the act of interpretation, the opening of the imagination, not manipulation, and the human being is essentially a prophet, a witness, or a poet. "For me there is no question either of Physics or of theology," wrote Hamann, "but only of language, mother of reason and revelation, their alpha and omega." Reason, history, nature—speech itself—are one Logos, a single revelation or meaning, revealed individually and partially, and uniquely, in each encounter of the human soul with God. Each human life, each human vision and testimony, is infinitely critical and precious.

God and human beings—for Hamann everything comes into being and exists in and through that relation, including, above all, human beings themselves. "Human beings are not what they are because they were created by God, but because they are addressed by God. They do not live by the Word, but because the Word speaks to them. To hear is to live." But the hearing, the dependence, must be thought of not so much in terms of one will that obeys as an imagination that opens. Neither God, nor the world as it is in God, and as God speaks through it, can be rationally deduced. It can only be heard, witnessed.

For Hamann, reason is the equivalent of what St. Paul calls the Law. Just as sin increases by virtue of the law, so error grows by virtue of reason. The commandments of reason are blessed, just, and good, but reason is not given to make us wise. Everything it touches, it kills or puts to sleep, for it creates the illusion that the world exists internally as an act of faith. All one can say is, Lord, awaken us. The world, as God speaks through it, must be *witnessed:* it must be lived in one's being and heart by the heart—for while the four senses pass by the brain, the fifth sense, hearing, is said to pass directly to the heart. It is the heart that hears. For Hamann everything arises out of the conversation God holds with the human heart. Nothing finally matters but that: God and human being, speaking and hearing.

Put another way, everything created, the creature, is a living speech, a dynamic, communicating reality. But in that transaction, there is no duality: only a singular experience, a unity. What we call that unity is a matter of perspective. Hamann usually calls it God, as when he writes, "Without thee I am nothing; thou art all that I am." Reality is from God, by definition. All that is, is grace, revelation. "Our spirit can only be considered awake," Hamann writes, "when it is conscious of God, when it thinks and feels him, and it recognizes his omnipresence." But who or what in this is God? Hamann writes: "If one assumes that God is the cause of all effects great and small, both in heaven and on earth, everything is divine. Everything divine, however, is also human; because human beings can neither act nor suffer except according to the analogy of their nature, no matter how complex that machine may be. This *communicatio* of the divine and human *idiomata* is a fundamental law, the master key to all knowledge and to the whole visible economy."

Another fundamental law must be added: "I know and acknowledge," Hamann writes, "no other Archimedean point than his Word, his oath, and *his I am and I shall be,* in which consists the whole glory of his old and new name." The meeting between God and the heart is between two—as it were—I's, for only an "I," a living I AM, can speak, hear and respond authentically. "Not *cogito ergo sum,* but rather the reverse, or, to put it still more Hebraically, *est, ergo cogito.*" Being, which Hamann has named Word, he now names "I." To be is to speak. To speak is to be an "I." To be an "I" is to be a word—in the Word, of the Word. It is to be a word in a world of words. To be in the world is to be together—"I" to "I"—with other beings that are I's also, in whatever measure. It is what we call love. The Word is amatory discourse—for what is the appropriate mode of being with and knowing, understanding, another being like oneself, but love, which is the laying down of self for the sake of the other, for the sake of what does not yet exist? It is to create, and to create beauty, for beauty is the counterpart of love. Hamann writes: "The secret parts of our nature upon which all taste for and enjoyment of beauty, all truth and goodness are founded, bear relation, like that tree of God's in the midst of the garden, to knowledge and life. Both are causes as well as effect of love. The coals thereof are coals of fire and a flame of the Lord; for God is love, and the life is the light of men." This is the love that moves the stars. And who is the true subject of love? Ibn 'Arabi says, "A being does not truly love anyone other than his Creator."

"Speak that I may see you," Hamann writes. "This desire was accomplished by creation, which is a discourse from the creature to the creature; for day speaks to day, and night announces night. The Word of Creation crosses all climes to the end of the world, and one can hear its presence in every language." The creative and living Word is not of any particular language. It is the sheer, omnipresent, transparent communicability that traverses all things. It is the understanding that it is a speaking world, a world of images, beings, ideas—not things. Today, because of the ingrained nominalism of our times, we no longer understand this transcendence, the wordless word, the speech of angels and spirits that, as Swedenborg tells, gives human words life—this word that is not a name attached to a thing but the thing itself. "Who knows where the fault may lie," Hamann rhapsodizes, "within us or without us; the fact remains that there is nothing for us in nature but fragments, *disjecta membra poetae*. To gather these is the task of the scientist; to interpret them that of the philosopher; to imitate—or, more audaciously—to give them form, that of the poet."

What does Hamann mean? He means that the substance of things is language. He means that in the beginning, because of the primacy of the divine-human conversation, because God is a speaking God— "the powerful speaker," "the poet at the beginning of days"—and the human being is, in the image of God, a speaking-hearing, prophetic creature, all things spoke. And could still if we could only hear. "Each phenomenon of nature was a word, the sign, the symbol, the pledge of a secret union, inexpressible but no less intimate, a communication and a community of divine ideas and energies. All that man in the beginning heard, understood, and saw with his eyes, all that his hands touched, was a living Word, for God was the Word."

The echo of St. John is intentional, for Hamann is a Christian, and the primal Word of creation is the God who became incarnate. Creation and redemption are two moments of a single gesture of humility and condescension—the self-emptying of God to creation or humanity for the sake of coming near to him. "The poet of the beginning of days is the same as the thief at the end of days." Redemption is the key to creation: "The revelation in the flesh is the midpoint of everything." For Hamann, God's *kenosis*—his humility and self-emptying in Christ—is not the exception but the rule of creation. The whole beauty of the world is a "miracle of divine foolishness, a free descent of the Spirit into the hells of createdness and materiality," as von Balthasar puts it. The descent, humility, and poverty, are the spirit in the letter. Hamann writes:

That the spirit of God abases itself through the human pencil of the holy persons that it itself impels—divesting itself of its majesty just as much as does the Son of God through the servant figure—is an aspect of the unity in divine revelation. In the same way, the entire creation is a work of the highest humility. Merely to admire God, who alone is wise, in the creation is an insult akin perhaps to the abuse accorded to an intelligent man when the rabble estimates his worth by the coat he is wearing. If divine style—to shame the strength and ingenuousness of all profane scribes—chooses the foolish, the trivial, the ignoble, then we must admit that we need the eyes of a friend, a confidant, or lover, illuminated, armed with jealousy, if the rays of heavenly glory are to be penetrated in such a disguise.

How else could one see a God who must hide himself? The eyes of a lover are needed. Love alone teaches humans to read the hiddenness and mystery of things—the "contingent signs of the absolute that the absolute in its generosity allows to appear." It is not the thinking human being, but the loving one who is forced to recognize his or her ignorance, the limitations and fragility of human nature, the simultaneity of the highest and the lowest in all things. The human being is not God, the human is not the living Word, and the condescension and humility, the disguise of the divine in the human, the analogy in the creature, involves a continuous coincidence of opposites, a perpetual round dance or *perichoresis* of darkness and light, veiling and unveiling. God is everywhere; but the letter is not the Spirit. The Spirit quickens, but the letter still is flesh, not quickened flesh. "Every story bears the image of a human being, a body which is dust, and ashes, and empty," Hamann writes, "but it also has a soul, the breath of God, life and light, which shineth in the darkness and the darkness cannot comprehend it. The spirit of God reveals itself in his word in the form of a servant, but as its own master; it is flesh—and dwells amongst us, full of grace and truth." Spirit and letter, like divine and human, ignorance and knowledge, are not two. They seem two only because human beings are finite, sensible creatures, who, though they can perceive more than sense can discover, can perceive truth and essence only through images, signs, and paradoxes. Human knowing, divine showing forth—experience and revelation—are phenomenal and figurative. They are a word, a logos, a binding together of what is apart. "The sense and passions understand only images. All the treasure of human knowledge and happiness consists in images. The first explosion of creation and the first impression of its historian—the first appearance and the first communion with nature—are limited in this word, Let there be light. Thereby began the experience of the presence of things." Without this primal Word, which is Light, nothing can be revealed, seen, born witness to; for it is light that reveals. Light is all. "Every good thing is a grant and a gift from the Father of Lights."

For Hamann the light of creation, revealing all in the beginning, is also the light of redemption and of human beings. "Everything was created by him who redeemed us. If he has not desired to redeem us, nothing would have existed. This life, this existence in him, is the light of human beings; and light is everything that reveals and makes and makes manifest." In this light, we begin to see truly, to hear fully, no longer things, but reality, beings, the creative and primordial beauty of the world: God's glory, in which God's speech lives without shadow. In this light, the single eye—the heart—God and creation meet and are one.

For Hamann, as for Blake, Jesus, the union of the divine and human word, is the imagination, "the Spirit of prophecy," and "poetry is the mother-tongue of the human race." "After God had exhausted himself in nature and Scripture, creatures and seers, reasons and images, poets and prophets; and after he had spoken by his breath in the evening of days he spoke through his son—yesterday and today—until the promise of his future, no longer in the form of a servant, will be accomplished." Less than all will not satisfy. Redemption must continue until the last blade of grass is enlightened— becomes a living word.

In Novalis's words, "If the spirit sanctifies, every real book is a Bible." For, "Who has declared the Bible completed? Should the Bible not be still in the process of growth?" Writing is another kind of listening. The cycle of prophetic revelation may be closed, but the spirit of prophecy is still alive and may blow where it will. Indeed, as Corbin so profoundly noted, precisely because it is closed, the very fact of its closure requires the continued openness of prophetic understanding or poetic response. "Poetry," like "imagination," has become a derogatory word bearing the implication of something unreal, "subjective," superfluous. Nothing is more real or more necessary, when these words are understood as the Romantics—Hamann, Blake, Novalis, Hölderlin, Keats, and Shelley—understood them. Hamann's teaching of the living Word can help us. He insisted on the word-nature of human existence. He knew from experience that by participation in nature we are restored to a living wholeness that precedes our capacity to oppose ourselves to the world. These can help in the great restoration because they provide a foundation at once metaphysical, existential, and injunctive for the attempt. Hamann teaches us, in Keats' words, "To see as a god sees, and take the depth / Of things as nimbly as the outward eye / Can size and shape pervade" and to put it into words, living prophetic words.

Historically, there is much against the project. But the true word has always lived and lives still, because it is the nature of things. Poets have always borne and continue to bear witness to it. Lord Chandos, and Hofmannsthal himself, fell victims to the age. Others surmounted it. For these Orphic poets, "Song is being." In song, being reveals itself. It is.

I leave the last word to Paul Celan, the Jewish poet, who above all others struggled with the question of the recovery of the living word. His was a language that had been systematically abused, desecrated, and contaminated by the holocaust that took his whole family. What German has undergone, all modern languages also suffer in their own way as a result of the universal reduction of life to technology and mechanism. The battle is one. Celan's tragic example can light our way.

Once
    I heard him
    He was washing the world
    Unseen, neighborly,
    Really.
    One and unending
    Annihilated
    I-ed.
    Light was. Saving.
                *
Thread suns
    Over gray-black desolation.
    A tree—
    High thought
    Grasps a light-tone: there are
    Still songs to sing beyond
    Human beings.

12

Becoming Novalis

I equals not-I. This is the highest principle of all science and all art.

Actually, we are all identical—and only from this point of view does each identity divide. I is the absolute communal place—the nexus.

—Novalis

GEORG FRIEDRICH PHILIPP VON HARDENBERG was born on May 2, 1772, in Oberwiederstedt in Lower Saxony. Short in duration, his life was infinite in depth. Dead at twenty-nine, he left behind under the pen name of Novalis a body of work of such radiance, religious feeling, and philosophical depth that only now, more than two centuries later, can we hear his voice and understand the vision embodied in his texts.

He took the name of Novalis from the Latin for "newly ploughed fields," placing his work under the sign of the opening of a new era. "Novalis" or von Rode (from *roden,* to clear land with a mattock; to break new ground) was a family name on his mother's side. Already in the thirteenth century, von Hardenbergs had called themselves "von Rode" or "de Novali." This coincidence confirmed Friedrich's sense of mission, of being called "to cultivate the earth," to baptize and humanize it by love raised to the highest power, which is the productive or creative imagination.

Novalis presents himself as a prophet and example of human possibility. Sometimes the possibility seems so different from our present state, so pure and angelic, so transparent and lacking in personality in any negative sense, that we hardly believe it to be human. Yet none was more human than he. This too makes him elusive and terrifying. For the beauty of the poet is the beauty Rilke spoke of, which we can only just begin to bear. Rather than he, it is we who are hardly human, not fully real. Friedrich Hardenberg dedicated his life to the art of becoming human; for him there was no other art. Becoming human, he became "Novalis."

He was born in 1772, the first of eleven children, only one of whom outlived their mother. His father, Heinrich Ulrich Erasmus, was austere, ascetic, conservative—a good man, but a cold father. His first wife had died childless, the victim of smallpox. The experience of this loss opened his consciousness so that he felt elected, illumined. Turning to Pietism, he found the presence of grace, the interior kingdom, the ever-present possibility of new birth. Not wishing the movement of the heart to fade, he made a written contract with God, which he renewed with each communion: "I will improve myself and through a powerful transformation make that good in me which in my youth I spoiled."

In the midst of regeneration, he found a life-companion and spiritual partner in a poor cousin, Auguste Berhardine. She was an orphan who already lived beneath his roof. It was a happy match. Auguste Berhardine's gentle, motherly nature balanced her husband's dogmatic severity. Yet life was not easy in the cold and dark thirteenth-century-convent Hardenberg home. A mother's love could do little to assuage the essential dryness of a life that revolved around daily prayer and Bible study. Besides which, as his son later wrote, his father's overwhelming conviction of his own sinfulness, together with the asceticism he employed to control it, arose more from a deep-seated fear or weakness of soul than from strength or love. The result was a hard, perhaps bitter, puritanical man, inhibited in communicating love—not an easy combination to live with.

Until his ninth year, young Friedrich was dreamy and backward seeming. He was slow to learn and of delicate health. Then, in 1780, a great change occurred. A severe bout of dysentery was followed by an ailment of the stomach, which only the most painful and lengthy cure could heal. Parents and physicians expected the worst. It did not come. On the contrary, the illness proved a blessing. Friedrich's recovery was accompanied by a remarkable mental awakening. His ability to learn increased daily. His memory improved, his attention became more powerful, his gifts of observation truer and more precise. Above all, his spirit began to show, independent and high-minded, not about to accept passively and without thinking any authority or tradition.

With the change, Erasmus was forced to take a greater interest in his son, who now began to question everything. His tutor could do no more for him. Fearful above all for his son's faith, Erasmus turned to the Moravian brotherhood of Neudietendorf. But in that environment a free spirit could find no asylum. Though the creed was not uncongenial—with its emphasis on the joy of conversion and new birth, on the heart as the seat of religious experience, and on the marital relationship as the privileged analogue of the soul's relationship to Christ, it was and remained his lifeblood—Friedrich found the religiosity intolerable and refused to stay on until his confirmation.

Not knowing what to do, and harried by events at home, Erasmus turned for help to his brother, Friedrich Wilhelm, a Lord of the German Order of Knighthood, a man both of the world and of the Enlightenment, a skeptical rationalist, highly cultured, principled, and urbane. Sent to his uncle at Lucklum, the eleven-year-old Hardenberg discovered the conversation and culture with which Pietism had been unable to come to terms. Goethe, Wieland, Lessing, Shakespeare, the French Encyclopedists now became familiars. At the same time, he discovered a worldlier ambition—to be a poet.

With his twelfth year came yet another decisive turn. In December 1784, his father was appointed supervisor of the salt works at Weissenfels, a pleasant little town on the river Saale about twenty miles from Leipzig. Though family life was no less austere, there were neighbors and friends—even a certain warmth. Weissenfels became the heart of Hardenberg's life. Here, in Saxony and Thuringia, his destiny played out. He wrote his first verses, developed a deep affection for classical letters (he asked a friend to send him the works of Euripides, Aeschylus, and Theocritus, amongst others) and for poetry (Young's *Night Thoughts on Life, Death and Immortality* in German translation) and fairy tales. His brother wrote:

> He was very industrious in his studies and already knew Latin and Greek with a certain fluency by his twelfth year; there are also several

poems from this period. In his leisure hours his favorite reading was poems and tales, which last he also loved to tell his sisters. It is also of interest that, under Friedrich's direction, the three brothers were in the habit of playing the following game: each was assigned a spirit—the spirit of the sky, the water, or the Earth—and each Sunday Friedrich would recount the latest events that had occurred in their respective realms, which he knew how to unfold in the most graceful and varied manner.

In the spring of 1790, inwardly committed to a "poetic life"—he had already made contact with the literary world and written poems about Orpheus, with whom he was to have a lifelong identification—Friedrich left his home in Weissenfels to complete his education at the Lutheran Gymnasium in Eisleben. He translated portions of the *Iliad*, the *Odyssey*, Vergil's *Eclogues*, Pindar's *Odes*, as well as fragments of Horace. It was imitative work, but preparatory nevertheless.

In the autumn of the same year, he entered the University of Jena to study Law. Here he fell under the genius and tutelage of Schiller, whose work as a poet and dramatist he already knew. But the man who faced him now was a philosopher and a historian. Schiller was at a turning point in his life, about to enter the three-year study of Kant's philosophy that would culminate in the masterly *Letters on the Aesthetic Education of Man*. The encounter was providential—"His first look threw me into the dust and raised me up again"—for it demonstrated the revolutionary, life-transforming role of the marriage of poetry and philosophy on the path to self-knowledge.

The meeting was initiatory. With it Hardenberg passed from the rank of youth to that of apprentice and took his stand on the world stage. He saw in Schiller "one of those rare men to whom the gods have revealed face to face the high secret that beauty and truth are one and the same goddess.... I recognize him [he wrote to Reinhold, his teacher in Kantian philosophy] for the lofty genius who hovers over the centuries ... the teacher of the centuries to come ... a citizen of the world whose heart beats for more than humankind."

These were revolutionary years: the French Revolution was the context and the axiomatic, if implicit, starting point of discussion. Its connection with Kantian philosophy may be found in the universal concern for the meaning and reality of human freedom. The task of the age was to realize a conception of the human as a free, perfectible being in whom love and imagination conjoin in spontaneous creativity. For Schiller, the secret of this freedom lay in the state in which beauty is created and enjoyed. Only in this state is the human being perfectly free, poised on the creative edge between the world of the senses and that of the mind, obeying the dictates of neither, but freely choosing between them.

Reverberations of this impulse were felt across Europe, forming the creative ferment, the inner revolution, called Romanticism. The challenge, and the promise, thrown down by Kant binds together destinies as disparate as Goethe, Coleridge, and Hegel, as well as Novalis (and Novalis's teacher, Fichte, who wrote, "I am living in a new world"). After Kant, the world had to be made anew. Even those who knew nothing of Kant, like Blake and Keats, recognized the chief task of their age to be overcoming that false duality of subject and object, consciousness and nature, under whose illusion the world, and hence the soul, is torn apart.

Following his year at Jena, Hardenberg, still determined on a career in law, enrolled at the University of Leipzig with the resolution "to fast my soul with respect to the arts, so that I may seek to gain more firmness, more resolution, more purpose, more planning." But some things cannot be planned. Soon after arriving he must have met Friedrich Schlegel, for the latter wrote to his brother, August Wilhelm, in January 1792:

> Destiny has placed in my hands a young man of whom everything may be expected. He pleased me greatly and I went out of my way to meet him. Soon he opened the sanctuary of his heart to me. I have now taken my seat there and cast about for good things. He is still a very young man—of slender good looks, a fine face with dark eyes, and a charming expression when he speaks with fire of something beautiful—with unbelievable fire—he speaks three times more and three times faster than the rest of us. He has the swiftest powers of comprehension and receptivity. The study of philosophy has given him great agility in unfolding beautiful, philosophical thoughts—he follows not the true, but the beautiful.

His favorite authors are Plato and Hemsterhuis. On one of our first evenings he developed with tremendous, fiery zeal his opinion that evil did not exist in the world and that all things were drawing near again to the Golden Age. Never have I seen youth's brilliance so clearly. His perceptions have a certain chastity that has its ground in the soul and not in lack of experience. For he has already been much in society—in Jena—where he knew everyone, among them the finest spirits and philosophers, above all Schiller.

Schlegel, to whom Hardenberg showed his first poems, undertook to tame and tutor "in all the arts of companionability" his new friend, who seemed like a wild creature, "ever full of energetic, restless joy." Skeptical, ironic, and sentimental, Schlegel tested Hardenberg's deep-seated piety, his sense of devotion, thereby strengthening his inborn sense of inwardness, his unique depth. The relationship was marked by crisis, tension, and vacillation as Schlegel led the way from the Apollonian Greece of Schiller's "Gods of Greece" to the more Diony-sian, nocturnal, ecstatic world of Hellas. "You have been the high priest of Eleusis for me. Through you I have come to know heaven and hell—through you I have tasted of the tree of knowledge," wrote Hardenberg, and Schlegel replied: "You are a prophet—become now and evermore a man." At the same time, girls' names begin to appear in verses and letters. Then came debts and a family quarrel.

In desperation, Hardenberg decided to become a soldier, but the idea came to nothing. He returned to Weissenfels. In April 1793, he enrolled at the University of Wittenberg. Here Kant, Schiller, and the Greeks took their places against a background dominated by Luther and ecclesiastical history. He graduated in June 1794 and returned to Weissenfels to await the call of destiny.

Appointed a law clerk, Hardenberg moved to Tennstedt in north Thuringia, where he was to work and live with District Judge Coeles-tin August Just, a man renowned for his knowledge and culture, who lived with his niece, Caroline. Just was Hardenberg's first biographer; as such, he confessed, "I was supposed to be his teacher and leader, but he was my teacher." For him, Hardenberg was the first human being of whom it could be said, not that he had genius, but that he was genius. He wrote that Hardenberg freed him "from the fetters of one-sidedness to which a longtime businessman can so easily become fixed."

On November 17, 1794, Hardenberg set out with Just and his niece on "an expedition" to collect taxes. It was an ordinary morning when, without warning, in the midst of the unaffected simplicity of a country family, Hardenberg met his destiny—Sophie von Kuhn. It was a superhuman meeting. The place was called Grüningen. That Sophie was only twelve years old at the time made no difference. This was a love that transcended time and space. "In a quarter of an hour my mind was made up," he wrote to his brother Erasmus, explaining in a poem:

> It cannot be drunkenness—or I was not born for this star—…
>
> Is actual complete consciousness
> of moral grace intoxication? Is belief in humanity
> but the game of an idle hour?
> If this is intoxication, what is life?
> Must I be forever separate? Is this premonition
> not of future union, of what,
> already here, we recognize as our own
> but are as yet unable to possess entirely?

The vision of "moral grace" occurred in "full consciousness." "Sobriety" was the form of the experience, hope was its content:

> One day humanity will be what Sophie is
> to me now—perfect moral grace.
> Then higher consciousness will be confused
> no more with the fog of too much wine.

Three years earlier, Hardenberg had noted in a letter to Schiller: "[Moral beauty] lifts us above ourselves…. If I could only unite this love for moral beauty and grace into the purest, noblest passion which has ever permeated a mortal bosom with its fiery glow!"

Henry Corbin points out in his study of the dialectic of love in Ibn ʿArabi, "A being does not truly love anyone other than his Creator." If this is the secret of the real Beloved, who in reality is the Lover? These mysteries must be approached with circumspection. We can guess (following Corbin) that we have to do not with two heterogeneous beings, but with a single being, an *unus-ambo* or bi-unity, at once two and one. Love in this sense is an eternal exchange between God and creature, Heaven and Earth, Self and Other.

From this moment on, Grüningen is the sacred omphalos, the imaginal place of revelation, ecstasy, and transformation. It is paradise. Hardenberg dates letters from there "Elysium."

> A temple—wherein we kneel,
> A place—whither we draw near,
> A joy—for which we burn,
> A heaven—I and thou.

On Sophie's thirteenth birthday, March 15, 1795, she and Friedrich plighted their troth. Who was she? To Hardenberg, Sophie was what Beatrice was to Dante. She was a being apprehended directly by the Imagination and transfigured into a symbol by a theophanic light. She was a real woman transfigured by a celestial aura; a divine archetypal figure contemplated in a concrete form. Yet, in the flesh, we must not forget, she was an adolescent girl. Hardenberg described her in his diary:

> Klarissa. Her precocity. She wishes to please all. Her obedience, her respect for her father. Her decency, her innocent trustfulness. Her obstinacy of feeling, her malleability before others, whom she either treasures or fears …

The list continues. It names, among others, her capriciousness; her gentleness; the fact that she does not want to be anything, but is something; her musical nature, her love of dance; her natural sense of religion, her free *joie de vivre;* her openness, her lack of reflection; her fear of marriage; her orderliness; her talent for imitation, pretence, secrecy; her generosity.

It is a strange mixture—With whom has she passed her life? Where has she been? Hardenberg asks—and yet perhaps not so strange a mixture when we recall she is only thirteen. No wonder she seems not to have reached the age of reflection, nor to have any understanding of poetry. In many ways she is still a child. That Hardenberg declared himself so soon irks her. She does not like it that he is so open; she does not wish to be burdened by his love. Often it weighs upon her. Generally, she is cold. Yet she requests locks of his hair and is devoted to him.

For his part, Hardenberg could begin to say:

My favorite study has the same name as my bride. Her name is Sophie. Philosophy is my life's soul and the key to my true self. Since my friendship with Sophie I am bound to this study.

What he means is that with the same passion as he loved Sophie, at the same time, he began work on what he described as "pressing preliminary studies for my whole life ... necessary exercises of my powers of thought." Why he undertook the work is suggested by a diary entry: "One must exercise and build up in an orderly fashion all one's powers—the powers of imagination, of understanding, of judgment, etc. I am now building up the intellect, which must come first, for it teaches the way." During these "Sophianic" years Hardenberg's chief bedside book was Fichte's *The Science of Knowledge*. It begins: "Attend to yourself: turn your attention away from everything that surrounds you and toward your inner life; this is the first demand that philosophy makes of its disciple. Our concern is not with anything that lies outside you, but only with yourself." No poet since Dante (who drew so deeply from St Thomas) would be more closely associated with a philosopher than Friedrich von Hardenberg with Johann Gottlieb Fichte—not just by the embodiment of metaphysics in poetry, but with documented philosophical work and its conclusion: magic idealism.

The Science of Knowledge provides a philosophical directive for life—or rather, a directive for the *philosophical life*. To seek the ground of experience the student is led on a rigorous course of training in the observation of consciousness—what Coleridge called "the mind's self-experience in the act of thinking." Experience is the experience of something by someone. There is a subject and an object, a self and an apparent not-self. Which comes first? The idealist apparently sacrifices the independence of the thing for the independence and freedom of the self. The dogmatist (to use Fichte's term) sacrifices this independence—this primacy of mind or freedom of the intelligence—to the thing. What follows is materialism and determinism. Fichte will have nothing of either. He is uncompromising. Intelligence for him is active, primary; the self is free, ethical by definition. When the object is taken as fundamental, as it is by the materialist, mind is reduced to an epiphenomenon and the subject loses all moral responsibility and efficacy. Fichte wastes no time on such possibilities. His concern is above all with the morally active self. Behind Kant's retention of the thing-in-itself, Fichte sees lurking a hidden Spinozism, an exaltation of nature, a loss of essential human freedom. Without this freedom, how is ethics possible?

This is summed up in the central Fichtean experience of the I or Self. If we wish to found philosophy not in the world, but in intelligence or mind, then we must assume the existence of a higher, unfallen self or transcendental "I," the source of both the lower self or empirical I and the world. The first task on the Fichtean path is to realize, by intellectual intuition, the activity of the transcendent self—in traditional language, the philosopher's angel or the witness in Heaven—as the active principle in consciousness.

Intuitive participation in the transcendent I can be demonstrated neither logically nor conceptually. It can only be experienced. The object of the Fichtean quest cannot be known. It is knowing itself. Lived, it is life. It cannot be objectified; it is pure activity or self-enactment, in which there is no longer any foreign element to create a difference between enactment and accomplishment. "For idealism the intelligence is a doing and absolutely nothing else." The doing is the seeing referred to by Eckhart: "The seeing through which I know Him is the same seeing through which He knows me." Every act of objectification, each thing in the world, presupposes and confirms the action of the seeing that is the transcendent Self.

Activity derives from, and must be ascribed to, the transcendent Self, the I of one's I—this is the source and end of becoming human, the goal of human activity. Reality in this state is non-dual, without subject and object. Subject and object, the division of the I into consciousness and nature, exist only for the empirical consciousness of the divisible "I." When ordinary, empirical consciousness comes onto the scene, the work of creating the world has already been done. Beyond empirical consciousness lies some fundamental creative power, which Fichte, like many others, calls the power of productive imagination. Imagination is the Mediatrix. It is the interworld between the transcendent Self and the phenomenal, paradoxical dualized world with its ordinary I and not-I. It is everywhere at work. Distilled, this means, as Novalis later wrote:

> It is bad that poetry has a special name and that the poet represents a profession apart. Poetry is not anything special in itself. It is but the mode of activity proper to the human spirit. Are not the imaginations of the human heart at work every minute...?

More than that, insofar as it can be known by its effects, we can say that the imagination, which is the pure enactment of being, is the true self, the point-activity beyond subject and object that is the creative ground of both.

In the autumn of 1795 Hardenberg began his Fichte notebooks, working at these problems:

> The proposition "a is a" contains only a positing, a distinguishing, and binding together. In order to make "a" clearer, A is divided. "Is" becomes the general content, "a" the given form. The essence of identity can be established only apparently. In order to represent it we must leave it behind....
>
> Application of the above to the phrase, I am I.
>
> What is I? Absolute thetic power. The sphere of the I must include all else for us. Only as its own content can the I know content. Knowing points to its I-being.

Similar remarks follow, as Hardenberg moves on to consider consciousness and knowledge:

> Consciousness is a being outside being in being.
> But what is that?
> Something outside being cannot be true being.

Untrue being outside being is an image.

Therefore whatever is outside being must be an image of being in being.

Consciousness is thus an image of being in being.

Need to clarify images / Signs / Theory of signs.

It follows that "the I has a hieroglyphic power." The world is made of images. It is a continuous imagination or dream.

Hardenberg is not a philosopher like Fichte; he is a poet whose temperament is religious. His concern is not with Fichte's "not-I" but with "thou"—which opens up to frame the whole world. Two fragments from the notebooks sum up this move:

Instead of not-I—thou.

Spinoza reached to nature—Fichte to the I, or Person. I to the thesis: God.

Hardenberg's path, unlike Fichte's, is a *via negativa*. Philosophy must be a particular kind of thinking. In philosophizing there is a striving to think some fundamental ground to the bottom, but such a ground is never truly primordial. It is an inner state—a connection with the whole. The impulse to philosophize becomes unending activity—without end, because an eternal need for an absolute ground that could only be satisfied in a relative fashion would be present. Through the free renunciation of the absolute, endless free activity arises in us—which is the only possible absolute that can be given us and which we find through our inability to attain and know an absolute. The absolute given in this way lets itself be known only negatively, in that we enact and find what we are looking for—which cannot be attained through any action. Hardenberg seeks to realize this activity that mediates between and lives in the relationship—the unity—of subject and object. To do so, attachment to subject and object, self and world, must fall away. "The true philosophical act is self-murder. This is the real beginning of all philosophy, to it may be attributed all the requirements of the philosophical disciple, and only this act corresponds to all conditions and characteristics of transcendental action."

Such is the precondition for the realization of the imagination, the true poetic—demiurgic or creative—power. For it is the same imagination that unites as divides—the same I. "Dividing (separating) and uniting. The pure and the empirical I." "The imagination is the binding mean term (logos)—the synthesis—the power of exchange." To live there, at the midpoint between inner and outer, spirit and nature, became Hardenberg's aim.

In November 1795, eight months after the secret engagement, Sophie fell seriously ill "of a fever with pains in the side." The fever left, but not the pain. Five months later, with Sophie barely recovered, the engagement was made public on her fourteenth birthday. In July 1796, Sophie fell ill again, more seriously still. Following an operation in Jena, she lay for weeks within the shadow of death. Goethe visited her sickbed and was moved by her transparent purity. Had he not been so moved, Hardenberg remarked later, he would have lost all respect for Goethe as a connoisseur of beauty or knower of truth and goodness. Hardenberg's first love gradually flamed into an ecstasy.

In December, Sophie returned to Grüningen, Hardenberg remaining in constant attendance. Four days before her fifteenth birthday, Sophie asked him to leave; eight days later, on March 19, 1797, she was dead.

Hardenberg had spent the past year and a half wrestling with the Fichtean dilemmas, not as matters of speculation but as spiritual exercises. To understand what this means we need only recall the painful, heart-rending circumstances in which he lived. To strive to detach himself while yet remaining faithful with every fiber of his being, at a time when everything seemed intent on fastening its tentacles upon him and rendering love impossible, must have required superhuman effort. But Hardenberg had no choice. Every available moment he sought to experience the realities that Fichte had described. It was for him a question of vocation, in the religious sense. It was necessary to realize the transcendent I, to live in the full power of the productive imagination, in order "to become a perfected human being—a person," a free, moral agent. He wrote in his notebooks:

> Morality is the core of our being—when morality is what it ought to be. The ideal of being must be the aim and origin of all morality.

An unending realization of being should be the vocation of the I: its striving always to have increase of being. From the I am evil lessens and good increases. The highest philosophy is ethics. All philosophy of the I begins in ethics.

Precise self-observation went hand in hand with a continuous moral striving to become the I of one's I. What is even more astonishing is the place where this happens. Where the ethical and the philosophical come together, Hardenberg named now imagination, now person, the essential being—the person in the heart.

At the same time, life had to be lived, trips taken, work accomplished. Hardenberg even (in 1795–6) changed jobs, becoming the assessor of salt mines under his father, which meant both a return to Weissenfels and intense scientific studies in geology, chemistry, halurgy. No wonder then that in between philosophical entries we find admonitions like "Exercise patience," and "Equanimity—even in the most hopeless cases. E.g. in the case of Sophie." Also, "Perhaps the fault, because of which I attain no further, lies somewhat in this—that I cannot grasp and hold a whole." Finally, in a page of fragments originating around the moment of her death we find:

> I have religion for Sophie—not love. Absolute love, independent of the heart, grounded in faith, is religion.
> Absolute will can transform love into religion.
> The mixture of will and striving for knowledge is faith.

Sophie had died with perfect maturity, beauty, grace, and peace. So spiritually concentrated was she in her agony that, it is said, Hardenberg saw her immortal being shining out, hard and bright, like a diamond. To this being he vowed himself eternally. Sophie's death became the key to life, the revelation of a higher life—death-in-life—the promise of a higher birth or resurrection. From this moment on, death and life moved into inextricable proximity. Only love could make them one. He recognized his destiny:

> Whoever flees pain
> will love no more.

To love is always
to feel the opening,
to hold the wound
always open.

Transformation was his only prayer and hope. Four days after Sophie died, he wrote:

Let my sadness grow
to a delicate flame
which so consumes me
that a gentle gust of wind
might then transform me....

Two paths had led him to this: Sophie and philo-sophy. Finally, the two became one, "Christ and Sophie." With the death of Sophie von Kuhn, Hardenberg's final initiation was about to begin. He was twenty-five, the same age as Dante when Beatrice Portinari died. Less than a month after Sophie's death, on April 14, his brother Erasmus died. Death surrounded him. It became his reason for living—a form of his beloved. Hardenberg vowed to follow Sophie, to remain faithful to her and love her beyond time and the tomb. His faith would not allow life to divide them. On April 18 he began a journal, dating it: Day 31. It is a remarkable document. Extracts follow, for there is no substitute for the actual tone of the narration in which the mystery of the transformation of Friedrich von Hardenberg into Novalis is accomplished:

Day 31: Sensual stirrings early this morning. Many thoughts about She and I. Philosophy. Passably cheerful and bright. The object of my thoughts reasonably firm....

Day 32: Early: many things regarding my resolution—hesitation, vacillation—then philosophy. Midday cheerful. Upstairs about two. Philosophy.... Went to Grüningen. Showed Madame Just Sophie's portrait. Spoke a great deal about her. On the whole a cheerful, calm day.

Day 33: Thought much about Sophie today. Felt unwell on rising—a little improved toward midday....

Day 34: Sensual imaginings first thing in the morning. Then suitably philosophical.... I thought often of Sophie, but without intimacy or fervor; of Erasmus my thoughts were cold.

Day 35: Nothing.

Day 36: I wrote well. After lunch, coffee in the garden; for once felt a true calm in me.

Day 37: My head not exactly clear—and yet, early on, I did have an hour of bliss. My imagination was perhaps a little voluptuous—yet today I felt rather good. In the afternoon my head was clear. *Wilhelm Meister* occupied me all day. My love for Sophie appeared to me under a new light. In the evening I spoke openly—yet in between I thought much of my resolution. I hold to my determination courageously. Sophie will make it go ever better. I must only live in her more and more. Only in the thought of her am I truly well.

Day 38: Manly and well today.... Thought much of Sophie—freely and bravely.... In the evening, a lively impression of her death....

Hardenburg's verse jottings from this time give a more pointed emotional tone:

The petal
has now wafted over
to the other world—
The player in desperation throws the cards from his hand and
smiles as if waking from a dream....

*

The more uneasy the dreams
the nearer
the quickening dawn

*

My love has grown
to a flame
that has consumed
everything earthly.

*

She is dead—
die likewise—
desolate is the world.
        *

Who shuts her out
shuts me out.

Returning to the journal:

Day 39: On the whole I can be happy—true, I have not thought of
her with deep feeling—I have been almost jolly—but in a certain
way I have not been unworthy of her—I have thought of her sometimes in a manly way.... My resolution holds firm....

Day 40: ... I must treat myself in a more manly fashion—must
trust myself—I must not be childishly fainthearted and act weakly
and spoil myself. I must learn to bear pain and sadness better.

Day 42: ... Leafed through some old chemical pages after lunch.

Day 43: ... Rained continuously. Wept much in the morning
and again after lunch. The whole day completely sanctified in her
memory.... Very moved—went to her tomb to plant flowers....

Day 47: ... Now I seem rather cold and too much in the everyday mode. Let me strive only for higher, permanent reflections and
their mood. O how little I can dwell in the heights!

Day 48: ... Before my eyes I beheld the living image of my
Sophie—"in profile" on the couch beside me—in her green
shawl—it is always in characteristic situations and clothes that I
see her most easily. In the evening, in a general way, I thought of
her intimately, truly, deeply. I have good reason today to be happy
with everything. Up to now God has guided me with love—He
will continue to do so.

Day 49: I can be satisfied with my fidelity and my devotion. But
I did not go to bed as happy as yesterday: I was agitated, anxious.

Day 50: I was not much together with Sophie in my thoughts
today—but occasionally was so, intensely and with fervor, especially in church.

Day 51: The weather was magnificent—a living memory of
her—then I walked a little—picked flowers and laid them on her

grave. I felt well—if a little cold—yet I wept—The evening was beautiful—I sat by her grave for a time.... In the morning my resolution was distant, in the evening it was close.

Day 54: Philosophical in the morning.... I gathered flowers—laid them on her tomb—I felt close to her—during this half-hour I was very happy, serene—animated by her memory.

Day 55: Lust stirred from early morning till midday.... On the tomb of my beloved—stayed there until 7 o'clock—in a state of true closeness, without weeping....

Day 56 (May 13): I rose early at five. The weather was good. The morning passed without my doing much. Captain Rockenthien came with his sister-in-law and the children. I received a letter from Schlegel, with the first part of the new translation of Shakespeare. After lunch a walk—then returned for coffee—the weather changed, first a storm, then cloudy and tormented—full of desire—I set to reading Shakespeare—continued engrossed. In the evening I went to Sophie. There I was indescribably happy—moments of dazzling enthusiasm—I blew the grave aside like dust—The centuries were like moments—Her nearness was palpable—I believed she would always come forward before me.... In the evening I had a few good ideas. Shakespeare gave me much to think about.

In this entry lies the germ of the Third Hymn, the oldest, of *Hymns to the Night*. Different influences on this seminal experience have been proposed—Herder, Schleiermacher, Jean Paul—but as it stands in the context of the journal, what is most remarkable is the framing of the event by Shakespeare. The volume that Hardenberg received from Schlegel contained, amongst other plays, *Romeo and Juliet*. Hardenberg was resolved to join his Sophie in death. Clearly *Romeo and Juliet* would strike a responsive note. In his note to Schlegel accompanying the return of the volume on May 25, Hardenberg wrote:

I am beginning to suspect what makes Shakespeare so unique. He has been allowed to develop divinatory structures. The contrasts did not disturb me as they used to—I enjoyed the piece just as it was. Much of what I experienced I cannot yet express.

The structure is magnificent—With what expiatory sacrifice the old feud ends—The wild hate is undone in consuming love.

Returning to the journal:

Days 57–58: ... Much lasciviousness.... In the evening, I went to the tomb and enjoyed moments of wild joy....

Day 59: I went into the portrait room (the room much loved by Sophie)—I opened the cupboard and stood gazing at my Sophie's things—reading my letters and her correspondence in general. Afterwards, I was completely close to her. Then I went downstairs to walk in the garden. Went to get a glass of milk and took Ferguson's *Moral Philosophy,* and went to the cemetery, where I read Ferguson and drank my milk.... My resolution took on a new vigor—a new firmness.

Days 60–61: Thought joyfully of my resolution, full of happiness—thinking of Sophie a great deal. On her tomb, passably fervent.... I must live more and more in her will—I am now only for her—not for myself, nor for anyone else. She is the height—the only one—My chief task must be: to bring everything into connection with the idea of her.

Day 62: The idea came to me at her grave—that by my death I would provide humanity with faithfulness unto death—that in some sort I would make possible a like love for her.

Day 63: Without her there is nothing in the world for me—Actually I should give nothing else any value.

Day 64: Reread some Fichte extracts in the morning—Some stirrings of desire.... Inwardly very active, walking endlessly in the corridor.... Then I went to the tomb, where I reflected much and experienced an ineffable peace.

Day 64: In the measure that the sensible pain diminishes, the stronger the spiritual sadness grows, the higher ascends a kind of peaceful despair. The world grows ever stranger—things around me ever more indifferent—And proportionately all grows brighter in and around me. With regard to my resolution, I must only not begin to rationalize—every reasoned motivation, each speculation on the heart's reasons is already doubt, hesitation, infidelity.

Day 66: As to the resolution, I must no longer reason about it—and as I seek to think certain thoughts so also I should strive to voluntarily arouse in myself by certain means specific moods....

Day 68: I must absolutely seek, learn to affirm my I as best I can through life's vicissitudes and emotional transformations—Unceasingly to think of myself, and what I am experiencing and doing.

Day 69: Fichte ... Thought of S. assiduously—and above all it became clear to me that neither the most beautiful scientific visions nor anything else should retain me on Earth. My death will be the confirmation of my feeling for what is highest, an authentic sacrifice—not a flight—not an act of desperation. I also noted that it is manifestly my destiny—that there is nothing here for me to attain—that I must separate myself from all....

Day 72–73: Between the turnpike and Grüningen I had the joy of discovering the true Fichtean concept of the I.

This moment of enlightenment, so long awaited, occurred as if by design on the same spot from which Hardenberg first glimpsed the house where he was about to meet Sophie.

Day 80: Who flees pain no longer wishes to love. The lover must feel the gap eternally, must hold the wound always open. May God ever maintain in me this indescribably beloved pain—this sadness and memory—this brave longing—this manly resolution and faith strong as a rock. Without my Sophie I am nothing; with her, everything.

Day 83: Today I found the sole good—the idea of unspeakable solitude—that has surrounded me since Sophie's death—with her the whole world died for me. Since then, I no longer belong here.

Day 87: She is dead—hence I die also—the world is waste. Even my philosophical studies should no longer detain me. In deep, calm peace I await the moment that calls me.

Day 88: Who excludes her, excludes me. Our betrothal was not for this world. I shall not be perfected here....

Days 90–103 (Weissenfels, 16–29 June): To have perpetually before my eyes my darling little Sophie ... Christ and Sophie.

Finally, in the margin, written sometime in early summer:

> A union concluded also for death, these are the nuptials that give us
> a companion for the night. Love is sweetest in death; death is a wed-
> ding night for one who loves; a most sweet secret of the mysteries.
>   Is it not wise to seek a hospitable resting place for the night?
>   Therefore he is well advised—who loves his sleeping one.
>   The twilight of evening is always a melancholic hour, as that of
> morning is a joyful one, full of expectation.

Here, for the first time, we hear the authentic voice of Novalis. A turn
had been made. He wrote to Wolfmann:

> My powers have waxed rather than waned. I often feel now that it is
> meet that it is so. I am wholly content. I have gained anew the
> power that rises above death. My being has taken on unity and
> form. Even now a new inner life is growing within me.

No wonder then that, on June 14, just a month after his great experience at Sophie's tomb, he had written to Schlegel: "Perhaps I shall
give you an epithet to my name, when and whenever God wills it, and
also provide you with the special occasion connected thereunto."

Though, in a sense, the practical function of a pseudonym is to
eschew biography, the bearer continues to have a life and a history. In
the case of Novalis, there is no "biographical problem" in that materials for the life of von Hardenberg abound. Yet the problem still exists,
for the biography of Hardenberg and the phenomenon of Novalis
exist in different, though related, universes, just as do, in a precisely
correspondent manner, the empirical I and the transcendent I.

Already in the period immediately following Sophie's death Hardenberg had realized that "the sciences have wonderful powers of
healing—at least, like opiates, they still the pain and raise us into
spheres where the sunshine is eternal." He therefore now embarked
on a career in mining, and chose Freiberg as his place of study. But
Hardenberg is also Novalis, and at the same time he composed "A
Tractate on Light," whose imminent completion he announced to

Schlegel in December 1797. The tractate, of which all record is lost, can be none other than the opening movements of *Hymns to the Night,* poetic and artistic gestures of an almost unbearable purity of thought and feeling.

On December 1, 1797, Hardenberg arrived in Freiberg to study under the famous geologist Abraham Gottlob Werner. This was a return to life. He became a student again, a novice in the higher sense. His devotion to work, his penetration, was extraordinary. He studied "with a higher aim, from a higher point of view." It was the "invisible" world that interested him. Late into the night, he read Plato and the hermetic masters, Hermsterhuis, Plotinus, and Spinoza; during the day, he attended lectures, went on field trips, and read deeply in the scientific literature of the time.

On the way to Freiberg, he had met the nature-philosopher Schelling, a new impulse, as was his providential welcome, almost upon arrival, into the home of the Inspector of Mines, von Charpentier. A year later, he became engaged to Julie von Charpentier. For her birthday, on January 22, he wrote a gnostic poem of exile, "The Stranger." Hardenberg stayed in Freiberg until Whitsuntide 1799, deepening his appreciation and grasp of both the natural sciences of chemistry, medicine, psychology, physics, and mathematics, and the sacred sciences of theosophy and alchemy.

On February 24, 1798, Hardenberg sent Schlegel in Jena a package of "miscellaneous remarks" or fragments, the first fruits of transforming all into Sophia. Schlegel had for some time contemplated founding a review. Hardenberg's package of seed thoughts called "Pollen" provided the moment for *The Athenaeum,* the most vital, transformative organ of German Romanticism. At the heart of *The Athenaeum* lay the fragments, the first works to appear under the name "Novalis." In them, poet, philosopher, and priest have become one—Novalis, the new man.

Poet and priest were one in the beginning—only later times have separated them. The true poet is however always a priest, just as the true priest has always remained a poet. Ought not the future to bring back this ancient condition of things?

Many have a familiar ring, but now they speak with a new authority, as befits their author, Novalis, one who knows, rather than Hardenberg, one who seeks:

> Everywhere we seek the unconditioned, and find only the conditioned. [By a play of words the German for "conditioned" also says "things."]
>
> The seat of the soul is where the inner and outer worlds touch. Where they interpenetrate—it is in every point of their interpenetration.

In some fragments, we recognize the new tone only: "We are on a mission: we are called to form the Earth." The philosophy implicit in the exalted moments of consciousness is the seed philosophy of Novalis himself, poet-priest of the new era. It is present from here on in all his writing. The fragments represent a radical transformation of speech into pure thought—the essence of speech into the essence of thought. According to Maurice Blanchot, the fragments represent "poetry affirmed in the purity of the poetic act ... pure consciousness in the moment of being." They are not aphorisms so much as affirmations of the power of poetic consciousness.

> Each word is a word of enchantment. Whatever spirit calls—such a one appears.
>
> ... The resolution to philosophize is an invitation to the empirical I to remember itself, awake and become spirit. Without philosophy, there is no true morality, without morality no true philosophy.
>
> ... Philosophy raises poetry to the level of principle ... Philosophy shows us what poetry is, that it is all and everything.
>
> Poetry is the great art of constructing transcendental health. The poet is therefore the transcendental doctor.
>
> Transcendental poetry is mixed from poetry and philosophy....
>
> The first human being was the first clairvoyant. To him, all appeared as spirit. What are children, but the first humans? The fresh eye of a child is more prolific than the insight of the most determined seer.

What is a human being? A perfect spiritual metaphor. All true communication, then, takes place in images—and are not caresses therefore true communications?

What is nature?—A systematic, encyclopedic index or plan of our spirit....

The true poet is all-knowing—he is an actual world in miniature.

The idea of the microcosm is the highest for humankind. We are cosmometers.

The world is in every case the result of an exchange between myself and the Godhead. Everything that is and arises—arises out of spiritual touching.

Everything that we experience is a communication. So the world in fact is a communication—a revelation of the spirit. The time is no longer when God's spirit is comprehensible. The sense of the world is lost. We have been left standing among the letters of an alphabet.

The key is the celebrated "Monologue":

Actually, there is a foolishness about speaking and writing. True speech is pure wordplay. One can only wonder at the comical error people make when they think they are speaking about things. No one knows precisely what is most distinctive about language, that it is concerned solely with itself. This is why it is so marvelous and fruitful a mystery that when someone speaks simply in order to speak he utters the most magnificent and original truths. But if he would speak of something specific, the capricious nature of language will make him say the most ridiculous and mistaken things.... It is with language as with mathematical formulas. They constitute a world by themselves, they play only among themselves, express nothing but their own marvelous nature, and for that reason they are so expressive and mirror the singular interplay of things. It is only by their freedom that they are parts of nature, and only in their free movement does the world soul express itself, and make them a delicate measure and abstract plan of things, So it is too with language....

In summer 1798—mid-July to mid-August—Hardenberg went to Teplitz in Bohemia to take a water cure. Fragments from Teplitz give evidence of the transcendental life, the life in the spirit or the higher I, which now could call itself Novalis. Three interrelated themes emerge in the fragments of the period: woman ("Sophie, or on women"), Christianity ("thetic cultivation of the New Testament, or the Christian Religion"), and daily life ("notes on the edge of life").

> The heart is the key to life and to the world. If our life is as precarious as it is, it is so in order that we should love and need another. From the fact of one's own insufficiency, one becomes open to the intervention of another, and it is this intervention which is its goal. When we are ill, others must look after us, and only they can do so. From this point of view, Christ is indisputably the key to the world.
>
> Daily life is a priestly life, like that of the Vestal Virgins. We are concerned only with keeping alive a holy and secret flame....
>
> Our whole life is divine service.

Much else was occupying Hardenberg at this time. He returned to Freiberg, where essential strands of life and interest began to converge. Philosophy was becoming clearer to him as the free practice of the imagination, which he called "magic idealism"—an "experimental physics of the human soul"—based on the absolute correspondence of inner and outer worlds: "Everything is magic or is nothing.... Our inner world must correspond with the outer world completely, down to the smallest detail."

As the theory and practice of the study grew stronger within him, Novalis's penetration of the invisible world—his transformation of the visible into the invisible—flowered into an epic project. It was nothing less than a universal encyclopedia or compendium of knowing. The new epoch could rest on nothing less than the understanding, transformation, and communication of the full fruit of the interpenetration of the sciences. Not that Novalis wished in any sense to reduce knowledge or nature to a system. Such a Cartesian enterprise would have been alien to him and quite opposed to his philosophy. Like his great contemporary Goethe, Novalis proposed a "hermetic" science, an empiricism or phenomenology of conscious-ness and love as the healthy antidote to the mechanical, death-dealing science that already had the ascendancy in his time.

Poetry, medicine, teleology, pedagogy, aesthetics, history, logic, psychology, philosophy, chemistry, archeology, physical history, cos-mology, theosophy, morality and religion, doctrine of the person, human relations, the future, anthropology—such themes and more occupy the more than one thousand fragments that make up the "Encyclopedic Material." For example:

Medicine—Usefulness of every illness: poetry of every illness. Ill-ness would not be part of life if, by uniting with illness, our exist-ence were not elevated.

Psychology—Love is the final goal of the World: the amen of the universe.

Anthropology—The child is love become visible. And we our-selves, we too are a germ of love which has become visible. A germ of love between nature and spirit, or art.

Theosophy—God is love. Love is the supreme reality, the first cause.

Encyclopedia—A "theory" of love is the highest science—the science of nature—or the nature of science.

Grammar—Language is Delphi....

Human sciences—Everything the human being does is the human being—or (what amounts to the same) is a constituent part of humanity, something essentially human.

Magic—The magus of physics should be able to animate nature and lead her, just as he does his body, at will.

Doctrine of spirits—The world of spirits is, in fact, already open: it is always manifest. If we were suddenly to have the necessary elas-ticity, we would find ourselves among them, in the world of spirits....

Politics—We are more closely bound to the invisible than to the visible....

Biology—Life is a moral principle. (Moral imperfection: imper-fection of life.)

Every science becomes poetry—after it has become philosophy.

Thoughts, like flowers, are certainly the most refined "evolution" of the power of plasticity—the most universal power of
nature, carried to the highest power.

The organs of thought are the generative parts of nature—the
genital organs of the world.

On May 12, Whitsunday, 1799, Friedrich von Hardenberg graduated with a degree in mining from Freiberg. He was in his twenty-
eighth year. As Novalis, he had already made his mark. He was a leading light of German Romanticism, the colleague of Schlegel, Schelling,
and Ritter. He had dined with Goethe. The *Sistine Madonna* in the
Dresden Gallery had had its transformative effect. He was engaged to
Julie von Charpentier.

He returned to Weissenfels to be Director of the Salt Mines, a job
he worked at with energy and devotion.

July found him in Jena, visiting Schlegel. There he met the poet and
novelist Ludwig Tieck. It was Tieck who, out of his own poetic soul
and his devotion to Jacob Boehme (to whom he introduced Hardenberg), was able to divine the secret meaning of Novalis as expressed
both in the fragments—"Pollen" and "Faith and Love"—and in the
still fragmentary, unpublished, but nevertheless complete, *The Disciples* [or Novices] *of Sais*.

In the latter, the poet, the "true decipherer," is the liturgist of
nature, its priest. As a poet, and Fichtean, his path to the understanding of nature is inward, but the end, whatever the way, is always the
same: "One reached the goal at Sais; he lifted the veil of the Goddess, /
Only to see, wonder of wonders, himself!" The human being and
nature are a unity; the way in and the way out are one, but humanity
alone is the key, the sacred bond.

However, humans have been cut off from nature, and the way back
must be found. But what is the way, which are the means? They must
lie to hand.

Attentiveness to subtle signs and traits, an inward poetic life, practiced senses, a simple, God-fearing heart—these are the requisites
of a true friend of nature.

Feeling and attention; and the interplay of these:

> Will we ever learn to feel? This divine, most natural of all senses is
> but little known to us. Yet feeling would bring back the old time for
> which we yearn. The element of feeling is an inward light that
> breaks into stronger, more beautiful colors. If one would feel truly,
> then stars would rise within one; one would learn to feel the whole
> world....
>
> To everything that humans undertake they must give their
> undivided attention, their self; once they have done this, miracu-
> lously thoughts arise, or a new kind of perceptions, which appear
> to be nothing more than delicate, abrupt movements of a colored
> pencil, or strange contractions and figurations of an elastic fluid....

Only through the play of attention (shades of Fichte) do humans
become aware of their uniqueness, their special freedom, and learn to
think and feel at once. The outer world becomes transparent; the
inner varied and meaningful. Poets have always lived in this state.
Long and detailed instructions in meditation are given, which make it
seem as if one "were awakening from a deep sleep, as though one had
just begun to be at home in the universe, as if the light of day had just
broken in on one's inner world."

Hymns to the Night, which had their origin in Sophie's death, were
composed during this time, at first in free verse, then in prose with
rhymed verse passages. This is one of the high, prophetic moments of
Romanticism, showing its spiritual origin and end. The night or
darkness that the Hymns extol is a higher light—the northern light
of the Midnight Sun, "night's lovely Sun." For there are two dark-
nesses. The first is a darkness that is only darkness, concealing and
holding light captive—this is a dark night of unconsciousness. But
there is also a mystical darkness, a luminous night of superconcious-
ness. Sufi masters refer to it as the dark Noontide, the black Light. It is
a suprasensory reality, an innerness of light that, now left outside,
appears dark. The Night of Novalis is the *mundus imaginalis,* the concrete spiritual universe of Hurqalya. As Henry Corbin says, "To see

beings and things in the Northern Light is to see them in the earth of
Hurqalya, that is, to see them in the light of the Angel." This is the esoteric night of hidden meanings, theophanies of the *deus absconditus*.

Here poets, sages, or philosophers encounter their "perfect
nature," the angel of their being, who bore them and to whom they
give birth. Here the hierogamy occurs. When the lover becomes the
substance of love, he or she becomes both lover and beloved—"for I
am yours and mine." By this union, this encounter, one becomes a
perfected being: "Calling the night to life you made me fully human."
Spiritual organs appropriate to the epiphanies manifested by the angel
now open up—as many eyes as there are worlds. To live beyond space
and time in the night of light and love that is the Imaginal World is the
dream, the goal of human existence.

But how difficult it is! The vision contains and sustains all. To enter
it one needs to be reborn: delivered from this world into the next—by
which is meant: the birth in the Imagination. Then light's chains, the
bonds of space and time, are ripped apart. Matter turns to dust, centuries evaporate. The visible becomes invisible; the human being
becomes an angel. Its allegiances become angelic; its heart is true to
the inner light—"to the Night, and to creative Love, her daughter."
Now the human being acknowledges the true source of things, "the
chaste, wise world of Archetypes."

The last three Hymns change focus. The experience at the grave,
the power of earthly love transfigured, transformed the poet. The
earthly token of transforming love is Sophia, but its heavenly, cosmic
archetype is Christ. As the poet awakens to higher consciousness, the
love of Sophia reveals itself to be the love of Christ. The fourth Hymn
turns to the divine Logos with breathtaking daring:

> Unending life
> rocks powerfully within me,
> I look from above
> down upon you....
> O breathe me, beloved!
> Ravish me,
> that I may fall asleep
> and love.

I feel death's
rejuvenating flood
transform my blood—
I live by day
full of courage and faith
and die nightly
in holy fire.

Then the poet turns to sing of the age of the gods that the horror of death interrupted. The heart's joy departed; sadness and longing took its place. "The old world bowed…. The gods with their retinue disappeared—Nature stood alone and lifeless…. Sworn faith left too, and with it its all-changing, all-relating divine twin, Imagination." The divine light withdrew within, into the highest reaches of the soul. There, within the veil of Night, it awaited humanity's awakening. Then came "the youth who through the length of Time stood upon our graves in deepest contemplation"—Christ, the death that would reveal life's meaning. He remains, and with him his Mother, the Night—Mary, the Mother, the Bride, Sophia.

The *Hymns* end with "Longing for Death." It is an ambiguous conclusion, dealing with the difficulty of returning to this world once one's heart has tasted that one. Old things are put aside; where to find the energy to take up new ones? What to do with the things of time in the light of eternal things? The great urge is to return to sleep and death. What can this world hold? The answer is that it must be transformed: "A dream will break our bonds apart / And sink us into the Father's lap."

The epitome of Novalis's idea of transformation lies in his vision of the "blue flower" in the first chapter of *Heinrich von Ofterdingen,* his great unfinished Orphic novel of poetic education. As the story opens, Heinrich is lying in bed, thinking of stories a stranger has just told:

"It is not the treasures that have awakened such inexpressible longings in me," he thought. "There is no greed in me; I only yearn to catch a glimpse of the blue flower. It is always in my mind. I can think and write of nothing else…. I feel rapturously happy; and inner turmoil only overtakes me when I do not have the flower before my eye."

He falls asleep and dreams of immeasurable distances, wild and unfamiliar regions. Like the initiate in the *Corpus Hermeticum,* and in a paraphrase of Hardenberg's own life,

> He wandered over oceans with inconceivable ease; he saw wild creatures; he lived with many kinds of people, in war, in wild tumult, in quiet huts. He fell into captivity and ignominious afflic- tion. Sensations rose in him to unknown heights. He went through an infinite variety of experiences; he died and came to life again, loved most passionately, and was then separated from his loved one forever.

Toward daybreak Heinrich's soul grew calmer. He found himself walking through a dark forest that led to a rocky gorge. He started climbing. The forest grew sparser. He reached a small meadow, behind which jutted a crag with a cavelike passageway cut into it. He followed it until it opened out into a great space, filled with a shaft of light ris- ing from the floor like a great fountain. It reached up to the ceiling, and then came tumbling down in innumerable drops like water into a basin. A holy stillness filled the place.

Heinrich approached the basin. Emitting a faint blue light, it surged and quivered in endless colors. He dipped his hand in and wet his lips. A breath passed through him. He felt refreshed. He longed to bathe; so he undressed and stepped into the basin. A heavenly sensa- tion flowed through him. The waves lapping at his chest were damsels dissolving at his touch. Intoxicated, he swam with the stream as it flowed from the basin. Then sweet sleep fell upon him and he found himself by a fountain, on a gentle sward. Blue, veined cliffs lay before him; the light was bright and mild. The sky was blue, clear. His atten- tion was drawn to a tall light-blue flower that stood near the spring, touching it with its broad shining leaves. Around it were innumerable flowers and a delicious perfume filled the air. He saw nothing but the blue flower. Inexpressible tenderness filled him. He moved toward it. As he did so, its leaves became glossier and laid themselves closely around the stalk. The flower then leaned toward him, and within its petals, upon a great blue corolla, hovered a delicate face.

This blue flower, unveiled in a dream within a dream, in the innermost depths of the soul, speaks of the archetypal human being: the eternal priestess of the heart, the "visible spirit of song" in the human soul. In a sense it is what Novalis called in German the *Gemüt*, which the dictionary defines as "mind; heart, cast of mind; disposition, nature; temperament, emotion, feeling, sentiment." For Novalis, the *Gemüt* was the initiated human soul in its full inwardness, its wholeness as microcosm and universal key.

> In our *Gemüt* everything is bound together in the most original, pleasant and vital fashion. The strangest things come together there in a single place, a single time, in a particular analogy, or by peculiarity or chance. In this way marvelous unities and strange associations arise, in which one thing recalls all and becomes the sign of many, and is itself in turn symbolized and called forth by many. Understanding and imagination are united in the most astonishing way through time and space, and each thought and every appearance of our *Gemüt* is the most individual member of a thoroughly original whole.

Heinrich von Ofterdingen, which contains the celebrated tale of "Eros and Fable," ends with the birth of Astralis, the spiritual child of Heinrich, the poet, and his departed love, Mathilda—revealing the blue flower to be "the sweet birth in the beating of the heart":

> … Mathilda and Henry were no longer alone
> but were now united in a single image.
> Newborn, I raised myself to the heavens.
> In a blessed moment of illumination
> earthly destiny was fulfilled.
> Time had now lost its rights,
> what it had lent, it now reclaimed.
>
> The new world breaks in,
> darkens brightest sunshine,

from mossy ruins now one sees
a wonderfully strange future shimmering,
and what once seemed commonplace,
now seems just as wonderful and strange.
One in all and all in one,
God's image in plant and stone,
God's spirit in men and beasts:
all this must be taken into one's soul.
No more the order of time and space,
but now the future in the past.
The kingdom of love has begun,
the fable begins to spin.
The primordial game of each nature begins,
people plan words of power,
and the great soul of the world
moves everywhere, blooms ceaselessly.
All must reach into one another,
each through the other thrive and ripen,
each in all represented....
World becomes dream, dream becomes world,
what one believes happens,
one can see it from afar.
Here fantasy first freely commands
at will the weaving of the threads,
here concealing, there unfolding,
floating off in magic mist.

Dream has become the world. The human soul has recognized itself in the world, as the world. The last fragments, besides those on science, particularly mathematics (whole studies have been written on Novalis's Romantic Pythagoreanism), and on history (his last work was the apocalyptic essay "Christendom or Europe"), have as a hidden thread the self-subsistent soul or interior world in its totality, the heart of the being—the *Gemüt*. Poetry, the highest philosophy, becomes its expression. "The innocence of your heart makes you a prophet," Heinrich is told. "All things will become intelligible to you. The world and its history will become Holy Scripture."

Hardenberg spent 1799 in geognostic and literary work. He made new friends—besides Tieck, Henrik Steffens (the Norwegian Romantic philosopher and naturalist) and Jean Paul, the apostle of the I. In December his appointment as Assessor of Mines became official. In April, he finished the first part of *Heinrich von Ofterdingen*. Five days later, he applied for a post of district judiciary in Thuringia. He would carry out these duties in addition to his responsibilities in the salt works; the two jobs together would allow him to establish a household of his own with Julie von Charpentier. From the middle of May to the middle of June, he was in Thuringia, on a mineralogical expedition. Then Tieck visited, briefly, before Hardenberg was off again, inspecting salt works. Finally, at the end of August, destiny showed its hand for the last time. A hemorrhage wracked his delicate body, and the feverish presence of tuberculosis made itself known.

Seven months of struggle followed. Bowing before his fate, accepting it as given by God, he gave himself nevertheless to hope and surrendered to the will for life. It was not easy. As he noted, he had no gift for martyrdom. Yet he knew he chose his life. Nothing came by chance. He would live it out. A late fragment reads:

When they are properly understood the law of grace and the law of free will are not at all contradictory; both belong to a single whole and often need each other.

In October 1800 his younger brother drowned in the Saale River. From November to mid-January, he lay in Dresden, scarcely a shadow, no longer recognizable. In December, he received his appointment to the district judiciary in Thuringia. But his strength was failing. Late in January, he returned home. On March 19, the fourth anniversary of Sophie's death, he began to slide perceptibly toward another world. Early in the morning of March 25, 1801, after breakfast, listening to music played on the piano by his brother, in the presence of his parents, his friend Schlegel, and his betrothed, Hardenberg fell asleep in perfect harmony, never to reawaken. Among his last fragments we find:

It is most understandable why, in the end, all will become poetry— will not the world, in the end, become soul?

13

Romanticism and the Evolution
of Consciousness

$\mathcal{T}$HE LATE NINETEENTH CENTURY—it seems long ago, but it is the birthplace of all we know today—still showed the day-bright face of materialism, its terrifying optimism. Everything seemed possible. But with the twentieth century, we entered what Jan Patocka, Vaclav Havel's mentor, called "the century of night." It was a century of wars, mass death, dehumanization, and fatal fragmentation. Patocka thought that this night had been approaching since the disintegration of Christendom which, despite its many sins, was still organized upon the traditional understanding of human beings and the human community as striving to incarnate divine realities on Earth. The twentieth century (and now the twenty-first) show us the sheer horror of what happens when being, knowing, and loving become owning and controlling rather than striving to enter ever more deeply into being. All meaning is reduced to domination and manipulation; and sheer matter—that figment of the dragon's imagination—is made autonomous and given free reign.

It is no paradox, then, that the question of the evolution of consciousness seems given to us to think with a special urgency at this time. The philosopher Martin Heidegger would say that this question is our historical destiny—that in responding to it we allow Being, what is given, to come to presence and be received as history. If we respond authentically, then something authentic will be given in Being's history, which is the history or evolution of consciousness itself. But for this to occur, as Heidegger says, we must submit to, endure, and give birth to a great change. Perhaps all the suffering is for the sake of this great change. We may call it a universal *metanoia* or transformation of consciousness. Heidegger calls it the end of philosophy as metaphysics and the beginning of thinking in a non-metaphysical way—poetically. He spoke of a radical turn. He quotes the poet Hölderlin: "We have been a discourse; soon we shall be song." Much is at stake and we—and the planet we inhabit—are it.

But why Romanticism? Because, as Owen Barfield has pointed out, the Romantics were our forerunners. They were the first to experience that with the Renaissance the right opportunity had been wrongly used, that a wrong turn had been taken or, better put, a new freedom had been abused, as new freedoms often are. The Romantics first foresaw the full consequences of the "victorious analysis" that we endure:

> A dark and abstract night, indefinite, immeasurable, without end,
>   Abstract philosophy warring in enmity against Imagination.
>   (Blake, *Jerusalem*)

The Romantics experienced prophetically what fragmentation and alienation, what fear of freedom and responsibility, what death and sleep and loss of will lay ahead if our course were not changed. "Jerusalem [human nature] is scattered abroad like a cloud of smoke through non-entity," wrote Blake. And Keats' fallen divinity, the frozen, sleeping God Saturn, awoken by the immortal truth of human nature, moaned, "quiet as a stone, still as the silence round about his lair," his hand "nerveless, listless, dead, unsceptred," his "realmless eyes" closed:

> I am gone
> Away from my own bosom; I have left
> My strong identity, my real self,
> Somewhere between the throne and where I sit.

The Romantic response was not an ignorant gesture of unsophisticated revolt. Whether we consider poets like Blake, Keats, and Hölderlin, philosophers like Fichte, Schelling, and Hegel, or "Renaissance" figures like Swedenborg, Goethe, Novalis, and Coleridge, the Romantics were the leading figures of their age, the most powerful thinkers,

with whose insightful, imaginative thinking we have not yet caught up.
Imaginative thinking, as we shall see, is the key.

Part of the reason for their power resides in their moment. They
were the first to reap the full fruits of the Renaissance, itself a reaping
of the fruits of Hellenism, and so a fruiting of the seed of Western culture. In the Romantics, for the first time since the original impulse at
the axial period of Pythagoras and Plato, the fullness of the Western
tradition, having passed through the crucible of Christ, was available
and open to be rethought. What had previously come into being
sequentially was now present simultaneously—the earliest Greek philosophers, poets, and dramatists and the Hebrew tradition; the Platonic, Hermetic, and Gnostic traditions; and the tradition of the
Church Fathers, Greek and Latin, scholastic and mystic. Finally, and
most importantly, the Romantics were able to view dispassionately
both Renaissances—that of Paracelsus, Bruno, Ficino, Dee, and the
Rosicrucians *and* that of Descartes, Bacon, and Newton. They were
given a fullness of vision—Heraclitus and Plato, Aristotle and St.
Paul, St. John and Plotinus, Bruno and Leibniz, the Hermetic writings
and St. Augustine, Meister Eckhart and Thomas Aquinas, Newton and
Boehme.

The result was a renewed understanding of *the primacy, unity, and
universality of human beings and nature in consciousness or mind,*
together with a profound sense of the ambiguity of the powers that
abstract calculating rationality had rendered self-conscious in the process. It was evident to the Romantics that in the evolution of Western
philosophy and culture the development of rational abstraction—the
mathematicization and systemization of certainty and the laws of
thought—had caused an apparently irresoluble separation (and
objectification) between the knower and the known. Subject and
object were split apart, one result of which was a suspicion and fear of
the actually lived and experienced phenomenon.

More than that, the Romantics realized that the divorce of subject
and object that gave rise to the idea of limits to knowledge also
appeared in other guises. There was, for instance, the objectification
of time, as well as the consequent separation between meaning and
experience, quality and quantity, value and fact, humanity and nature,
the gods and the world. The Romantics recognized that the subjectivity

of calculating intelligence produces an energizing sense of individual identity based upon the mind's self-experience in the act of thinking—an experience of thinking as identity. They saw as their task the transformation, even redemption, of calculating reason by thinking identity as imagination. They realized that reason, swept away by its newborn power, had destroyed the unity of time and eternity, sensible and supersensible, the whole and its parts. "The Reasoning Spectre / Stands between the Vegetative Man and his Immortal Imagination," says Blake. It is not evil in itself, but when it arrogates all power to itself as technological thinking and takes on an independent existence under the illusion that, like the Cartesian ego, it is self-constituted and autonomous, then, as Blake says:

> When separated
> From imagination and closing itself as in steel in a Ratio of
>   things of memory, it thence frames laws and moralities
> To destroy Imagination, the Divine Body, by Martyrdoms and
>   Wars.

Reason becomes for Blake an evil, even the Antichrist, because for him imagination and imaginative thinking are the Body of Christ, which Christ must interpenetrate and in which we must dwell. Blake knows "of no other Christianity and of no other Gospel than the liberty of both body and mind to exercise the Divine Arts of the Imagination."

Romanticism, whether in the person of Novalis or of Hegel, Blake or Coleridge, is always concerned—metaphysically, cosmologically, psychologically—with the recovery of the true Christianity of the poetic, creative Word. From Hazlitt to Heidegger, poetry is the method of Romanticism. "Poetically man dwells on Earth," wrote Hölderlin in a fragment much meditated upon by Heidegger. For the Romantics, all human endeavor—science, mathematics, religion, morality—was essentially poetry and to be lived poetically. Poetry was both a theory and a means of knowing. It was a way of dwelling and worshipping, praying, and being at home on Earth in a truly human way. Heidegger claims that poetry is "the setting-into-work of truth," its revelation, "the saying of the world and Earth ... the saying of the unconcealedness of what is." For Heidegger, the nature of poetry is the founding of truth—"founding" understood as bestowing, grounding, and beginning. Hazlitt, for his part, writes:

> Poetry is the universal language, which the heart holds with nature and itself.... Many people suppose that poetry is something to be found only in books ... but wherever there is a sense of beauty, or power, or harmony, as in the motion of the wave of the sea, in the growth of a flower that "spreads its sweet leaves to the air, and dedicates its beauty to the sun," there is poetry in its birth.... Poetry is that fine particle within us, that expands, rarifies, refines, raises our whole being: without it "man's life is poor as a beast's."

To juxtapose Heidegger and Hazlitt in this way proposes a convergence. Novalis called it "magic idealism," Goethe "experienced idealism." Both meant an Imaginative Consciousness, with roots in Christianity and Hermeticism, but transformed to propose a restoration of the universal triad of Heaven, Earth, and Humanity in free human giving—as the beginning of the giving back, the return of what has been given. "The human being is the Messiah of nature," wrote Novalis, who would not rest till the last blade of grass had been enlightened. He also said, "The greatest secret is the human being itself. The solving of this endless problem is in very deed the History of the World. We seek the purpose of the world. We ourselves are this purpose." But who are we?

Ancient Gnostics, early Christians, spoke openly of the Heavenly Anthropos, of Divine Humanity. Sethians, for instance, told of a "first light in the power of the deep, blessed and incorruptible, which is the Father of all and is called the First Man [Anthropos]." Others, Valentinians, asserted that "the Forefather of all things, the Pre-Beginning and the Pre-Unthinkable is called 'Anthropos,' and that this is the great and hidden mystery, namely that the power which is above all and embraces all, is termed *Anthropos*. And because of this the Savior designates Himself the 'Son of *Anthropos*.'" For this reason, when Adamic humanity was created,

> Fear fell on the angels in the presence of this creature ... because of the One who had invisibly deposited in him seed of the substance

above ... for Adam, being fashioned in the name of *'Anthropos'* inspired fear of the pre-existent *Anthropos*, because *Anthropos* was in him.

This vision, which we find also in Plato's *Timaeus,* in Philo, and in the Adam Kadmon of Kabbalistic tradition, did not cease with the institutionalization of the church. It remained the foundation of alchemy, and it was always part of Christian theology in its more Platonic aspect—as exemplified for instance in the cosmic theology of Maximus the Confessor and Scotus Eriugena. Above all, it was the hidden, radiating center of Christian liturgical life. It animated the building of the great cathedrals and monasteries of the Middle Ages. We find it recurring in the true Renaissance of Paracelsus and Boehme and of those attempting to bring to birth a new human spirituality in the face of the church's conservatism and of the rising swansong of rationalism. The *Anthropos* is the cornerstone of Romanticism, prophetically articulated in Swedenborg, who, echoing and amplifying Paracelsus's "Heaven is human and human is heaven and all humans one heaven and heaven but one human," wrote:

God is true human. In all the heavens the conception held of God is that he is human. The reason for this is that the heaven as a whole, and in every part, resembles the human form, and the Divine, present with the angels, constitutes heaven. It is because God is a Human that all angels and spirits are humans in perfect form.

As Blake put it:

All are human beings in eternity, Rivers, Mountains, Cities,
    Villages
All are human beings.

Novalis said, "The idea of the microcosm is the highest that human beings can attain to," and Goethe, more circumspectly:

The teachers of utility would think that they had lost their God if they did not worship Him who gave the ox horns to defend himself.

But I hope I may be allowed to worship Him who, in the abundance of His creation, was great enough, after making a thousand kinds of plants, to make one more, in which all the rest should be comprised; and after making a thousand kinds of animals, a being comprising them all—the human being.

That was in 1831, when he was an old man. In 1795, younger and more ingenuous, he is more direct:

All perfect organic beings, among which we see fishes, amphibia, birds, and mammals, and at the top of the ladder, human beings, *were formed after one model,* which in its constant parts only varies in one or other direction and still develops and transforms through propagation.

Here we approach the hidden core of our subject. Before doing so, however, we must ask why we place it in the context of "evolution"— "evolution of consciousness"—rather than "history of ideas" or even "history of religion." What does it mean to make consciousness primary? Why do we need to speak of the transformation of the structure of understanding rather than simply discussing once again yet another change in its content?

This is a vast question. To make consciousness primary is to place the question of who we are, where we are going, and how we should respond to the needs of our time within the most fundamental metaphysical question, *Why is there something rather than nothing?* If there were no process such as evolution and no awareness—or "existence" or "life" or even "divine presence"—such as consciousness, would there be anything at all?

In its etymology, *consciousness* proposes a "knowing with" or, better, a "to-gethering knowing," a knowing that gathers together two elements of a *polarity*—Nothing and Something, a cause and an effect, a duality—*together with* the experience of a mean term, a pattern that connects them. Consciousness is the ternary connecting pattern of experience, a seeing that binds. There must be an Activity, which *differentiates* (distinguishes or severs), carries itself away from itself, and simultaneously carries itself back to itself, *relates.* This mutuality of ground, difference, and relation is consciousness—an informing triadic identity. It is informing because it is formative, causal, and patterning. It is identity because it determines the unity a thing is or makes with itself, without which it is nothing. Without consciousness, there is nothing. Consciousness must be primordial. As Meister Eckhart, countering St. Thomas, asserts, God must exist because he understands.

As for evolution, most generally it purports to explain how things got to be the way they are. Since we have just said things are the way they are by virtue of consciousness, evolution must refer to some kind of logic or process whereby consciousness "consciousnesses." Evolution would then be what consciousness does.

In its original meaning, however, "evolution" suggests what is now called epigenesis or embryology (ontogeny)—that is, the unfolding of a principle, as a book is unrolled or a bud opens. From this perspective, evolution is more like the analysis of the implications of an initial axiom or tautology. Another metaphor would be the unfolding metamorphosis of an implicate order contained in a seed or primordial synthesis. Appearing from a temporal perspective to be an orderly succession of stages from seed to fruit, each moment builds on the previous one. Ontogenetic evolution is repetitive and conservative, while the more general so-called evolution is more innovative and refers to the complex, creative processes of learning and change whereby a nexus of relations maintains itself over time within ever widening nets, up to and including the whole.

But what evolves? Here, present theories falter. "Transformism," which is the evolution of material entities as presently conceived, seems logically and empirically untenable, since it is by definition impossible for two material forms to occupy the same space at the same time. The first must be destroyed for the second to appear. If there is to be continuity between the first form and the second—any relationship or metamorphosis between them—it must be nonmaterial by our present understanding. Bodily life as presently conceived must be a means and not an end in any evolutionary process: it must be a state of transition. Hence the unsatisfactoriness of Darwinian attempts to account for some interpenetrated activity of another order than the material as presently conceived. One creature cannot turn into another any more than one phenomenon can explain another, as Coleridge knew when he wrote, "The solution of phenomena can never be derived from phenomena."

From this point of view, any theory of evolution must be spiritual (nonmaterial), and the consciousness that understands it must also be "spiritual" and seek to unify the spiritual in humanity with the spiritual in nature. Any such theory must overcome the Cartesian dichotomy between mind and matter, human and nature, and must at the same time re-conceive or re-experience the relations of time and space as a unity. Time and space unified produce a unity at once mind and matter, distinguishable but indivisible. The activity is primary, a pathway through space, creating matter. But that movement itself, giving rise to time, space, and matter, is only another name for consciousness, the creative Word. "In the beginning was the Act," said Goethe. "All is activity," said Novalis.

Our problem is, which world do we belong to? Jesus said, "My kingdom is not of this world." Of which world is his kingdom? The ecological crisis has led many to the misinterpretation of human nature as ordinary nature presently conceived, thereby confirming not only the status of Darwin's "trousered ape" but also the vision of the next evolutionary stage as silicon-based intelligence. The two go together—Darwinian evolution and human beings, or bacteria if you prefer, as the launching pad for a new computerized intelligence. There is a desperate need for a creative alternative. The evolution of consciousness, spiritually conceived, can perhaps provide some guidance.

The evolution of consciousness is not new; it is universal. It is the inevitable expression of the Egypto-Judeo-Christian tradition, the so-called Hermetic stream, which proposes a different model of evolution. Humanity, rather than deriving from the so-called physical universe, precedes it, includes it. It gave rise to it and now must pass beyond it while redeeming it. D. T. Suzuki wrote, "Nature is already man, otherwise no man could come out of it. " Rather than the last thing, humanity is the first—the first and the last—the whole both preceding the parts and arising from them.

Evolution, hermetically considered, is the incarnation, the unfolding, and emergence of a supersensible organism, *natura naturans*. This is consciousness, traces of whose progressive "working out" we recognize in the now material record, not of things, *relata*, but of rela-tionships, functions, and modes of knowing to which human cogni-tive, moral, aesthetic, and other faculties correspond. Nature is a tapestry of hieroglyphs. It is the finished work of the gods, represent-ing critical moments that must be contained synthetically, as identity and totality, not only in the initial seed, but also in the present fruit, twentieth-century humanity. Humanity, as consciousness learning to think, innately contains the totality of the universe. Humanity is at once evolution and consciousness, the key to the mysteries of both matter and spirit.

Human nature is the Divine Water of the ancient alchemists, the unique root, substance, and operation of their Great Work, which fools ever despised and the ignorant held to be of no value, not know-ing what a treasure it was. And this single Principle, the Divine Water and perennial Fountain, whose perfection was knowledge and health, is available to all. Again and again, ancient alchemical texts speak of the humiliating treatment accorded the greatest of treasures, how it is cast into the street and trampled in the dung. What were they talking about? What was the matter whose realization was a "philosophical stone" and was called by the Middle Ages "Christ"? Blake knew, when he wrote of Jerusalem, the human soul, and the emanation of Albion/Cosmic Humanity:

> I am outcast: Albion is dead:
> I am left to the trampling foot and the spurring heel:
> A harlot I am called: I am sold from street to street:
> I am defaced with blows and with the dirt of the prison,
> And wilt thou become my husband, O my Lord and Saviour.

What has "evolved" is human nature, which we are. Evolution of consciousness is the only reality. We are it. It is our fall and return. It is at once the ocean and all the water drops constituting it—from the first scission that gave rise to the originary dissipative structures and the primordial cells to the complex present moment called thinking humanity, with whose "fall" and "redemption" the return begins. The return situates our quandary and accounts for our ambiguous rela-tions toward the rest of nature. As Goethe wrote:

Nature! We are encompassed and embraced by her—powerless to withdraw yet powerless to enter more deeply into her being. Uninvited and unforewarned, we are drawn into the cycle of her dance, and are swept along until, exhausted, we drop from her arms.... We live within her, yet are foreign to her. Conversing with us endlessly, she never divulges her secret.

Such is the experience of reason, which situates the human fall and return. Reason looks out upon phenomenal nature, "evolution," to which the human body belongs, and realizes that, as body, phenomenal nature means death, the destruction of bodily form. At the same time, reason realizes with Kant that, as reason, it can never know nature, or history, but only its own forms of knowing. Reason submits to a double alienation, and so its products, which include orthodox evolutionary theory, are doubly alienated—alienated by a lack of understanding both of matter and of consciousness. Without understanding these, how is it possible to found any human moral or social life? Life itself escapes us. Rudolf Steiner was clear on this. To begin to find an answer to these questions is to begin to awaken from the deep sleep of reason that breeds only monsters.

Not only Goya, but all the Romantics realized this. Coleridge above all struggled through a difficult life to express what I have been struggling to express. As a "transcendent philosopher," Coleridge does not say, like Descartes, "Give me matter and motion and I will construct for you the universe," but "Grant me a nature, having two contrary forces, the one of which tends to expand infinitely while the other strives to apprehend or find itself in this infinity, and I will cause the world of intelligences with the whole system of their representations to rise up before you." In common with alchemists and Platonists of old, Coleridge believes that "every power in nature and in spirit must evolve an opposite as the sole means and condition of its manifestation." Matter becomes, not a thing, a fixed preexistent entity or container, but "a Product—*coagulum spiritus*—the pause, by interpenetration, of opposite energies." Matter in this view is a momentary synthesis, a crossing, of opposing tendencies, complements or contraries. *Contraries, however, are not negations.* As Blake well knew it is the same "Reasoning Spectre" that

Separated the stars from the mountains, and the mountains
  from man.
And left man groveling root outside himself that created negations where there had been "contraries":
Negations are not contraries: Contraries mutually exist but
  negations exist not.

Goethe and Coleridge call the contraries "polarity." Goethe speaks of "polarity" and "ascension," and out of their crossing derives "evolution":

Polarity is a property of matter insofar as we conceive of it as material; ascension is a property of spirit insofar as we conceive of it as
spiritual. The first is in continual attraction and repulsion, the latter is constant upward striving. But since matter never exists without spirit, and spirit never exists without matter, matter is capable
of advancing and spirit has the power to attract and repulse....
Only an individual who has analyzed sufficiently is in a position to
do the thinking prerequisite to synthesis, and only one who has
sufficiently synthesized is in a position to do a reanalysis.

This indicates, in Coleridge's words, that for Goethe, as for the Romantics, generally what acts in nature *as* nature is "essentially one with the intelligence which is the human mind above nature." There is nothing in nature for which there is not a key in the human being. There is nothing in nature whose meaning is not open to us and the potential of whose creation or co-creation does not reside in the human totality.

The crux, as Coleridge realized, is the subject-object distinction. It was the task of the Romantics to overcome it. The distinction of sub-ject and object is the alienation of reason. How to overcome it? In the famous twelfth chapter of *Biographia Literaria*, Coleridge points out the coincidence of subjective and objective in every act of knowing: "In every act of conscious perception we at once identify our being with that of the world around us, and yet place ourselves in contradis-tinction to it." Things exist and we perceive them: there is the paradox. Things outside seem to be inside, and conversely. But which has prior-ity? Are we a projection of the world or is the world our projection?

Both cases may be argued, but neither may be demonstrated conclusively. All that seems conclusive is the "I AM," the "I"—for if that does not exist, neither of the other hypotheses would have validity. Either as cause or as effect, "I" seems to be central.

The subject-object distinction now dissolves into the prior problem of identity. As Schwaller de Lubicz points out, it is not "my" identity or "I" that is in question, but identity or I-ness as such. The problem is universal. We are faced with the question of the identity, the "I," of anything at all. The principle of identity states that A is A. By virtue of it, things make their claim—that there are things, that there is something rather than nothing. All things make their claim by virtue of being identical with themselves. A stone makes its claim as stone insofar as it is "I"-Stone, that is, in a relation of self-identity. The stone has no self-consciousness of its identity, but nevertheless makes a unity with itself, and in that self-relation resides its "I." This "I" has nothing to do with a psychological ego, or what Blake calls the great Selfhood, Satan. Identity in this sense is what Blake calls "Minute Particulars, every one in their own identity." Recall that for Blake, "the infinite alone resides in definite and determined identity." "He who wishes to see a vision, a perfect whole, / Must see it in its minute particulars." Why? "States change: but individual identities never change or cease."

Heidegger, in his famous essay "The Principle of Identity," points out, first, that the apparent tautology of identity—a stone is a stone, A = A, A is A—conceals a mediation. Plato was dimly aware of this when he said of motion and rest that each of them is different from the other, but is the same *for itself*. Concealed in the "for itself," the dative, is the fact that in identity each thing is returned upon itself, is with itself, togethered, before itself. Heidegger writes:

> The more fitting formulation of the principle of identity A = A would accordingly mean, not only that every A in itself is the same, but rather that every A is itself the same with itself. Sameness implies the relation 'with,' that is a mediation, a connection, a synthesis: the unification into a unity.

Here lies the correspondence between the "with" of identity and the "with" of consciousness, between the mediation that, since the era of speculative idealism, is characteristic of identity and the mediation that is characteristic of consciousness.

In the same essay Heidegger goes on to affirm that it is by virtue of this mediation, which is *being* as expressed in the *is* of A is A, that things make their claim upon and for Western thinking. As he puts it, precisely echoing Schwaller de Lubicz,

> Everywhere, wherever and however we are related to beings of every kind, we find identity making its claim upon us. If this claim were not made, beings could never appear in their Being. Accordingly, then there would not be any science. For if science could not be sure in advance of the identity of its object in every case, it could not be what it is.... The claim of the identity of the object *speaks*, whether they hear it or not.

To whom does it speak? How does one hear it? Heidegger does not say, but it cannot speak other than to the identity or consciousness in us, that we are. Being speaks to Being; Identity to Identity.

I have first suggested that "identity" is related to consciousness, while Heidegger has just proposed it to be related to "being." Are these one or two? Heidegger quotes Parmenides, as the first and most perspicacious teacher regarding identity: "For the same [are] thinking and being." According to Parmenides being belongs together with thinking or perceiving in the Same. By virtue of the Same, being and consciousness belong together. The Same is the primordial unity of thinking and perceiving, concepts and percepts, in what Goethe calls *einem lebendigem Ur-Auge*, a living Primitive Eye. Meister Eckhart says, "The eye with which I see God is the same eye with which God sees me."

Should we seek a principle, says Coleridge, "some truth capable of communicating to other positions a certainty that it has not itself borrowed; a truth self-grounded, unconditional and known by its own light," which is neither subject nor object but "the identity of both," we have but one choice: the Sum or I AM. In this alone, being and knowing are identical, each supposing the other. Just so, too, he says, in the Divine I AM "the principle of being and knowledge, of idea and reality, the ground of knowledge and the ground of existence are absolutely identical."

The leap to theology is not accidental. "In the beginning was the Word and the Word was with God and the Word was God. The same was in the beginning with God." In the ineffable *Arche*, the Origin, was the Distinction, the Ratio, the Relation, the Mediation, the *Logos*, and the Logos was the Origin and was *with* the Origin, that is, was the Self-Identity, the Image, the Consciousness of the Origin. The Divine Nothing came before Itself. It sacrificed Itself to Itself in an act of sacrifice that is the meaning of Divine Love, the Heart of the Father, its Light and the Word, its Identity—and the Divine I AM was. And was made flesh. Through this Word or Identity that was in the Origin *in* this Identity, all things were made. In the logic and unfoldment of the Divine Self-Presentation all things were made and contained. This is the great mystery of Christianity. As Scotus Eriugena says, "Through him who was begotten but not made, all things were made but not begotten." The generation of the Divine Identity was *life*—divine presence—*the presence of the Divine Identity*. This presence was the light of humanity. Christian tradition, in harmony with Hermeticism, is unerring. All that was made, that was life in Him, was that whose light He was. Such is primordial humanity or human nature. God said, Let there be light, and there was light. Light speaking is the Divine Identity, Light spoken is primordial cosmic humanity. This is why Coleridge can speak of the imagination as "the living Power and prime agent of all human perception, and as the repetition in the finite mind of the eternal act of creation in the infinite I AM." This is why Christ for Blake is the Human Imagination and the Imagination is identical to the universe. It is why Coleridge could write in a notebook:

> In looking at objects of nature while I am thinking, as at yonder moon dim-glimmering through the dewy window-pane, I seem rather to be seeking, as it were *asking* for, a symbolical language for something within me that already, and forever exists, than observing anything new. Even when that latter is the case yet still I have always an obscure feeling as if that new phenomenon were the dim awakening of a forgotten and hidden truth of my inner nature.

After which, he exclaims: "It is the *Logos*, the Creator and Evolver!"

The stage is now set to situate what Romantics like Keats and Goethe were trying to do.

Keats and Goethe seem very different, at least on the surface. Keats was pure poet—"He is with Shakespeare," said Matthew Arnold. Blessed, indeed graced, he achieved a miracle of conscious development from Cockney medical student to great poet in four intense years stretched between the constant presence of death and the fatality of impossible love. Goethe, on the other hand, lived to the ripe old age of eighty-three, leading a staggeringly full life of perpetual growth and transformation while pursuing a vast range of pursuits and activities. He lived many lives in one. Not only a poet, dramatist, novelist and autobiographer, he was also a practicing scientist in botany, osteology and comparative anatomy, optics, mineralogy, geology, and meteorology, as well as an active public servant and statesman. Nothing could be apparently more different than these two lives, yet their method was similar in revealing ways.

The distinguished critic Bernard Blackstone has suggested that the English Romantic movement be viewed as one of disintegration and integration: "Blake presenting a synthesis, which breaks up in Wordsworth, Coleridge, Byron, and Shelley to be restored, as far as was permitted, in Keats." One may argue with the details of this view, but it is useful as a generalization. In Blake we are presented with a fully realized synthesis of the *Sophia perennis,* expressed in timeless, mythological language. Blake presents the Gospel or Holy Writ of Romanticism, leaving it to the other Romantics to live out and think through this wisdom in the conditions of the time. Their task was to make a new synthesis, not as prophets but as ordinary mortals. This is the effort of a Coleridge and a Wordsworth. In Coleridge especially, the sense of effort is palpable. It is also, and supremely, the effort of Keats. Whether he achieved any synthesis, or whether, as Blackstone is forced to conclude, the disintegration was a historical process no poet could reverse, is irrelevant. He presents a spiritual attempt to unify and to know that, at the level of practical achievement, is matched only by Goethe.

Keats was the poet. Poetry and to be a poet was the substance of his life, a vocation. It was his calling and his character. From the beginning, he was distinguished by a combination of courage, sensitivity, generosity, and daring. He was incapable by nature of taking a step forward in knowledge without advancing three steps in development. Those who knew him at school are unanimous. His friend Holmes refers to the "generosity;" while his brother George writes:

> John was open, prodigal and had no power of calculation whatever. John's eyes moistened, and his lip quivered at the relation of any tale of generosity of benevolence or noble daring, or at sights of loveliness or distress—he had no fears of self thro interference in the quarrels of others, he would at all hazards, without calculating his power to defend, or his reward for the deed, defend the oppressed.

"When his love of poetry and books manifested itself ... about a year before he left school," his biographer Walter Jackson Bate writes, we do not get the impression that he was bookish. Rather, he illustrates the same qualities his brother recognized: "a union of energy, courage and absorption in something outside himself ... a capacity for commitment, for imaginative identification." In a word, *selflessness*.

When Keats was eight, his father died. His mother remarried quickly, against the wishes of her parents. The result was that the Keats children went to live with their grandmother. Within a year, the new husband was dead, and soon after Keats' mother began to sicken with the disease—consumption—that was to test her children so sorely. Soon she was gravely ill; John, the oldest, suddenly responsible, sat up with her, giving her medicine, reading to her, even cooking for her.

This was the Christmas break, 1809. Within three months, his mother was dead. John felt the loss deeply. He was fourteen, going on fifteen: an orphan. He was now reading, voraciously, indefatigably, but it was time for another change. From this point on, he will never know stability. His grandmother, feeling her age and anxious for the future of her grandchildren, now made two men, Abbey and Sandell, trustees of her money, appointing them to be the children's guardian. Within a year, they decided that the two eldest boys should support themselves. John left school and was apprenticed to a nearby surgeon and apothecary. He accepted this change without resentment: the hours of surgical duty were short and left much time free to his passion for reading. Reading, not in the sense of "accessing information," but of a passionate, almost clairvoyant, imaginative identification. This led, naturally, within about three years (1814), to the awakening of poetry and the writing of poems.

About the time Keats completed his apprenticeship, his grand-mother died. A month short of twenty, he enrolled at Guy's Hospital for further studies in surgery, attending courses in anatomy, physiol-ogy, chemistry, and medicine. He became a "dresser," dressing the wounds that before antiseptics inevitably became infected. He also pulled teeth, set bones, witnessed operations—the patient held down, often screaming with pain. But Keats' heart, though he successfully completed his studies, was not in medicine: "Poetry was to his mind the zenith of all his Aspirations. The greatest men in the world were Poets and to rank among them was the chief object of his ambition."

In July 1816, Keats took his apothecary examinations. Since he could not practice until he was twenty-one, at the end of October, he seized the opportunity and left immediately for the seaside town of Margate, where in solitude he might begin the soul-making process of becoming a poet. The fruit of this moment is contained in three verse epistles in which we find the first indication that poetry, which for Keats is the equivalent of "soul-making" lies in the shedding of literal vision. Though he fears he will never hear "Apollo's song" or feel it in his being, at other times the elements themselves seem naught "but Poesy." Then, as in a trance, he sees and knows. The "portals open wide," hidden treasure is revealed.

Keats returned to London at the end of September. Shortly after-ward, he visited his friend Cowden Clarke, who had a copy of Chap-man's translation of Homer. The friends began to read together the shipwreck of Ulysses in the fifth book. At the line "The sea had soak'd his heart through," Keats stopped with a "delighted stare." Within a few hours the famous sonnet "On First Looking Into Chapman's Homer" was written, unselfconsciously, naturally: "Then felt I like some silent watcher of the skies / When a new planet swims into his ken." Keats, now twenty-one, was committed to poetry. His life was strong; he made new literary and artistic friends—Leigh Hunt, Rey-nolds, Haydon. He felt his destiny drawing him on. Keats moved in with his two brothers—Tom, only seventeen but already on terminal sick leave because of consumption, and George, who became the housekeeper, nurse and companion to Tom, and agent for John. Family, friends, society were necessary for Keats to generate the warmth—the passion, the intensity—needed about his heart to make poetry.

The offer came to publish a book, and he decided to complete it by writing two longer poems. One of these, "Sleep and Poetry," allows us a glimpse of what poetry means to Keats. Poetry is Apollo's song, but a song that is a way of seeing. It is the poet's feeling eye, his seeing heart, that, opening, opens to and opens the poetry, the heart in things. In "Sleep and Poetry," sleep—"Soft closer of our eyes! / Low murmurer or tender lullabies!… / Most happy listener!"—is first praised as gentle, soothing, tranquil, healthful, secret, and serene, "more full of visions than a high romance." Sleep, though a great restorer, creator, and teacher, is *unconscious*. Higher than sleep, but with the same transformative, restorative, healing power, is poetry:

> The thought thereof is awful, sweet, and holy,
> Chasing away all worldliness and folly;
> Coming sometimes like fearful claps of thunder,
> Or the low rumblings earth's regions under;
> And sometimes like a gentle whispering
> Of all the secrets of some wond'rous thing
> That breathes about us in the vacant air.…
> No one who once the glorious sun has seen
> And all clouds, and felt his bosom clean
> For his great Maker's presence, but must know
> What 'tis I mean, and felt his being glow.…

Poetry comes to one who is prepared, purified, and spiritualized—who has made the heart clean. It comes through the heart, but it enters and is entered *through the senses*. It is a supersensuality, an exaltation of the sense world, through the heart.

"O for ten years," Keats cries,

> that I may overwhelm
> Myself in poesy; so I may do the deed
> That my own soul has to itself decreed.
> Then will I pass the countries that I see

In long perspective, and continually
Taste their pure fountains.

He names these countries: first the kingdoms of nature, of the elements, earth, air, fire, and water, the realms of Flora and Pan—Keats will write of all these. Bidding the joys farewell, having resumed and lived through them, the poet must move to a nobler life, where he may live, as he loved "the agonies, the strife of human hearts." Apollo descends and passes before him, strengthening his resolve, even though he is forced to bewail the fact "that the high Imagination cannot freely fly as she was wont of old." Keats knows only too well her power:

> Has she not shown us all?
> From the clear space of ether, to the small
> Breath of new buds unfolding? From the meaning
> Of Jove's large eye-brow, to the tender greening
> Of April meadows?

The imagination contains all genetic wisdom, creative thought, and certain knowledge. It is the organ for the comprehension of Nature. Could all this be forgotten? "Yes, a schism / Nurtured by foppery and barbarism, / Made great Apollo blush for this his land." People now are thought wise who cannot understand the glories. They sway upon a rocking horse and think it the same as Pegasus. The winds blow, the ocean rolls: they see, but they *feel* it not. Beauty is awake, but they are asleep. Yet poetry is ever present, and Keats will dedicate himself to it and to meaning and beauty:

> … though I am not wealthy in the dower
> Of spanning wisdom; though I do not know
> The shiftings of the night winds that blow
> Hither and thither all the changing thoughts
> Of man: though no great minist'ring reason sorts
> Out the dark mysteries of human souls
> To clear conceiving: yet there ever rolls
> A vast idea before me, and I glean

Therefrom my liberty; thence too I've seen
The end and aim of Poesy.

What the vast idea is, Keats never says. It has to do with an act of
knowing, gnosis. The knowing comes first; only then comes the
poetry. The idea is liberating. It frees the poet, but only as he or she is
able, by poetry, knowing, and imagination, to set free nature's own
imagination. It is a single act. Keats' vast idea has to do with realizing
Blake's "Body of Divine Analogy"—"nature" is the outside whose
inside is the "imagination" or the fullness of the human heart, its
power of thought and perception. The poet becomes the expression of
the universe, which, just like he, is an integrated, dynamic, whole. In
the identity of the human heart with the heart of the world, the Imagination, lesser identities are contained. The poet is all-embracing, a
magus, without fixed, or limited, identity, because he contains all
identities. Thus, Keats can say, as he does in "The Poet," that the poet
is one with any person,

> ... be he King,
> Or poorest of the beggar-clan,
>   Or any other wondrous thing
> A man may be 'twixt ape and Plato;
>   Tis the man who with a bird,
> Wren or Eagle, may find his way to
>   All its instincts; he hath heard
> The Lion's roaring, and can tell
>   What his horny throat expresseth,
> And to him the Tiger's yell
>   Comes articulate and presseth
> On his ear like mother-tongue.

Or, as he puts it in another poem:

> He passes forth into the charmed air
>   With talisman to call up spirits rare
> From plant, cave, rock and fountain. To his sight
> The husk of natural objects opens quite

> To the core, and every secret essence there
> Reveals the elements of good and fair,
> Making him see where learning hath no light.

The poetic power allows the poet

> To see as a God sees, and take the depth
> Of things as nimbly as the outward eye
> Can size and shape pervade.

Summing all this up, Blackstone says:

> The poet is not a philosopher: he is a wizard, whose function it is
> by virtue of his art to unlock the imprisoned essences of things and
> make use of them for creative purposes. The goal is transfor-
> mation.... This to me is the sense of Keats' poetry, taking it as a
> whole and taking it as sincere. It is a poetry of magic.... For with
> Keats the poetic experience is emphatically a *poesis,* a making. And
> this is what it has in common with nature. Art is nature working in
> man at its highest intensity. Not *ut pictura poesis:* neither poetry or
> nature is a picture. Each is an opus, an *operatio,* a working.

Poetry is not words on a page. It is closer to "the vast idea." It is
not an object, something out there and over against a subject. Rather,
it is a way of seeing, a way of experiencing or being. Yet it is not subjective. It is the experienced organization of the world. Poetry for
Keats is a *method,* more particularly a method of knowing, which is a
participative identifying, a qualitative exaltation, through the senses,
in phenomena.

The struggle is to find such a method. How does Keats set about it?
First, one puts on the world like one's own self; one sheds one's own
temporal self and assumes the world. He writes to his friend Jane Rey-
nolds, visiting the seashore:

> In truth the great Elements we know of are no mean Comforters—
> the open Sky sits upon our senses like a Sapphire Crown—the Air
> is our Robe of State—the Earth is our Throne and the Sea a mighty

Minstrell playing before it—able like David's Harp to charm the evil Spirit from such Creatures as I am.

But how, as he says, "to have a *heart* always open to such *sensations*"? How to prepare oneself to inhabit such a state perpetually? He writes to Bailey:

> I wish you knew all that I think about Genius and the Heart.... I must say of one thing that has pressed upon me lately and increased my humility and capability of submission, and that is this truth—Men of Genius are great as certain ethereal Chemicals operating on the Mass of neutral intellect—[for] they have not any individuality, any determined Character.

To be a poet, to open and to assume the Poetic Genius, which is Nature's understanding of itself, requires humility, submission, and an *openness,* that is, a *selflessness.* Keats will come to this again and again in his letters, each time in a different way. "As to the poetical Character," he writes to Richard Woodhouse,

> (I mean that sort of which, if I am any thing, I am a Member; that sort distinguished from the wordsworthian or egotistical sublime; which is a thing per se and stands alone) it is not itself—it has no self—it is every thing and nothing—It has no character—it enjoys light and shade; it lives in gusto, be it foul or fair, high or low, rich or poor, mean or elevated—It has as much delight in conceiving an Iago as an Imogen.... A Poet is the most unpoetical of any thing in existence; because he has no Identity—he is continually in for [informing]—and filling some other Body.

Keats could even fill a billiard ball. He lives in gusto. "Gusto" is a word Hazlitt uses to connote the quintessential activity of a thing, its essential gesture. Listen to Keats' disinterestedness, his inhabiting and identifying with determining gestures.

> I go among the Fields and catch a glimpse of a Stoat or a field mouse peeping out of the withered grass—the creature hath a

purpose and his eyes are bright with it. I go amongst the buildings of a city and I see a Man hurrying along—to what? The creature hath a purpose and his eyes are bright with it. But then, as Wordsworth says, "We have all one human heart."

Keats invokes the same faculty when he writes to another correspondent: "The setting of the sun will always set me to rights—or if a sparrow come before my window, I take part in its existence and pick about in the gravel." This is Keats' great gift—the ability to identify himself with the very being of even inanimate objects. As he writes in another letter: "I lay awake last night listening to the rain with the sensation of being drowned and rotted like a grain of wheat."

"I live in the eye and my imagination, surpassed is at rest." The heart of Keats' method lies in the surpassing of "imagination," in the collapsing of time and space into a single "haven of intensity," a single concentrated perception or "feel" in which perceiver and perceived are united in a "trembling and delicate snailhorn perception of Beauty." This is a thinking that is a touching. "Imagination is spiritual sensation," says Blake.

Let us now approach selflessness from another point of view, the ability to think in paradox and tautology, which Keats called "Negative Capability":

> ... that is, when a man is capable of being in uncertainties, mysteries, doubts, without any irritable reaching after fact and reason— Coleridge, for instance, would let go by a fine isolated verisimilitude caught from the Penetralium of mystery, from being incapable of remaining content with half-knowledge.

In another letter, writing of his friend Dilke, Keats makes this a little clearer, for Dilke did not have Negative Capability:

> Dilke [is] a man who cannot feel he has a personal identity unless he has made up his Mind about every thing. The only means of strengthening one's intellect is to make up one's mind about nothing—to let the mind be a thoroughfare for all thoughts. Not a select party. The genus is not scarce in population. All the stubborn

arguers you meet with are of the same brood. They never begin
upon a subject they have not preresolved on.... Dilke will never
come at the truth as long as he lives; because he is always trying at it.

Selflessness, the patient, nonjudgmental, nonrepresentational capacity
to *wait*, and see, requires the surrender of our analytic faculty in favor
of some more synthetic and receptive attitude or organ. This receptivity is a great clue, but it must not be confused with mere passivity. It is
rather the receptivity of affirmation. Reason negates, but the imagination and the heart affirm; they are a great Yes.

Such receptivity is selflessness or openness. To hold the heart open
to the image, the poetic character—the soul-making character, not
"the wordsworthian or egotistical sublime"—must have no character
of its own. Openness is the receptivity of the flower, rather than the
activity of the bee, as Keats so beautifully expresses in a famous letter
to Reynolds:

> It has been an old comparison for our urging on—the Beehive;
> however, it seems to me that we should be rather the flower than
> the Bee—for it is a false notion that more is gained by receiving
> than by giving—no, the receiver and the giver are equal in their
> benefits. The flower, I doubt not, receives a fair guerdon from the
> Bee—its leaves blush deeper in the next spring—and who shall say
> between a Man and Woman which is the most delighted? Now, it is
> more noble to sit like Jove than to fly about like Mercury—let us
> therefore not go hurrying about and collecting honey, bee-like
> buzzing here and there impatiently from a knowledge of what is to
> be aimed at; but let us open our leaves like a flower and be passive
> and receptive—budding patiently under the eye of Apollo and tak-
> ing hints from every noble insect that favours us with a visit.

These thoughts, Keats says, came to him "by the beauty of the
morning operating on a sense of idleness," and with his letter he
encloses a poem about a thrush, in which the thrush advises:

> O fret not after knowledge—I have none,
> And yet my song comes native with the warmth.

O fret not after knowledge—I have none
And yet the Evening listens. He who saddens
At the thought of idleness cannot be idle,
And he's awake who thinks himself asleep.

The paradox of "experience," of thinking that is lived and not manipulated, is that it must come to us. We must not fret after it. Between a fully experienced thought and ourselves there exists a chasm of unknowing that "fretting" will not bridge. Plato speaks of it as a spark that comes only after a long period of preparation, attendance, or waiting; then "suddenly, like a blaze kindled by a leaping spark, it is generated in the soul." For Keats the patient waiting is akin to wonder, the true beginning of philosophy, as the Greeks knew. Keats strove to return to that wonder, to reawaken the faculty that rational thought had all but extinguished.

Negative Capability, selflessness, disinterestedness, these were Keats' way to wonder—willed surrender leading to reverence and a sense of harmony, a loss of self in beauty, which is knowledge—a knowledge that for him is always "heart knowledge," for as he says most famously:

I am certain of nothing but the Holiness of the Heart's affections and the truth of Imagination.—What the imagination seizes as Beauty must be truth—whether it existed before or not—for I have the same Idea of all our Passions as of Love, they are all in their sublime, creative of essential Beauty.... The Imagination may be compared to Adam's dream—he awoke and found it truth. I am the more zealous in this affair because I have never yet been able to perceive how anything can be known for truth by consecutive reasoning.... However it may be, O for a Life of Sensations rather than of Thoughts!

I shall let Keats be his own commentator. The following lines resume what has gone before, but at a higher level. When he sent them to his publisher he did so with a letter. In it, he wrote: "The whole thing must I think have appeared to you, who are a consecutive man, as a thing almost of mere words—but I assure you that when I wrote

it was a regular stepping stone of the Imagination towards a Truth....
It set before me at once the gradations of Happiness even like a kind of
Pleasure Thermometer." The lines are from *Endymion:*

> Wherein lies happiness? In that which becks
> Our ready minds to fellowship divine,
> A fellowship with essence; till we shine,
> Full alchemiz'd, and free of space. Behold
> The clear religion of heaven! Fold
> A rose leaf round thy finger's taperness,
> And soothe thy lips; hist, when the airy stress
> Of music's kiss impregnates the free winds,
> And with a sympathetic touch unbinds
> Aeolian magic from their lucid wombs;
> Then old songs waken from enclouded tombs;
> Old ditties sigh above their father's grave;
> Ghosts of melodious prophesyings rave
> Round every spot where trod Apollo's foot;
> Bronze clarions awake, and faintly bruit,
> Where long ago a giant battle was;
> And from the turf, a lullaby doth pass
> In every place where infant Orpheus slept.
> Feel we these things?—that moment have we stept
> Into a sort of oneness, and our state
> Is like a floating spirit's. But there are
> Richer entanglements, enthrallments far
> More self-destroying, leading, by degrees,
> To the chief intensity; the crown of these
> Is made of love and friendship, and sits high
> Upon the forehead of humanity.
> All its more ponderous and bulky worth
> Is friendship, whence there ever issues forth
> A steady splendour; but at the tip-top,
> There hangs by unseen film, an orbed drop
> Of light, and that is love; its influence,
> Thrown in our eyes, genders a novel sense,
> At which we start and fret; till in the end,

> Melting into its radiance, we blend,
> Mingle, and so become a part of it—
> Nor with aught else can our souls interknit
> So wingedly. When we combine therewith,
> Life's self is nourished by its proper pith,
> And we are nurtured like a pelican brood.

The heart is the organ—of sensation—with which essences or identities may be touched, the past and future known free of time and space. The medium, as light is the medium of physiological vision, is love. For Keats, it is love that discloses and permits Truth and Beauty. Love is to the imagination what light is to the physical world. In his *Theory of Colors,* Goethe recalls "a significant adage in constant use in the ancient Ionian school—'Like is known only by Like;' and again, the words of an old mystic, 'If the eye were not solar, how could we perceive light? If God's own strength did not live in us, how could we delight in Divine things?'" Just so is the imagination, whose organ is the heart, akin to love, in which it dwells and in which it is drawn forth. Love is the impulse hidden behind all we have uncovered of Keats' method, for love—the meaning of love, as the great Russian philosopher Vladimir Solovyov defines it—is "the justification and salvation of individuality through the sacrifice of egoism," the Satan Selfhood. Solovyov says, "The meaning and worth of love, as a feeling, consists in this, that it effectually constrains us, in all our nature, to acknowledge for another the unconditional central significance, of which, in virtue of our egoism, we are conscious only in our own selves." This "acknowledgement of the unconditional significance of another creature" requires the surrender of our egoism, which is the means of the disclosure of our identity. It rests, as Solovyov shows, on *faith,* for it is not the actual creature sensuously received in its empirical being that is of unconditional significance, but that creature or being as it is in God, in its everlasting significance. Love as knowing unites three—myself, another, and God—in living Unity in a world of material impenetrability and separation. If evolution is conceived of as the progressive realization of Spiritual Unity, Love is the prime mover.

Be that as it may, Keats proposed love as a mode of knowing, which has interesting consequences. At its simplest, love as cognition, fully entering into another, grants the other perfect freedom. It is a hard fact that one can love only another like oneself—another living, thinking, feeling, willing being. One cannot love an object or even an idea. To do so, as Owen Barfield has shown, leads to idolatry and the fateful reification of the false self. One can only love another being: a being who is alive, spiritual, and cognitive as we are. This relation is inevitably two-way, and a learning experience. Keats looks forward to a spiritual science of beings and considered the world as a school for such, for the creation of identities or selves fit to know and love.

Keats applied his method only to poetry and to the creation and experience of poetry. His last poems, the great Odes, are as great examples of poetry as exist in English. Having written these, he died, at the age of twenty-five. What he would have gone on to do, had he lived, is unknown. All we can say is that, having perfected his sensibility in one direction, he would surely have gone on to deepen and expand it in others. In his last letters he speaks of philosophy, knowledge of the world in general, his medical past, and science. Keats was in the deepest and truest sense philosophical and scientific. But he died. The possibility of a Keatsian "science" must therefore remain a merely hypothetical question, without any interest as such questions are, except in one regard. Namely, his great contemporary, Goethe, did develop a "scientific" method or philosophy, one strangely similar to Keats' poetic method. Keats' prescriptions for poetry are uncannily like Goethe's prescription for science.

Goethe claimed never to have thought about thinking; he liked to present the appearance of one philosophically naïve. In his essay "The Influence of the New Philosophy," he wrote:

> As vegetation demonstrated its method to me step by step, I could not possibly go astray, and by letting vegetation tell its own story, I necessarily became acquainted with its ways and means of developing to completion the most obscure phenomena.
>
> In my study of physics I gained the conviction that one's highest duty in observing phenomena is to trace accurately every condition under which a phenomenon makes its appearance
>
> Kant's *Critique of Pure Reason* had long since appeared, but it lay completely beyond my orbit. Nevertheless, I was present at many a

discussion of it, and with some attentiveness I could notice the old question continually reappearing, namely, how much we ourselves and how much the outside world contribute to our intellectual existence. I had never separated the two, and when I did philosophize about subjects in my own way, I did so with unconscious naïveté, in the belief that I actually saw my views before my very eyes…. Whenever the familiar dispute arose I was inclined to align myself on the side that did greater honor to the human race.

This is the Olympian Goethe, very crafty and not at all naïve. It is not that he does not understand Kant but that on many, indeed most, fundamental issues he stands opposed to him. Kant attributed all we know of nature to the forms of knowing of the human mind, while Goethe considered everything, including the human mind and its forms of knowing, as aspects of nature. For Goethe human knowing was nature's knowing raised into self-consciousness of humanity. He was, as he said, "always unwilling to see the rights of nature infringed upon." Thus he was her great defender in the age of Kant and mechanism. For him nothing was to be torn out of the interconnected totality. Art and beauty were not apart from nature, or in any way opposed to it, but rather a higher expression of nature. The same "laws" should operate in art as operate in nature, laws that are in their essence "divine." In 1811 he wrote: "My mode of world conception—purely felt, deeply-seated, inborn and practiced daily as it were—had taught me inviolably to see *God in Nature, Nature in God,* and this to such an extent that this world view formed the basis of my entire existence."

The scientist was a priest and his laboratory, nature, was his altar and liturgy. And the study of nature was the way humanity could both raise nature into human consciousness and transform itself into a whole and healthy vehicle for the creative activity upon which both humanity and nature rest. Eckermann reports an interesting exchange between Hegel and Goethe on dialectics:

"They are, in fact," said Hegel, "nothing more than the regulated, methodically cultivated spirit of contradiction which is innate in all men, and which shows itself great as a talent in the distinction of the true and the false." "Let us only hope," interposed Goethe, "that these intellectual arts and dexterities are not frequently misused, and employed to make the true false and the false true."

"That certainly happens," said Hegel, "but only with people who are mentally diseased."

"I therefore congratulate myself," said Goethe, "upon the study of nature which preserves me from such a disease."

How did Goethe study nature? What was his method? He tells Eckermann: "All our efforts should be in the direction of eavesdropping on the methods of Nature herself, so that we may prevent her from becoming obstinate over enforced prescriptions, and yet not be deterred from our purpose by her arbitrary behavior." Elsewhere he speaks of restoring "to the intellect its old privilege of taking a direct view of nature" that, by the same stroke, will restore to nature her own freedom, which Kant had removed. It would also free the intellect from the prison cell of Kantian logic. As a Dr. Heinroth acutely observed, to Goethe's great pleasure, Goethe's thinking is "objectively active." It is never "divorced from objects," by which he means phenomena; anything given to the elements of the objects and his observation "interpenetrate." "What is seeing without thinking?" he asks, for if observation is itself thinking, his thinking is a way of observation. Nothing is inside, nothing is outside, for what is within is without.

Human and world for Goethe are one. He was skeptical of any subjective approach to the law of "know thyself." "Man knows himself only insofar as he knows the world, becoming aware of it only within himself, and of himself only within it. Each new subject well-observed opens up within us a new organ of thought." Nature is a world of thoughts or perceptions, and the thinking that appears to reveal itself in human thought is in reality equally revealed and inherent in the objects and processes of the sense world. The method of observation that will attune our thought to the thought in nature that we wish to observe must take its form from it. "Make an organ of yourself," he said. Goethe is a phenomenologist and his path lies through the lived experience of phenomena. His method trains perception to see things as they are. We can see him working at this in his *Italian Journey,* where at one moment he asks:

How far will my scientific and general knowledge take me? Can I learn to look at things with clear, fresh eyes? How much can I take in at a single glance? Can the grooves of old mental habits be effaced? This is what I am trying to discover.

A year later in Rome, we have evidence—besides the discovery of the *Urpflanze*, the Archetypal Plant—that the practice has born fruit. Goethe writes of the illuminated dome of the Castle Sant'Angelo:

> ... I am full of new thoughts; when I am left to myself and have time to reflect, I can recover the smallest details of my earliest youth, and then, when I turn to the external world again, the splendor of the objects by which I am surrounded makes me forget myself and carries me as far and as high as my innermost being permits. My eye is becoming better trained than I would have believed possible.

Goethe is seeking the principles whereby the multiplicity of nature is a unity, the understanding and perception of which would allow him to see that unity is multiplicity. This principle he calls *Ur Phenomena*, Primal Phenomena: they are the irreducible functions or activities through which nature creates and through which humanity must understand. They are direct traces of Divinity and of one nature with consciousness or mind. Eckermann reports:

> We then spoke of the high significance of the primal phenomenon, behind which we believe the Deity may directly be discerned. "I ask not," said Goethe, "whether this highest Being has Reason and Understanding, but I feel He is Reason and Understanding itself. Therewith are all creatures penetrated; and man has so much of it that he can recognize parts of the Highest."

Paradoxes abound here, chief of which is that the Primal Phenomenon is an "idea," which Goethe claims to be able to "see." The most famous evidence of this is the well-known exchange between Goethe and Schiller following a lecture on plants; the two men agreed that the lecturer's way of observing nature was not to be admired and that another method must exist. Goethe described the exchange:

> The conversation lured me in. I gave a spirited explanation of my metamorphosis of plants with graphic pen sketches of a symbolic plant. He listened and looked with great interest, with unerring comprehension, but when I had ended he shook his head, saying, "That is not an empirical experience, it is an idea." I was taken aback and somewhat irritated, for the disparity in our viewpoints was here sharply delineated.... The old antipathy was astir. Controlling myself, I replied, "How splendid that I have ideas without knowing it, and can see them before my very eyes."

What did Goethe sketch? What did he see? As far as one can gather, the Archetypal Plant is of the nature of a leaf principle, the set of relations defining a leaf. *The Metamorphosis of Plants* shows that every plant, from seed to seed, unfolds through seven varying embodiments of leaf—into which process, polarity and ascension enter. Yet Goethe went looking for the Archetypal Plant. He seeks it throughout his Italian journey, and apparently in the hope of finding it. He calls it an *En kai Pan,* a one-in-all, a principle of unity in multiplicity. Here is the paradox. After going through the Public Gardens in Palermo, Goethe writes: "Seeing such a variety of new and renewed forms, my old fancy suddenly came back to mind: Among this multitude might I not discover the Primal Plant? There must certainly be one. Otherwise, how could I recognize that this or that form was a plant if all were not built upon the same basic model?" Here he hopes to "discover" the Primal Plant, which he speaks of as a Platonic universal.

Later, in Rome, he wrote a reflection on his moments in Sicily that puts the first account into a different light:

> While walking in the Public Gardens of Palermo, it came to me in a flash that in the organ of the plant which we are accustomed to call the *leaf* lies the true Proteus who can hide or reveal himself in all vegetal forms. From first to last, the plant is nothing but leaf, which is so inseparable from the future germ that one cannot think of the one without the other.

> Anyone who has had the experience of being confronted by an idea, pregnant with possibilities ... will know that it creates a tumult and enthusiasm in the mind.

Since he can recognize when a flower is a flower, there must be a principle of flowerness by which he does so. Goethe seeks this universal flower in phenomena.

The Archetypal Phenomenon is at once a thought and a perception; an idea and a sensation. It is a fusion of thought and nature, concept and percept, in a timeless unity, to which the only appropriate human response is wonder. To try to look beyond the Archetypal Phenomenon, Goethe says, is childish. It is like trying to look behind a mirror.

Here is another *pons asinorum,* like the subject-object distinction and not unrelated to it, namely, the distinction between the timeless and the temporal. Goethe's method was aimed at living in the present moment so as to fuse timeless and temporal in a single perception. Archetypal Phenomena seem to have been such eternal percepts. But how to express this? Goethe was extremely sensitive, naturally, to the difficulty. It is not clear he ever overcame it. In a piece called "Reservations and Surrender," he writes that we feel God is operative in nature, nature in God, *"from eternity to eternity."* Intuition, observation, contemplation, he goes on, lead us closer to the mysteries; then, "we encounter a characteristic difficulty—one of which we are not always conscious—namely, that a definite chasm appears to be fixed between idea and experience." And he continues:

> Our efforts to overbridge this chasm are forever in vain, but nevertheless we strive eternally to overcome this hiatus with reason, intellect, imagination, faith, emotion, or if we are capable of nothing better—with folly.
>
> By honest persistent effort we finally discover that the philosopher might probably be right who asserts that no idea can completely coincide with experience, nevertheless admitting that idea and experience are analogous, indeed must be so.
>
> In all scientific research the difficulty of uniting idea and experience appears to be a great obstacle, for an idea is independent of

time and place, but research must be restricted within them. Therefore, in an idea, the simultaneous and the successive are intimately bound up together, whereas in an experience they are always separated. Our attempt to imagine an operation of nature as both successive and simultaneous, as we must in an idea, seems to drive us to the verge of insanity. The intellect cannot picture united what the senses present to it separately, and thus the duel between the perceived and the ideated remains forever unsolved.

In transforming rational analytic perception into a more biological-intuitive *seeing*, Goethe put his finger on the problem of time.

Whether or not Goethe ever solved it, it was the intention of his method to do so. That he did is indicated in that his method bore fruit—in his theory of plant metamorphosis, in his color theory, etc. I suspect that he realized his method more than just in theory, but that he could not speak of it, both because the words were lacking him and because he felt it would be inappropriate. It would be inappropriate *because* the words were lacking. We know that Goethe began his career with an intense and committed practical as well as speculative study of alchemy in deeply religious and pietistic circles. We know too that though he ceased his overt study of alchemy, he continued to employ alchemical principles and ideas. Therefore his science can be seen as "hermetic." At the same time, he looked upon himself as a spiritual pilgrim, whose life was to be a continual process of rebirth through renunciation, purification, and devotion. His aim, as he writes to Herder, was "the divesting of all personal will," the achieving of a timeless center, the realization of spiritual androgyny. Yet he says that idea and experience will never coincide in the center. Only art and action can effect a synthesis.

What is the action? What is the Primal Activity he seeks? Overtly, the foundation of Goethe's method, of his life and character, is his "objectivity"—his devotion to the object, whatever it be; his surrender to it and his permeation by it. His aim was the ever more realized permeation and interpenetration of self and world, the integration of thinking and intuitive seeing. This is true from the beginning and must have been given to him as a gift that he then strove to render ever more perfect. His early poems are remarkable for the "pantheistic" intensity with which he totally absorbed and was absorbed by "nature." But what was nature to Goethe? We have heard him speaking of it "scientifically" and philosophically, but something has been lacking—the other aspect of Goethe, the *Ewiglich Weiblich,* the Eternal Feminine.

The young Goethe writes nature and love poems; the old Goethe ends his *Faust,* upon which he has worked fifty years, among rocky mountain gorges, "at the holy shrine of love." The whole is an invocation to the "glow of love's pure empire … immortal love's core." This it is whose powers enfold the struggling inner life of human beings. Pure pilgrim souls rise, aided by love's powers, until they come to the Heavenly Queen. She sanctions "what in humans may move feelings tender and austere," which lifts them to her presence.

> Virgin, pure in heavenly sheen,
> Mother, throned above,
> Highest birth, our chosen Queen
> Godhead's peer eternal.

The souls rise toward her. She is invoked as "the visage of salvation." Through her gaze the pilgrims arise in "glad regeneration." Then the "mystical chorus" ends the play with its enigmatic coda:

> All things transitory
> But as symbols are sent
> Insufficiency
> Here becomes event.
> The inexpressible,
> Here it is seen,
> Here it is done;
> The Eternal Feminine
> Lures to perfection.

What drew him on? It was nature and the study of nature. However not the phenomenal time- and space-bound nature as constructed by the rational, sense-determined Kantian mind, but First Nature, at once the pure Bride of God and his own Original Human Nature. This was Goethe's guide and teacher, before whom his rational mind had to lay down its false claim to be self-constituted and constitutive of nature. What I have written of love and selflessness in thinking in relation to Keats holds true for Goethe too.

We might ask what the effort of Keats and Goethe toward a selfless thinking has to do with "evolution." Goethe would say that the law of life that both we and the universe are is transformation. In his poem "One and All" he writes: "An eternal living Activity works to create anew what it has created, lest it entrench itself in rigidity and what has not yet been seeks now to come into being.... It is meant to move, to act and create—first to form, then to transform itself; its moments of immobility are only apparent. In all that lives the eternal works on— for everything must dissolve into nothingness, if it is to remain in Being." Yet, in another poem he says, "Nothing that is can dissolve into nothingness! In all that lives the eternal works on: remain, rejoicing, in Being!" And at the end of the poem, he gives an answer to this paradox: *"What is fruitful, alone is true."*

To bear fruit a seed must be cast into the ground and die. It must suffer its loss of form; it must die into fruitful life. Whatever theory we prefer to explain how across the eons things got to be the way they are, we can imagine such a sequence of dyings-into-life accompanying the "evolution of the world." Closer to our own time, the agony of the ancient mythological-intuitive-holistic mind as it died into the birth of sense-based reason is palpable. Now it seems to be the turn of that dialectical, objectifying reason to transform itself in sacrifice for the sake of a higher birth. That, as Heidegger would say, is the task of thinking—of evolution. Metaphysics, reason, must transform themselves, die into a new life of higher reason or poetic thinking. The Romantics were the first to sense this.

14

Deserts and Gardens

AFTER MY FATHER DIED, my mother, brother, and I were sitting in dazed, silent shock in a little alcove in the corridor outside the Intensive Care Unit. He had had pneumonia. Just hours before we learned that, while he was in his small hometown hospital, he passed out from lack of oxygen. He must have been left unattended for a considerable time because lack of oxygen, it turned out, had left him "brain dead."

We did not know this. We knew only that he had passed a crisis and that they had seen fit to move him to a large metropolitan hospital. There, we had watched him sleeping peacefully for four days until the reality of the situation was revealed to us. Painfully, we made the decision to remove the life support systems. As we watched the life slowly drain out of him, the realization dawned that he had actually left several days before—exactly when we couldn't tell.

Sitting in the corridor, we couldn't talk about it. We just sat, filled with loss and disbelief, in a kind of expectant trance, waiting. As we did so, a man approached. He said he was the hospital chaplain. Addressing my mother, he asked whether he could sit with us. We said, "Yes, of course," and introduced ourselves. He sat in our silence. The silence intensified, another silence descending and enveloping us. Gradually, he began to talk about himself and his work at the hospital. We asked him questions. We were glad to talk about something else and to fill the void we felt beneath the surface of our consciousnesses. Haltingly, a conversation began to unfold, punctuated by repetitions and silences. Slowly and subtly, with great tact and tenderness, he drew us out. He focused on my mother, asking her this and that, about herself and about her life with her husband, my father. He responded with deep attention, feeling, and care to everything she said—so that, in the circle we formed, one thought, one memory, one piece of life circulated quietly and naturally into another.

Thinking back on it, what seems most remarkable is the way he was able to hear the feeling, the yearning—Augustine would say the "desire without an object"—in whatever was said. The verbal, informational content of the conversation became the trace of a deeper, more interior movement, one carried, sustained and embodied by the flow of life itself. Strangely, though we were bereft and surrounded by a sense of loss, as the conversation unfolded, a mood of confidence and trust, even praise, seemed to rise from the flow of memory images and the life-current of longing, momentarily fulfilled and then moving on. Round and round the conversation went. Slowly and gently, the story descended, clothed and carried by the sense that life is endless and filled with a longing that is its own satisfaction. As it did so, we began to feel as if we understood some new whole that was densely interconnected, almost recursive, each part connected to every other.

As this moment occurred, the chaplain asked my mother whether she would like to say a prayer together. She nodded; we all bowed our heads. The chaplain spoke the prayer. Remarkably, what he did was no more than articulate what we, and above all my mother, had just brought to experience and shared, in and through our conversation. He spoke for all of us. He expressed my mother, my brother, and me as if he had lived our lives. He did not speak for himself. Rather, it was as if out of our midst we all spoke through the words he spoke. Our speaking rose up and something came down to meet it. United in and through the speaking, we were united in a greater whole. As he spoke, an experience of deep peace, of questions answered, of life making sense and being its own meaning if only we listened without judgment or wishing it to be otherwise, descended upon us. In retrospect, I think of that moment as an experience of grace, as a great "Yes."

Until that moment, my understanding of the nature of the soul was more theoretical than actual. I knew James Hillman's famous essay on "Peaks and Vales," in which he distinguishes soul and spirit. I knew that soul was deep and dark and temporal. It was immanent, manifold, and grounded in desire; warm and wet, it was fecund in images. Spirit on the other hand was cool, transcendent, high, empty, absolute, and timeless. I knew these things but I did not yet have an experiential, existential understanding of what this meant and what the actual living relation of soul and spirit really was. Until this moment of prayer, I did not know what a soul-embodied spirituality would be. It was certainly not a question of either/or. I refused the choice. Either live a solitary mountaintop life, far from the world, in the divine darkness of the superabundance of light, or live soulfully in the world, in human love and relationships, in subjectivity, in the daily round of pain and joy, tears and laughter. That was no choice. I knew it was not either/or. Each could and should include both.

Over the years, I have come to think of the two paths not so much as "peaks and vales" but more as "deserts and gardens." The desert has been a primary metaphor of the spiritual path in the West at least since St. Anthony, the first Desert Father, in the third century. Anthony, in fact, did not go straightway to the desert, but began in simple solitude and reclusion not far from town. Yet for him, and for that time, that was not enough. At about the age of thirty-five, still seeking purity of heart and having battled the demons inwardly and now facing them outwardly, as Christ himself had done in the wilderness, he crossed the Nile into the solitude and emptiness of the true desert. He stayed twenty years and, during that time, the desert began to fill with others like him until there were tens of thousands seeking the same silence.

Thus began the tradition of the Desert Fathers. Cassian brought it to the West, and the model of the desert as the privileged metaphor of Christian spiritual life was born. Others before Anthony, such as the Hebrew prophets, had taken the same path. They too became models of the spiritual life, so that the Carmels of the Carmelites became known as "deserts" in honor of Elijah.

Using one's imagination, one may say that the desert is an essentially inhuman place, stark and arid, so dry that it could explode at any moment into flame, a barren place, empty of images, without plants or animals, not cultivable, and filled with demons. The desert is wordless, impersonal, and passionless. It is pure unremitting detachment. One becomes other in the face of overwhelming otherness. In the desert, human beings are naked, thrown upon themselves, caught between vast earth and vast sky, as between two infinite horizons, exhausted by day, frozen by night, alone before God upon whose unthinkable, unknowable being all hangs like a feather on a leaf. From the experience arose the notion that God, too, is a desert, whose glory is forever hidden from human sight, and that the self likewise is to be stripped bare and made empty like a desert. "When you are praying, do not shape within yourself an image of the deity," advised Evagrius of Pontus, one of the founders of monastic spirituality. If an image comes, whether of a loved one, or of Jesus or Mary or of an angel, it comes from the devil and is an illusion—*Makio,* the Zen Buddhists call it.

The spiritual tradition of the "desert" is a great, wonderful, and complex thing, and, like all Christian striving, it has as its beginning and end the practice of love: to become charity or love in action. But it is not primarily a soul path, and it is unclear, in the end, how successful such desert practice is in healing soul wounds—our own and those of others. The "desert"—negative theology, unknowingness, the emptiness of the self as of God—is real and true. It does not exist, however, apart from the world of created things and natural, human, and cosmic happenings, but with it. Likewise, soul can never be found without spirit (or body) but with it—and the Word, too, is always with God, in the beginning, now, and forever, and Christ similarly is with Mary, the bridegroom with the bride, for all eternity.

The desert path is not a path through the world, but seeks to transcend, to escape it. The Earth is lesser and less desirable than Heaven. Yet they go together and are inseparable, bound into a single destiny. Otherwise, what we do here would have no relevance; we would leave it behind. But that cannot be. Earth must be every bit as important as Heaven. Or else Jesus would never have been born of Mary and suffered and died and risen so that humanity, the Earth, and the whole universe, could become one with Heaven and the Godhead itself. What we do—how we walk, the path we take—must transform the world and not just ourselves, peeling us from it. Some healing or "wholing" of the split between us and the world, and between Earth and Heaven, must occur.

Nevertheless, for many years, I continued to follow the desert path. I learned much from it; I found it intellectually fascinating, paradoxical, universal; I became wise in the subtleties of the *sophia perennis.* I became very "spiritual." Yet I remained unchanged. Some fundamental primal wound remained untouched. In some ways I had grown, but psychologically I remained wounded, broken, filled with unresolved memories, rejected experiences, pain, blindness, and darkness.

Then I discovered another metaphor, image, or path—that of the garden—to place beside the desert. With it, I discovered a new "soul" way of experiencing the spirit, through the Rosary, Mary's Rose Garden. This taught me much about the healing field of the soul.

How different is the call to the garden from the call to the desert! The garden is a much more human place. It is the human place—suprahuman, yes, but human too because made for, with, and by us. The garden is our home. It is enclosed and surrounded by the desert, the wilderness that lies outside the garden. As I learned, the desert too is also a garden, but one we do not yet know, just as disorder is an order that escapes comprehension.

Gardens abound in our cultural imagination, beginning with the first garden, Paradise, which God planted "eastward in Eden," where he placed our first ancestors. A garden was our first home. Eden, like every garden, is an Earth in miniature, teeming with minerals, plants, and animals, beautiful to the senses and nourishing to the soul and body, with water flowing through it, the soil damp and fertile, the sun coming and going, warm periods alternating with cool. Our first home.

Complementing the first garden is the garden of the soul, portentous of the future—our future home. This so-called "celestial Paradise" is also the woman "black and comely," "the rose of Sharon and the lily of the valleys," of whom Solomon sings in his Song of Songs. Into this garden, for this woman, "a garden enclosed … a spring shut up, a fountain sealed," filled with the images of fruits, precious stones, and flowers, the lover of the soul, the bridegroom, comes down. "Awake, O north wind; and come, thou South," the woman sings. "Blow upon my garden, that the spices thereof may flow out. Let my beloved come into his garden, and eat his pleasant fruits." He comes, the beloved, "up from the wilderness"—out of the desert, in his own sweet time, in a cataclysm of grace. He comes "like pillars of smoke, perfumed with myrrh and frankincense, with all the powers of the merchant." He sings: "I am come into my garden, my sister, my spouse." She sings in response, "My beloved has gone down into his garden, to the beds of spices, to feed in the gardens, and to gather lilies.

I am my beloved's, and my beloved is mine: he feedeth among the lilies." He comes because it is spring and the garden is fertile, well tended, full of good produce. "For, lo, winter is past and the rain is over and gone; the flowers appear on the earth; the time of the singing of birds is come, and the voice of the turtle is heard in our land; the fig tree putteth forth her green figs, and the vines with the tender grape give a good smell."

There are other gardens, too, more familiar and closer to our time. In the Middle Ages, time and again, initiatory romances begin with mysterious encounters in gardens—eros and psyche, Christ and Sophia. Think of the Unicorn tapestries in the Musée de Cluny in Paris. Then there are a plethora of alchemical gardens, "philosophical gardens" Philalethes calls them, where the alchemists "imitate nature in her mode of operation." He speaks of the "hidden gardens of the virgins Hesperides," the daughters of Night who take their name from Hesperos, the evening star, the star of Aphrodite. In those virginal gardens one may find the Golden Apples given by Gaia for the marriage of Zeus and Hera, and guarded by two serpents.

> A River springs amidst a Garden fair
> With flowers many deckt,
> Whose drops are Crystal like, these into Air
> By central heat are checkt,
> This air condenses like Pearl Orient,
> Which on this Body falls,
> Whose lustre on its blackness being spent,
> To brightness it recalls.
> And both together make a Crystal spring
> Whose streams most strangely shine;
> These after are condensed, and with them bring
> Treasures of silver fine.

Like all good gardens, the gardens are full of life. They are filled with a multiplicity of forms, and are rich in individual creatures, all of which, to the gardener, are of infinite value. None is preferred above the others; each has its place and function—even the so-called weeds. Each in its own unique way has value and beauty; each is true and good. Like all gardens, the gardens are temporal rather than spatial organisms. They must be cultivated in time, living time. All depends upon the right gesture at the right moment, and each moment is alive and drawn beyond itself by the whole in which it participates. Living time is immanent in the seasons, in the daily, hourly rhythms of climate, weather, and the moon, sun, and stars. Such time is fecund and enclosed, like the garden itself is. It seems to flow backward and forward, and round about, continuously circulating, teleological, connecting seed and fruit. Throughout the garden, fruit calls to seed and seed calls to fruit, and through the stages between seed and fruit, time nurtures and proliferates the infinite, harmonious infolding of the vitality, the regenerative power, the freshness of nature. Hildegard of Bingen calls the invisible sap *viriditas,* "greenness"—"the greenness of a paradise that knows no fall" as Peter Dronke, the medievalist puts it.

I discovered this *viriditas* and the healing field of the soul implicit in Rosary at a very difficult period of my life. It was one in which, forced by circumstances I was powerless to change, I was metaphorically brought to my knees and taught that life was meaning—always, inevitably, and necessarily filled with meaning, whether I recognized it or not. I learned that life always knew best, and was wise, and would always lift me up and carry me, whether I wanted it to or not. I learned, too, that all I could do was respond, with gratitude, praise, and reverence for whatever life brought. I learned that this was healing. I learned it with the force of a revelation through the Rosary at the feet and in the presence of Mary Sophia.

Physically, the Rosary is a string of beads, hung from a Cross. A person praying or meditating the Rosary starts from the Cross and moves up through five beads. On them one prays the invocation of the Trinity, the Apostle's Creed, the Our Father, the Hail Mary, and the *Gloria*: "Glory be to the Father and to the Son and to the Holy Spirit, as it was in the beginning, is now, and ever shall be, world without end. Amen." This leads one onto the chaplet or round of beads itself, which consists of five sets of ten smaller beads, separated by single larger beads, set slightly apart. One goes around three times—one hundred and fifty beads—a full *psalter.*

On the smaller beads one prays: "Hail Mary full of grace, the Lord is with you, blessed art thou among women and blessed is the fruit of thy womb, Jesus. Holy Mary, Mother of God, pray for us sinners now and at the hour of our death." On the larger bead, one prays the Our Father. One goes round the five sets of ten beads three times. 150 Hail Marys in all. Each round—each set of fifty beads divided into five groups of ten—represents one of the Mysteries of the life of Christ:

—first, the Joyful Mysteries;

—then the Sorrowful Mysteries;

—finally the Glorious Mysteries.

The "Mysteries" present the person praying the Rosary with a sequence of fifteen, or three sets of five, images that depict Christ's life as seen from both Mary's and our point of view. The images accompany the Hail Marys and continuously reframe them.

We begin with the images of the five Joyful Mysteries:

—The Annunciation, in which the angel Gabriel comes to Mary;

—The Visitation, in which Mary visits her cousin Elizabeth, in whose womb John the Baptist leaps, to which Mary responds with her Magnificat;

—The Nativity or birth of Jesus;

—The Presentation in the Temple, in which the old man Symeon makes his prophecies including that "a sword will pierce [Mary's] own soul too";

—And finally, the finding of Jesus in the Temple.

From this, we move to the images of the Sorrowful Mysteries:

—the Agony in the Garden;

—the Scourging at the Pillar;

—the Crowning with Thorns;

—the Carrying of the Cross;

—and fifthly, the Crucifixion.

Next come the images of the Glorious Mysteries:

—the Resurrection;

—the Ascension;

—the Descent of the Holy Spirit;

—the Assumption of Mary into Heaven;

—and, finally, the Coronation of Mary.

The images are important, for it is their interaction, embedded in and enlivening the repetitions, rhythms, and harmonies of the prayer, that sustains the soul in entering the field or garden that is healing.

The images themselves constitute a field. Every image is connected to, and interwoven with, every other image. There is no hierarchical organization. The whole is a circle, moving simultaneously forward and backward, so that the totality is truly an "enclosed garden." Through this garden the images and the prayers circulate without end. There is no end, or that is the experience, because we are always every point, spread throughout the whole. In saying the Rosary, we enter a different kind of time: continuous presence.

It is the images that differentiate the Rosary from other kinds of bead practices that depend more single-mindedly upon the mystery of repetition.

The images are interesting from another point of view. Note that, in listing the fifteen Mysteries, I am listing the essential iconography of Western art from the late Middle Ages through the sixteenth century. This suggests that much of early Western art might be related to the Rosary and raises the question of how the Rosary functioned in its original sacred setting.

The early history of the Rosary is obscure. There seem to have been two traditions: a tradition of reciting Hail Marys (which functioned as a surrogate psalm book for those who could not read) and a tradition of meditating on the life of Christ. Among the Beguines, for instance, both these practices were used and we find, accompanying the meditation on the life of Christ, the creation of images—in this case, three-dimensional, tactile images, small sculptures, above all of the *Piéta*. From the Beguines who used the image as a plastic, tactile icon, the image spread into sacred art, where it provided support for devotion, meditation, working upon the soul as medicine.

The two meditative traditions—recitation and imagery—came together in the early fifteenth century in a book called *Our Lady Mary's Rose Garden* by a Carthusian, Dominic of Prussia. He attributed his inspiration to one of the great mystics of Helfta, Mechtild of Hackeborn, to whom Jesus showed in a vision a beautiful tree on whose leaves the whole life of Christ was written in golden letters. On this basis, Dominic composed a series of points on the life of Christ to be meditated while reciting. The new practice was looked on as a lay liturgy. It was intended for those who could not speak Latin and follow the Mass. They were encouraged to say the Rosary during the

Mass. From such humble beginnings, the practice of the Rosary took like wildfire, and illustrated Rosary books began to be printed in great quantities for the growing numbers of Rosary confraternities. By 1481, the Cologne fraternity had over 100,000 members.

The deeper significance of this began to come clear to me when I read a study by Karen Roberts on "The Influence of the Rosary Devotion on Grünewald's Isenheim Altarpiece." Mathis Gotthart Nithart (Grünewald) created this altar, one of the masterpieces of Western art, for the Antonite hospital at Isenheim. The Antonites were and are a healing order, specifically devoted to the cure of skin diseases and, above all, the plague known then as St. Anthony's Fire and today as ergotism. It was designed for the choir altar of the church attached to the preceptory where the patients would be. In her dissertation, Karen Roberts shows that the panels of the Isenheim altarpiece are directly related to the Rosary and suggests that prayer with images was part of the Antonites' mystery of healing. It was not the sole remedy. There was surgery; there were herbal, specifically alchemical, tinctures; there was the Mass; there was music; and there was prayer, the Rosary, in conjunction with images—the altarpiece itself. The Antonites regarded this use of the altarpiece, and of the Rosary, as critical to the healing process. The Antonites were not alone in using such images. The Hôtel-Dieu in Beaune, France, founded in 1451 by Nicholas Rolin, and run by the Hospital Sisters of Valencienne to care for poor and sick peasants, used Rogier van der Weyden's Last Judgment altarpiece as part of their healing program. Rolin, the founder, required that the hall of thirty beds be continuous with the chapel so that patients who were too sick to leave their beds would still be able to view the masterpiece.

Images are important because the soul lives in and through images.

As one says the Rosary—I say "one," but I can really speak only for myself, self-taught on the beads—my experience is that one moves rhythmically through a flowing moiré pattern of images, one within another, over another, through another. An image, as James Hillman aptly pointed out, is not so much a thing seen, as a way of seeing, a mood of soul. In the Rosary, one begins with a mood of encounter, of reception, of being face-to-face with otherness, with newness— ultimately with resurrection, even redemption. The angel comes to Mary. She must have felt something akin to Rilke's overwhelming sense of a beauty that is the counterpart of an awe that we can barely begin to bear. The angel, the otherness, is full of reassurance. Mary responds with complete openness and radical acceptance. "Be it unto me according to thy word." Fundamental trust—which is implicit in the angelic salutation whose repetition accompanies the flow of images—is the ground for the entire field set up by the Rosary, the soil of the garden of the soul. It is the feeling that, no matter what, life is good, a transformative gift that will carry us forever forward, through joy and pain, longing and desire, on our endless journey to be at home where we are.

The ground of trust moves, in the next image, into praise—"My soul doth magnify my Lord and my spirit exults in God my savior"— conjoined with the sense of being blessed: "From this day forth, all generations will call me blessed." Then a third virtue or mood is added to the amalgam of trust and praise already set in motion: gratitude. "The almighty has done great things for me…. His mercy reaches from age to age."

We begin with trust, praise, gratitude.

I should point out an extraordinary feature of the field, the Rose Garden of Mary. First, as one repeats the angelic salutation—with each repetition or invocation—Mary is there. She is present, over-lighting and infusing the whole field with enormous love and compassion. She is filled with trust, praise, and gratitude, and forms our souls in her likeness. We ourselves, as it were, become Mary—we follow Mary's course through the life of Jesus, and we witness and participate in his life from her point of view. This point of view may be thought of as the epitome of service. Service is as selfless a "living with" as we can accomplish, an accompanying without, as the great psychoanalyst Wilfred Bion would say, "memory, desire, understanding, or even sense perception." It is a silent walking together in the invisible.

There is more as the field comes more and more into being. I can call this a sense of solidarity or community with all humanity and with the Earth. This solidarity grows from two sides—from Mary and from Christ.

From the side of Mary, we pray, "Holy Mary, Mother of God, pray for us sinners now and at the hour of our death," invoking all human beings and their mortality, our mortality. Since the world of the soul is also the world of the dead, we sense the presence of all the dead with Mary, praying for us and with us. It is as if in this prayer we unite with all human beings on both sides of the threshold. Our soul expands to include the heavens and the heavenly beings and begins to be a place where Heaven and Earth may intermingle and unite.

From the side of Christ, we move through the stages of his life. The crucifixion, the resurrection, and the ascension are perpetually before us and around us—behind us, above us, below us, as St. Patrick would say. We begin to understand that Christ Jesus, the first new human being, not only died, suffered, and rose for us, but that we, too, in all our ecstasies and travails, suffer and rejoice for, in, through, and with him. We feel at one with all suffering and rejoicing humanity, and understand the great saying of Julian of Norwich that, "in heaven, our sins will be glories to us."

With the shepherds and the angels, we are filled with praise and awe and joy. With Symeon, we understand and live in the paradoxical nature of this garden—that joy and suffering, life and death, living and dying are inextricably bound, two sides of a single reality: that healing salvation must "like a sword" also pierce the heart. With the twelve-year-old Jesus, teaching in the Temple and announcing to his mother that he must be about his Father's business, we recognize what life will require of us. It will require of us, as it does of Mary, a perfect letting go and dying to the little self for the sake of openness to facing reality as it is, without holding onto it or trying to change it.

Thus prepared, we may enter the Sorrowful Mysteries, which, paradoxically, are secretly the most truly joyful. From Mary's perspective, we witness the betrayal in the garden and the disciples' sleep. We witness Jesus' perfect submission—in response to which he receives angelic strength. We witness the scourging, which is the price of truth, of bearing witness to the truth. We often think of truth as something easy, but the truth is a purifying fire that burns away all old untruth. We must bear it with equanimity. Mary's witnessing is likewise in the same fiery furnace. She must stand by and see her son, whom she bore, mocked. She must watch as the crown of thorns pierces his brow. She must do all this in full identification, without understanding, and continue to trust, praise, bless, and thank—for the world of the garden is not linear, but simultaneous, all coexisting and conversing.

So, too, with the carrying of the Cross and the crucifixion. The paradox intensifies the coincidence of opposites—life and death, end and beginning, the totality of pain and the totality of joy, of possibility and impossibility, of complete hopelessness and absolute, certain trust and hope. We watch with Mary as if we did not know the end of the story—with radical openness, unthinking, unsaying. We watch with a mother's love and a mother's heart broken open, the clear salt of our tears mirroring the dark salt of his blood. But we are filled with unspeakable gratitude because we are loved before all else—that, as St. John wrote for Mary's community in Ephesus, God "loved us first" and that we exist and have our being within that love. "Your love reaches unto folly," Thérèse of Lisieux wrote. The love is without judgment, for the sake of our lives—no matter how messy, how strewn with falls. It is given to us—the ultimate gift—that we might rise into meaning.

Before he dies, Jesus says to the beloved disciple, and to us, standing with her at the foot of the Cross, "This is your mother." To Mary, he says, "This is your son." We understand that this garden, which is our soul and Mary's garden, will nurture and care for us when we are sick, will heal us and ultimately give us birth. Then Jesus dies, echoing Mary's "Be it unto me according to thy word." "Father, into thy hands I commend my spirit."

I am describing the echoing images, mysteries, sequentially, but when one is saying the Rosary they are present simultaneously, each reflecting the others. As soon as you invoke one, the others are there, a little like the Buddhist idea of "codependent origination" or Indra's net of jewels, each one of which reflects the others. As we move through the crucifixion into the resurrection, ascension, Pentecost, and so on, we are not moving forward, for these have been present all along—making possible what we have been doing.

The resurrection is thus a perpetual, continuous event. "The great life," in Joa Bolendas's phrase, is always present. This is one meaning of the Christian Mystery. Christ is always being crucified. He is in all suffering and pain, so that whenever we suffer or witness suffering, that suffering is always part of Christ's passion. Likewise, he is always rising. The resurrection is always present as a reality we are in, whether we are aware of it or not. The deaths we die are important—the falls,

the betrayals, the separations, the losses—but equally important are
our risings, our experience of new life flooding in. In a garden, though
spring comes but once a year, in another sense it is always spring,
always the greenness in the sap. Metamorphosis, death and resurrection, are continuous. Resurrection is different from rebirth. In resurrection, new life is continuous with old life. The Jesus who rises is the
same Jesus who dies. He bears the same marks and wounds. He takes
his human life with him into the resurrection. The soul, too, takes it
all with it, through and around its changes. What is different is the
context. We move from the context of the small life to that of the great
life—in Christian terms the life in Christ, in universal terms the life
that is the I AM we all are.

Saying the Rosary, entering the healing field of the garden, we live in
two currents of time flowing simultaneously. The great life, the future,
the resurrection flow into the small life of dying, becoming open, letting go, the two currents crossing at every moment, in every image, so
that they become one. In traditional terms, this is the marriage or
union of Christ with Mary. Living at the juncture, we are healed.

Next, we meditate the ascension—Jesus taken up to Heaven to take
his place at the right hand of God. Mary, too, will be assumed into
Heaven, and crowned, and sit at the left hand. This is a present reality.
It is the destiny of human beings to become children of God, of the
Earth to become a sun. This is the infinite possibility of our human
nature, the nobility and divinity of our humanness, which are central
to any healing of the soul.

What makes all possible, in the garden of the Rosary and in the
Christian Mystery as such, is the presence of the Holy Spirit in our
lives. And so we meditate the Descent of the Spirit at Pentecost. The
disciples are in an upper room, sitting in a circle around Mary; a powerful wind blows in from Heaven, and the Dove descends on Mary
and tongues of fire on each person present, a unique, individual
tongue of fire for each one.

This is the Holy Spirit, the spirit of love who is also the spirit of
truth who selflessly unveils the meaning of all things. The Holy Spirit
is like a fine rain that falls forever on the garden like a heavenly dew,
making it rich and fertile and bursting with new life: healing, meaning, insight. It falls on our life, for our life is an enclosed garden, a

whole, a round. Praying the Rosary, I have found that the healing field
it reveals is not limited to the practice of telling the beads but extends
to reveal the transformative meaning of my life as I live it, as a whole
and in its particulars, whether joyful or painful or glorious.

Like the Rosary, my life enacts a continuous conversation and intricate blending of images that—so long as I live in the threshold experience of trust, praise, gratitude, and openness to and identity/solidarity
with all that comes to meet me—unfold with wonder as well as with
sadness and pain. Underlying them and intensifying the never-ending
quality of the string of continually interacting and mutually reflecting
beads that is my life is the miraculous phenomenon of death and resurrection. We are always dying and rising again and, if we can let go of
our linear, spatial scenarios and enter into the living, sacred time of
the garden, the holy rain of grace will water and heal us as we go. That
is what is meant when, in the Gnostic Acts of John, Jesus invites us to
join his "round dance." Round dance or Rosary, the soul is healed
when it enters its own being. When we are at home in the garden,
tending and nurturing its plants, animals, and minerals, living
through all the seasons and days, so that even the cosmos becomes
part of our garden, healing comes like a gift and makes us whole.

This is what the Rosary reveals. It is true of all the phenomena of
our lives. I began with a conversation with a hospital chaplain that
ended as prayer, but I could have begun with any true encounter or
meeting with another human being or other human beings. For the
possibility of Mary's mediating presence exists in every moment.
Every moment gives the opportunity for the miracle of the Rosary to
occur. "Every moment," wrote Walter Benjamin, "is a moment the
Messiah could appear." Finally, it is conversation—in the sense of
Mary's Rose Garden—that makes possible the realization of Christ's
saying "When two or more are gathered together in my name I AM
there." At that moment, healing—the healing field—is also there.

15

Washing the Feet

> There is one body, and one Spirit, even as ye are called in
> one hope of your calling; one Lord, one faith, one baptism,
> one God and Father of all, who is above all, and through
> all, and in you all.
>
> —Ephesians 4:4–6

If we examine our relationship to the ground of our being, we
find a paradox. One side builds upon the grace by which each living
individual human being is potentially in contact with the eternal,
uncreated ground of all. This is the divine spark in each person to
which Meister Eckhart refers when he writes, "There is something in
the soul which is uncreated and uncreatable; if the whole soul were
this it would be uncreated and uncreatable; and this is the intellect."
Intellect is the Latin *intellectus,* synonyms for which are *spiritus,* spirit,
and *animus,* mind. A spiritual ferment exists in the soul, says Eckhart,
which, under certain conditions, can transform and spiritualize it. "In
this power, God is fully verdant and flowering, in all the joy and honor
that he is himself." Each particular has potentially a unique connection to the universal; but the connection must be made.

This is the relation of the individual to God—alone before the
alone. But the uncreated ground present in each has a similar relationship of identity to all other human beings—to all of creation. We are a
whole. This is the other side of the paradox. Both relationships are
"religious" in the sense that they "bind together" to re-form the
whole—religion and reformation being one. Nowadays, however,
there is a tendency to emphasize the mystical spirit immanent in each
human being and to ignore the aspect of the whole—humanity itself
(and the cosmos) as a mystical body. Yet the two aspects cannot be

separated, any more than the many can be separated from the one, or the body from the spirit. All things in the universe are essentially two—uncreated and created, creator and creation—and the two must be made one or, at least, not two. Such is the paradoxical work of creation. In the phrase of Maximus the Confessor, "Always and in all his Word God wills the mystery of his embodiment."

Everything hangs upon the soul, the *anima*.

Contrary to what one might expect, the soul or *anima* is traditionally taken to be our individualized and individualizing aspect. This is the separative, discursive faculty that establishes the line between this and that, past and present, self and not self, I and other. By such distinctions, we feel ourselves at first distinct; later, isolated; and finally, opposed to each other in fear, greed, envy, lust, etc. Faith, according to this tradition, is the hidden virtue and cure. It is the eye, the opening of the soul, by which she first sees and gives birth. For this reason, in Christianity, the exemplar of faith in its purest form is Mary, the "handmaid of the Lord," whose perfect surrender, epitomized in the phrase, "Be it unto me according to thy Word," echoes down the centuries to instruct us.

"Virgin," according to Meister Eckhart, "designates a human being who is devoid of all foreign images, and who is as void as he was when he was not yet." "Listen closely to the instruction that I am going to give you," he continues:

> I could have so vast an intelligence that all the images that all human beings have ever received and those that are in God himself were comprehended in my intelligence; however, if I were in no way attached to them, to the point that in everything I do or fail to do I did not cling to them with attachment—with its before and after—but if in this present now I kept myself unceasingly free and void for the beloved will of God and its fulfillment, then I should be a virgin, without the ties of all images, as truly as I was when I was not yet.

By images Eckhart means the contents of consciousness, the finished, fixed forms—past thoughts and memories—which we take to be the world, but are not the world in its immediacy and presentness, but only our own past, our own habits and fixed tendencies. Immured within the images, we feed upon ourselves and take our self-feeling for the world. These images interpose themselves between us and the world. They break the continuum of being, making any true meeting or true knowledge impossible. The antidote to the attachment, the normal condition of human consciousness, Eckhart calls *Gelassenheit*, releasement or detachment. Attachment imprisons us in the past, dismembers and fragments us. Detachment releases us for and to the present. Surrendering what is dead, materialized, and arrested in us—our mineral body—we become open to a genuinely new body.

Such detachment and openness is faith, the body of faith. Voidness is its activity; dematerialization, spiritualization, is its effect. "Faith cometh by hearing and hearing by the Word of God." Hearing is listening, attending. It requires silence and patience. If you are talking or in a hurry you cannot listen. Faith is inner silence. Listening in silence, renouncing and dissolving the categories of thought which rule us, relinquishing our ego's claim to be self-constituted and autonomous, we become open to the true awareness of things as they are. We hear the word spoken in silence, hear the word that silence speaks. In this way, as Eckhart says, the Virgin becomes a wife, a mother.

In the words of St. James: "Faith, if it hath not works, is dead, being alone.... For, as the body without the spirit is dead, so faith without works is dead also." What this might mean is suggested by the fact that Eckhart's "Hymn to Detachment," quoted above, explicitly echoes St. Paul's "Hymn to Love," with its refrain that whatever gifts I may have "and have not love" I am nothing, a sounding brass or a tinkling cymbal:

> Love is patient; love is kind and envies no one. Love is never boastful, nor conceited, nor rude; never selfish, not quick to take offence. Love keeps no scores of wrongs; does not gloat over other men's sins, but delights in the truth. There is nothing love cannot face; there is no limit to its faith, its hope and its endurance. (1 Cor. 13)

Love in this tradition is the fruit of faith. "For the beginning is faith and the end is love and when the two are joined together in unity it is God" (Ignatius). Faith is, in Krishnamurti's phrase, "freedom from the known," the *sine qua non* of unmediated knowing. The openness of faith or active release dissolves the carapace of habitual images and fixed circuits which we took to be the boundaries of the self. The objectified, materialized self opens into an experience of a provisional, contextual, "empty" self. Who we are becomes immanent in the network of relations we are engaged in. For a moment, we seem to be constituted by those relations, determined wholly by our recognition of an "other." Who we are becomes whom we are *with*, as the Word is with God. In the space of our relations we first come to be, and awaken.

To truly meet another one, as we are one, to feel something or someone in our inmost being as truly *real*, is very rare. We do not have *Gelassenheit*, and feel ourselves as more real than what surrounds us. We are the center of our attention. If we are honest, we rarely attend to anything else. Love, as St. Paul means it, begins with the recognition of the reality of something, someone, truly "other." Love and beauty are closely allied—beauty, which, in Rilke's words, "is the beginning of a terror we can hardly bear." They are the sudden, overwhelming presence of a reality greater than we are. Love recognizes the unconditional significance of an other. We have a carefully cultivated sense of our own importance—which we reinforce by projecting the world in our own image and then acting in it like a god. Then, suddenly, standing before a great work of art, a beautiful landscape, a person, we lay down the objectified self in recognition of something larger that, momentarily, takes possession and makes us feel more fluid and less bounded. This is well known. Lovers, like mystics, "melt" into their surroundings. Of the miracles of the everyday, love is the most available—each time we meet. "When two or three are gathered together in my name I am there." The mystery is, if this is so, what *body* shall he/she have, shall I have?

St. Paul can best guide us here, for he makes the right distinctions, separating flesh (*sarx*) and body (*soma*). Flesh refers to the outward, visible, mortal condition—to creation in the solidarity of its dismemberment, pain, and solitude. Flesh is the letter, the law, idolatry, by virtue of which sin (unfreedom, ignorance, suffering) comes to be. "Flesh" connotes human beings in their distance and difference, their isolation. It is sin because, denying the consubstantiality of humanity, creation, and God, it distorts the fundamental relationship of the universe, which is harmony, wholeness, and unity. Only by virtue of the spirit are humanity and human beings open to and together with the whole. St. Paul contrasts walking "after the spirit" with walking "after the flesh." He contrasts "carnal-mindedness," which is death, division, strife, and envy, with "spiritual-mindedness," which is life and peace.

St. Paul also uses the word "body"—with the connotation of wholeness or unity—to refer to the outer being, Wholeness is the essence of what a body is, and body means what is essentially whole or has become so. It is the body, not the flesh, that is the Temple of the Holy Ghost, the place of God's manifestation or glorification, where his Word is magnified.

St. Paul uses the term "body" collectively as well as individually. He moves freely from the one to the other, speaking now of the "individual" body, now of "the redemption of *our* body," of Christ reforming "the body of *our* humiliation." By this, body comes to connote what human beings have in common, irrespective of what appear to be individual differences. Mystically, we may take the consubstantiality to refer to human nature as a whole. The "body" connects human beings to each other and to the universe. Whereas "flesh" establishes human solitude and otherness, "body," joining human beings together, is the bearer of the resurrection. There is a body of sin, death, and humiliation, but there is also an immortal, resurrection body. There is no resurrection of the flesh. It is the body that is for the Lord and the Lord that is for the body.

Looking more closely at this body, which is the bride whose disunity is fragmentation and exile, we find that it is made up of beauty and love—it is a body of beauty and love. Call it *Shekhina* or Sophia. Love binds together what is separated, overcomes what separates, and brings parts together into a whole, a body. Love makes the body. But this love is not *eros;* it is *agape.* Platonic *eros,* though beginning with the soul movement inspired by the beauty of sensible things, leads the Platonist out of this world, intensifying desire into a single-pointed heavenly desire, whereby what is human is raised up. Platonic love, unlike Christian love, proposes as its end not identity-in-difference (i.e., relation) but identity-in-union. Its last term is death. But for *agape* or *caritas* (charity), death is the beginning. Love, which was death, becomes life, particularity. As God's love is particular—"He first loved us"—human love too must be particular, specific, from moment to moment.

"A new commandment I give you, that you love one another as I have loved you." There were two old commandments—to love God with all one's heart and all one's mind, and to love one's neighbor as oneself. These are human loves; they derive from the human point of view and indicate the path from the human to the divine. Such is the activity of *eros,* by which all things yearn for unity. The new commandment, fulfilling but not eliminating the old, proposes an inversion: that one love, not from a limited, human perspective, but from an absolute, universal, limitless point of view. The inversion is profound; by it "human" love is "divine presence." To love one's neighbor as oneself means to love one's neighbor *as if* he or she were oneself. The new commandment inverts this. It enjoins one to love for the sake of the other alone, to give oneself unconditionally, to empty oneself utterly: to go beyond oneself, out of oneself, so that one becomes, as it were, "nothing." It is to act as God acts, to love as God loves—God who loved us first.

Such action, which does not imitate but makes present, has been called by J. Edgar Bruns "the Christian Buddhism of St. John," who is the great teacher. For John, what humans *do* reveals God's presence, and is God's presence, just as for the Mahayanist it is the understanding that is the Buddha-nature—not conversely. "No one has seen God," but the Son has "acted him out." Similarly, "No man hath seen God; if we love one another, God abides in us"—because, for St. John, God *is* love. God is not some thing; he does not do anything; rather he is the doing. God cannot be identified with any faculty or any entity— in our activity we reveal him, he is there. Consequently, to be born of God means to bear God—in both senses of giving birth to and carrying. If we "love" we make "God" present, because "God" is "love." "God is love, and whoever abides in love, abides in God, and God abides in him." If we abide in love, remain in and one with it—if it becomes our body—our activity becomes what is divine. There is no dualism—no difference between the love that is our body and our spiritual unity with God, because God, Spirit, True Self, is another name for the love which is our body. Most important is that the activity of love, which allows for presence and realization, requires the recognition, the presence, of another. Making God present is an interhuman, relational activity. It is not achieved on the mountaintop. St. Basil had this in mind when, after a trip to the eremitical settlements of the Egyptian desert, he remarked, "That is all very well, but whose feet will they wash?"

To wash the feet, an activity paradigmatic of love, means laying down our own sense of unconditional value in recognition of the unconditional value of another. We shift the center of our lives away from ourselves as objects of our own attention; we change the direction of our attention and we become other. Forced to acknowledge the reality of another, we are forced to relinquish the sense of ourselves as isolated, atomic, selfish beings, to abandon the selves we have constituted by materializing past memories, thoughts, and desires into the complex artifact with which we have identified. As the Russian philosopher Solovyov puts it, "The meaning of human love, speaking generally, is the justification and deliverance of individuality through the sacrifice of egoism." Inversely: "The truth, as a living force, taking possession of the inward essence of human beings, and effectively rescuing them from false self-assertion, is termed love." As to the difference between true individuality and the false individuality of egoism, Solovyov is clear. The fundamental illusion of egoism does not lie in the absolute self-assertion and self-estimation of the subject, but rather in the subject's denial to others of the unconditional significance accorded to himself, relegating them to the circumference of his being and giving them only an external and relative value.

Washing of the feet is more than simple humility or ordinary selflessness. By its active identification with the other, the love it manifests overcomes "materiality" and affirms the consubstantiality of creation, the body of the whole. "Materiality," material existence, which is opposed to the consubstantial unity of the world, presents us with a twofold impenetrability:

1. Impenetrability in *time*, by power of which every successive moment of existence does not preserve the preceding one within itself,

but excludes it or dislodges it from existence, so that each new thing in the sphere of matter originates at the expense of, or to the detriment of, what preceded it.

2. Impenetrability in *space*, by power of which two parts of matter (two bodies) cannot at the same time occupy one and the same place, i.e., one and the same part of space, but necessarily dislodge one another.

By this we define ourselves, our bodies, and irrevocably make the world a place of dismemberment and conflict. Unmaking this view, transforming ourselves by love, we become consubstantial with one another. We become many persons in one body.

What is this body? According to one view it is *Sophia* or Divine Wisdom. Pavel Florensky, as we saw, speaks of Sophia as "the great root of the created world in its wholeness and unity," and "the original substance of creatures, the creative Love of God in them." Sophia is at once the ideal substance of the created world, its truth or meaning, and its spirituality—its holiness, purity, sinlessness, and beauty. She is the beginning and center of the redeemed creation, the Body of the Lord. In Christian terms, she is the Virgin Mary, the purified human soul. The mystery is that there is an another, uncreated Sophia. This Sophia is "God's revelation and the Holy Spirit's corporeality, the body of the Holy Trinity." As on Earth Sophia is the unity of creation, so in Heaven she is the Godhead's unity.

The unity of the Godhead, of the Persons, brings us closer to understanding the unity or body that human beings have and are— that allows them to become true persons likewise. For the self or intellect to manifest, said Eriugena, the soul, whose virtue is faith and whose vice is egoism, must summon it. By faith it must, in Eckhart's words, overcome egoism and become virgin, imageless, a perfect mirror. Considering the Virgin in her activity, we find her the exemplar of the human virtues of chastity, poverty, and obedience. Such must we be also. She lays down her will in order to live from moment to moment the will of the Divine. According to the Christian story, by that activity of perfect love and surrender, the Virgin was able to form a body for the Logos, God's Word—to become his mother and his bride. Christian tradition takes her for the true type of the church or mystical body—the universal body redeemed at once from below and from above: from below by the human activity of the renunciation of selfishness; from above by the descent of the Holy Spirit. But the two activities are one, as body and spirit, soul and spirit are one. The place of their meeting is who we are.

Have I dissolved the body by some metaphysical sleight-of-hand? Have I denied the unique relationship each one of us enjoys with the unfathomable ground of being? I hardly think so. There is no body outside the body we cognize, perceive, think about—and that body is the projection of the self we think we are. We only see ourselves. All the great traditions teach us to become other—our body must become other. We are our body, but not the body we think we are. Realizing our true self through the laying down of our selves, we become one with each other, we realize the single body of all humanity and become truly one for the first time.

Cumulative Selective Bibliography

1. The Way of Wisdom

Allen, Paul M. *Vladimir Solovyov: Russian Mystic.* New York, 1978.

Bock, Emil. *The Childhood of Jesus.* Edinburgh, 1997.

———. *The Three Years.* Edinburgh, 1987.

Bulgakov, Sergei. *Sophia, The Wisdom of God.* Hudson, N.Y., 1993.

Corbin, Henry. *Avicenna and the Visionary Recital.* Dallas, 1980.

———. *Creative Imagination in the Sufism of Ibn 'Arabi.* Princeton, 1969.

———. "The Eternal Sophia." *Harvest,* vol. 31, 1985.

Florensky, Pavel. *The Pillar and Foundation of the Truth.* Princeton, 1997.

———. *The Salt of the Earth.* Platina, Calif., 1988.

Foerster, Werner. *Gnosis: A Selection of Gnostic Texts.* Oxford, 1972.

Matthews, Caitlin. *Sophia, Goddess of Wisdom: The Divine Feminine from Black Goddess to World Soul.* London, 1991.

MacDermott, Violet. *The Fall of Sophia: A Gnostic Text on the Redemption of Universal Consciousness.* Great Barrington, 2001.

Newman, Barbara. *Saint Hildegard of Bingen: Symphonia.* Ithaca, 1988.

———. *Sister of Wisdom: St. Hildegard's Theology of the Feminine.* Berkeley, 1987.

Prokofieff, Sergei O. *Eternal Individuality: Towards a Karmic Biography of Novalis.* London, 1992.

———. *The Spiritual Streams of Eastern Europe and the Future Mysteries of the Holy Grail.* London, 1993.

———. *The Twelve Holy Nights and the Spiritual Hierarchies.* London, 1990.

Robinson, James M., ed. *The Nag Hammadi Library in English.* San Francisco, 1990.

Schäfer, Peter. *Mirror of His Beauty: Feminine Images of God from the Bible to the Early Kabbalah.* Princeton, 2002.

Schipflinger, Thomas. *Sophia-Maria: A Holistic Vision of Creation.* York Beach, Maine, 1998.

Solovyov, Vladimir. *Lectures on Divine Humanity.* Hudson, N.Y., 1995.

Steiner, Rudolf. *Building Stones for an Understanding of the Mystery of Golgotha.* London, 1972.

———. *Christianity as Mystical Fact.* New York, 1976.

———. *From Jesus to Christ.* London, 1973.

———. *The Gospel of St. John.* Hudson, N.Y., 1992.

———. *Isis Mary Sophia: Her Mission and Ours.* Great Barrington, 2003.

———. *The Redemption of Thinking.* New York, 1983.

———. *The Spiritual Hierarchies and the Physical World.* Hudson, N.Y., 1996.

Thérèse of Lisieux. *Her Last Conversations.* Translated by. John Clarke. Washington, 1977.

———. *Letters*, Washington, 1982
———. *Story of a Soul.* Translated by. John Clarke. Washington, 1976.
Versluis, Arthur. *Theosophia: Hidden Dimensions of Christianity.* Hudson, N.Y., 1994.
———. *Wisdom's Book: The Sophia Anthology.* St. Paul, Minn., 2000.
———. *Wisdom's Children: A Christian Esoteric Tradition.* Albany, 1999.
Von Balthasar, H. U. *The Glory of the Lord: A Theological Aesthetics.* 7 vols. San Francisco, 1982.
———. *Theo-Drama: Theological Dramatic Theory.* 5 vols. San Francisco, 1988.
Von Speyer, Adrienne. *Handmaid of the Lord.* San Francisco, 1985.

2. Our Daily Bread

Lubheid, C., trans. *Pseudo-Dionysius: The Complete Works.* New York, 1988.
Nicholson, R. A., trans. *Rumi, Poet and Mystic.* London, 1978.
Prabhavananda, Swami, and Christopher Isherwood, trans. *The Song of God: The Bhagavad-Gita.* New York, 1972.
Radhakrishnan, S., ed. and trans. *The Principle Upanisads,* London, 1968.
Rilke, Rainer Maria. *Selected Letters.* New York, 1988.
Schwaller de Lubicz, R. A. *Esotericism and Symbol.* New York, 1985.
Swedenborg, Emanuel. *The Divine Love and Wisdom.* London, 1933.
———. *Heaven and Hell.* New York, 1979.

3. The Hermetic Tradition

Aniane, Maurice. "Notes on Alchemy, the Cosmological 'Yoga' of Medieval Christianity." *Material for Thought,* Spring, 1976.
Bateson, Gregory. *Mind and Nature, A Necessary Unity.* New York, 1988.
———. *Steps to an Ecology of Mind: Collected Essays in Anthropology, Psychiatry, Evolution, and Epistemology.* Chicago, 2000.
Burckhardt, Titus. *Alchemy.* Louisville, Ky., 1998.
Eliade, Mircea. *The Forge and the Crucible: The Origins and Structure of Alchemy.* Chicago, 1978.
Evola, Julius. *The Hermetic Tradition.* Rochester, Vt., 1995.
Faivre, Antoine. *The Eternal Hermes: From Greek God to Alchemical Magus.* Grand Rapids, Mich., 1995.
———. *Theosophy, Imagination, Tradition: Studies in Western Esotericism.* Albany, 2000.
Festugière, A.-J. *La Révélation de Hermès Trismégiste.* Paris, 1944.
Fulcanelli. *The Dwellings of the Philosophers.* Boulder, 1999.
———. *The Mystery of the Cathedrals.* London, 1971.
Guénon, René. "Hermes." In *The Sword of Gnosis,* edited by Jaacob Needleman, 370–375. Baltimore, 1974.
Hirst, Désirée. *Hidden Riches: Traditional Symbolism from the Renaissance to Blake.* London, 1964.
Holmyard, E. J. *Alchemy.* Harmondsworth, Middlesex, 1957.

Jones, Rufus. *Spiritual Reformers in the 16th and 17th Centuries.* Boston, 1959.

Kühlewind, Georg. *Becoming Aware of the Logos: The Way of St. John the Evangelist.* West Stockbridge, Mass., 1985.

———. *The Logos Structure of the World.* Hudson, N.Y., 1992.

———. *Stages of Consciousness: Meditations on the Boundaries of the Soul.* West Stockbridge, Mass., 1984.

Lindsay, Jack. *The Origins of Alchemy in Greco-Roman Egypt.* London, 1970.

Lossky, V. *The Mystical Theology of the Eastern Church.* London, 1957.

———. *On the Image and Likeness of God.* Crestwood, N.Y., 1974

———. *Orthodox Theology.* Crestwood, N.Y., 1978.

———. *The Vision of God.* London, 1963.

Mead, G. R. S. *Thrice Greatest Hermes: Studies in Hellenistic Theosophy and Gnosis.* London, 1964.

Meyendorff, John. *A Study of Gregory Palamas.* London, 1964.

Olson, Charles. *Collected Poetry.* Berkeley, 1997.

———. *Collected Prose.* Berkeley, 1997.

Pagel, Walter. *Paracelsus, An Introduction to Philosophical Medicine in the Era of the Renaissance.* Basel, 1958.

———. *Joan Baptista Van Helmont: Reformer of Science and Medicine.* Cambridge, 1982.

Schwaller de Lubicz, R. A. *The Egyptian Miracle.* New York, 1985.

———. *Nature Word.* West Stockbridge, Mass., 1984.

———. *Sacred Science.* New York, 1982.

———. *Symbol and Symbolic.* Brookline, Mass., 1978.

———. *The Temple of Man: Apet of the South at Luxor.* Rochester, Vt., 1998.

Scott, Walter. *Hermetica: Ancient Greek and Latin Texts which Contain Religious or Philosophic Teachings Ascribed to Hermes Trismegistus.* 4 vols. Oxford, 1924.

Stavenhagen, Lee, ed. and trans. *A Testament of Alchemy: Being the Revelations of Morienus to Khalid ibn Yazid.* Hanover, N.H., 1974.

Steiner, Rudolf. *The Case for Anthroposophy.* London, 1974.

———. *The Secret Stream: Christian Rosenkreutz and Rosicrucianism.* Great Barrington, 2000.

VandenBroeck, André. *Al-Kemi, A Memoir: Hermetic, Occult, Political, and Private Aspects of R. A. Schwaller de Lubicz.* Great Barrington, 1987.

Van den Broek, Roelof, and Wooter J. Hannegraaff, eds. *Gnosis and Hermeticism: From Antiquity to Modern Times.* Albany, 1998.

Yates, Frances A. *Giordano Bruno and the Hermetic Tradition.* Chicago, 1979.

4. Orpheus's Perpetual Return

Athanassakis, Apostolos N. *The Orphic Hymns.* Missoula, Mont., 1977.

Burkert, W. *Lore and Science in Ancient Pythagoreanism.* Cambridge, Mass., 1972.

Chadwick, Norah K. *Poetry and Prophecy.* Cambridge, 1942.

Deck, J. *Nature, Contemplation and the One.* Toronto, 1967.

De Santillana, Giorgio, and Hertha von Dechend. *Hamlet's Mill.* Boston, 1969.

De Vogel, C. J. *Pythagoras and Early Pythagoreanism.* Assen and New York, 1966.

Findlay, J. N. *Plato: The Written and Unwritten Doctrines.* New York, 1974.

Guthrie, W. K. C. *Orpheus and Greek Religion.* New York, 1966.

Hamilton, Edith, and Huntington Cairns, eds. *The Collected Dialogues of Plato.* Princeton, 1980.

Harrison, Jane. *Prologomena to the Study of Greek Religion.* New York, 1955.

Iamblichus. *Life of Pythagoras.* Translated by Thomas Taylor. London, 1965.

Mead, G. R. S. *Orpheus.* London, 1965.

Proclus. *The Commentaries of Proclus on the Timaeus of Plato.* Translated by Thomas Taylor. London, 1820.

———. *Diadochus, A Commentary on the First Books of Euclid's Elements.* Translated by G. R. Morrow. Princeton, 1970.

Weil, Simone, *Intimations of Christianity among the Ancient Greeks.* Edited and translated by Ruth Chase Geissbuhler. London, 1976.

Westerinck, L. G. *The Greek Commentaries on Plato's Phaedo:* Vol. 1, *Olympiodorus;* Vol. II, *Damascius.* Amsterdam, 1976, 1977.

5. The New Song

Merton, Thomas, trans. *Clement of Alexandria: Selections from The Protreptikos.* New York, 1962.

Rosenstock-Huessy, E. *The Fruit of Lips or Why Four Gospels.* Pittsburgh, 1978.

———. *Speech and Reality.* Norwich, Vt., 1970.

6. The Mystery of Celtic Christianity

Anderson, A. O., and M. O. Anderson, eds. *Adamnan's Life of Columba.* Oxford, 1991.

Armstrong, A. H. *The Cambridge History of Later Greek and Early Medieval Philosophy.* Cambridge, 1970.

Bamford, Christopher. *The Voice of the Eagle: The Heart of Celtic Christianity, John Scotus Eriugena's Homily on the Prologue to the Gospel of St. John.* Great Barrington, 2000.

Bergin, Osborn. *Irish Bardic Poetry.* Dublin, 1970.

Bett, H. *Johannes Scotus Erigena: A Study in Medieval Philosophy.* London, 1925.

Bieler, L. Ireland. *Harbinger of the Middle Ages.* Oxford, 1966.

Bitel, Lisa M. *Isle of the Saints: Monastic Settlements and Christian Community in Early Ireland.* Cork, 1990.

Carabine, D. *John Scottus Eriugena.* Great Medieval Thinkers. Oxford, 2000.

Carey, John. *King of Mysteries: Early Irish Religious Writings.* Dublin, 2000.

———. *A Single Ray of the Sun: Religious Speculation in Early Ireland.* Andover and Aberystwyth, 1999.

Carney, James. *Early Irish Poetry.* Cork, 1965.

———. *Medieval Irish Lyrics.* Dublin, 1967.

Chadwick, Norah K. *The Age of the Saints in the Celtic Church.* Oxford, 1961.

———. *Studies in the Early British Church.* Cambridge, 1958.

De Paor, Liam. *St Patrick's World.* Blackrock, Dublin, 1996.

De Paor, Maire B. *Patrick, the Pilgrim Apostle of Ireland*. Dublin, 1998.

Eriugena, John Scotus. *Periphyseon: On the Division of Nature*. Translated by I. P. Sheldon-Williams and John O'Meara. Montreal and Washington, 1988.

———. *Treatise on Divine Predestination*. Translated by Mary Brennan. Notre Dame, Ind., 1998.

Finley, Ian. *Columba*. London, 1979.

Flower, Robin. *The Irish Tradition*. Oxford, 1970.

Gougaud, L. *Christianity in Celtic Lands*. London, 1932.

Herbert Maire. *Iona, Kells, and Derry*. Oxford, 1988.

Howlett, D. R. *The Book of Letters of Saint Patrick, the Bishop*. Dublin, 1994.

Hughes, K. *Early Christian Ireland*. Cambridge, 1979.

Kenney, J. F. *Sources for the Early History of Ireland*. New York, 1968.

Macleod, Fiona. *Iona*. Edinburgh, 1982.

Merry, Eleanor. *The Flaming Door*. Edinburgh, 1990.

Maher, Michael, ed. *Irish Spirituality*. Dublin, 1981.

McCone, Kim. *Pagan Past and Christian Present in Early Irish Literature*. Maynooth, 1990.

Moran, D. *The Philosophy of John Scottus Eriugena*. Cambridge, 1989.

O'Donnel, Manus. *The Life of Colum Cille*. Edited by Brian Lacey. Blackrock, Dublin, 1998.

O'Donoghue, Noel Dermot. *Aristocracy of Soul: Patrick of Ireland*. London, 1987.

O'Fiannachta, Padraig, ed. *Saltair: Prayers from the Irish Tradition*. Translated by Desmond Forristal. Dublin, 1988.

O'Meara, J. *Eriugena*. Oxford, 1988.

O'Meara, J, and L. Bieler, eds. *The Mind of Eriugena*. Dublin, 1973.

Poole, R. L. *Illustrations of the History of Medieval Thought and Learning*. London, 1884. Reprint, New York, 1960.

Rees, Alwyn, and Brinley Rees. *Celtic Heritage*. London, 1961.

Steiner, Rudolf. *Mystery Knowledge and Mystery Centres*. London, 1973.

Ryan, John. *Irish Monasticism*. Dublin, 1931.

Taylor, John W. *The Coming of the Saints: Imaginations and Studies in Early Church History and Tradition*. London, 1906.

Walsh, John R., and Thomas Bradley. *A History of the Irish Church 400-700 AD*. Dublin, 1991.

Whiteside, Leslie. *In Search of Columba*. Blackrock, Dublin, 1997.

7. What Ails Thee?

Ashe, Geoffrey. *Avalonian Quest*. London, 1982.

Goodrich, Norma Lorre. *The Holy Grail*. New York, 1992.

Heline, Corrine. *Mysteries of the Holy Grail*. Los Angeles, 1977.

Loomis, Roger Sherman. *The Grail: From Celtic Myth to Christian Symbol*. Princeton, 1991.

Matthews, John. *The Grail: Quest for the Eternal*. Illustrated Library of Sacred Imagination. London, 1981.

Seddon, Richard. *The Mystery of Arthur at Tintagel*. London, 1990.

Stein, Walter Johannes. *The Ninth Century and the Holy Grail*. London, 1983.

Steiner, Rudolf. *Christ and the Human Soul: The Mystery of the Holy Grail*. London, 1992.

Von Eschenbach, Wolfram. *Parzival*. Translated by A. T. Hatto. Harmondsworth, Middlesex, 1980.

Weston, Jesse L. *From Ritual to Romance*. New York, 1957.

Wyatt, Isabel. *From Round Table to Grail Castle*. Sussex, 1979.

Williams, Charles, and C. S. Lewis. *Arthurian Torso*. Oxford, 1948.

8. The Troubadours and the Cultivation of Eros

Blackburn, Paul, trans. *Proensa: An Anthology of Troubadour Poetry*. New York, 1986.

Bogin, Meg. *The Women Troubadours*. New York, 1976.

Carson, Anne. *Eros, The Bittersweet*. Princeton, 1986.

Dronke, Peter. *Medieval Latin and the Rise of the European Love Lyric*. 2 vols. Oxford, 1965, 1966.

———. *The Medieval Lyric*. London, 1968.

Goldin, Frederick. *German and Italian Lyrics of the Middle Ages*. New York, 1973.

Guénon, René. *Fundamental Symbol: The Universal Language of Sacred Science*. Cambridge, 1995.

Lacan, Jacques. *Ecrits*. Translated by Bruce Fink. New York, 2002.

———. *On Feminine Sexuality, the Limits of Love and Knowledge: The Seminar of Jacques Lacan, XX, Encore 1972–73*. Translated by Bruce Fink. New York, 1998.

Makin, Peter. *Provence and Pound*. Berkeley, 1978.

Nelli, René. *L'Erotique des Troubadours*. Toulouse, 1963.

Plummer, John F., ed. *Vox Feminae: Studies in Medieval Women's Song*. Kalamazoo, Mich., 1981.

Pound, Ezra. *Literary Essays*. London, 1960.

———. *The Spirit of Romance*. New York, 1968.

Roché, Déodat. *Le Catharisme*. 2 vols. Narbonne, 1957.

———. *L'Eglise romaine et les Cathares albigeois*. Arques (Aude), 1957.

Spitzer, Leo. "The Mozarabic Lyric and Theodore Frings' Theories." *Comparative Literature* 4, 1952.

Surette, Leon. *A Light from Eleusis: A Study of Ezra Pound's Cantos*. Oxford, 1979.

Topsfield, L. T. *Troubadours and Love*. Cambridge, 1975.

9. The Meaning of the Rose Cross

Allen, Paul M., ed. *A Christian Rosenkreutz Anthology*. Blauvelt, N.Y., 1968.

Arnold, Paul. *Histoire des Rose-Croix et les origines de la Franc-Maçonnerie*. Paris, 1955.

Barnes, Robin Bruce. *Prophecy and Gnosis: Prophecy in the Wake of the Lutheran Reformation*. Stanford, 1988.

Burckhardt, Titus. *Fez, City of Islam*. Cambridge, 1992.

Chacornac, Paul. *Grandeur et Adversité de Jean Trithème.* Paris, 1963.

Case, Paul Foster. *The True and Invisible Rosicrucian Order.* York Beach, Maine, 1989.

Clulee, Nicholas H. *John Dee's Natural Philosophy.* London, 1988.

Debus, A. G. *The Chemical Dream of the Renaissance.* Cambridge, 1968.

Edighoffer, Roland. *Rose-Croix et Société Idéal selon Johann Valentin Andreae.* Neuilly sur Seine, 1982.

French, Peter J. *John Dee: The World of an Elizabethan Magus.* London, 1972.

Gertrude of Helfta. *The Herald of Divine Love.* Translated and edited by Margaret Winckworth. New York, 1993.

———. *Spiritual Exercises.* Translated and introduced by Gertrud Joan Lewis and Jack Lewis. Kalamazoo, Mich., 1989.

Godwin, Joscelyn, trans. *The Chemical Wedding of Christian Rosenkreutz.* Grand Rapids, Mich., 1991.

Guénon, René. *Initiation and Spiritual Realization.* Ghent, N.Y., 1999.

———. *Perspectives on Initiation.* Ghent, N.Y., 1999.

King, Margot H, trans. *The Life of Lutgard of Aywières.* Toronto, 1987.

Lapoukhin, I. V. *Some Characteristics of the Interior Church.* London, 1912.

McGinn, Bernard, ed. *Apocalyptic Spirituality.* New York, 1979.

McIntosh, Christopher. *The Rose Cross and the Age of Reason.* Leyden, 1992.

———. *The Rosicrucians.* Wellingborough, 1987.

Merkur, Dan. "The Study of Spiritual Alchemy." *Ambix* XXXVIII, no. 1, 1990.

Montaigu, Henri. *Paray-le-Monial: Synbole et Prophetie du Sacré Coeur.* La Place Royale, 1979.

Montgomery, John Warwick. *Cross and Crucible: Johann Valentin Andreae, Phoenix of the Theologians.* The Hague, 1973.

Newmann, William R. *Gehennical Fire, The Lives of George Starkey, an American Alchemist.* Cambridge, Mass., 1994.

Obrist, Barbara. *Constantine of Pisa: The Book of the Secrets of Alchemy.* Leyden, 1990.

Reeves, Margerie. *The Influence of Prophecy in the Later Middle Ages, A Study in Joachiism.* Oxford, 1969.

———. *Joachim of Fiore and the Prophetic Future.* London, 1976.

Ritman, Joseph R. "The Key to Hermetic Philosophy." *Hermetic Journal* 35, 1987.

Robin, Jean. *Le Royaume du Graal.* Paris, 1993.

Sédir. *Histoires et Doctrines des Rose-Croix.* Paris, 1932.

Steiner, Rudolf. *Esoteric Christianity and the Mission of Christian Rosenkreutz.* London, 1984.

———. *Rosicrucianism and Modern Initiation.* London, 1982.

———. *The Secret Stream: Christian Rosenkreutz and Rosicrucianism.* Great Barrington, 2000.

Toulmin, Stephen. *Cosmopolis: The Hidden Agenda of Modernism.* Chicago, 1992.

Szydlo, Zbigniew. *Water Which Does Not Wet Hands: The Alchemy of Michael Sendivogius.* Warsaw, 1994.

Waite, A. E. *The Brotherhood of the Rosy Cross.* New Hyde Park, N.Y., 1961.

———. *The Real History of the Rosicrucians.* Blauvelt, N.Y., 1977.

Waldenses, Vaughan, Ashley McFadden, et al. *A Rosicrucian Primer*. Edmonds, Wash., 1994.

Yates, Frances A. *The Occult Philosophy in the Elizabethan Age*. London, 1979.

———. *The Rosicrucian Enlightenment*. London, 1972.

Woohouse, C. M. *George Gemistos Plethon: The Last of the Hellenes*. Oxford, 1986.

10. The Love that Moves the Stars

Aeldred of Rievaulx. *Spiritual Friendship*. Translated by Mary Eugenia Laker. Kalamazoo, Mich., 1974.

Cassirer, Ernst. *The Individual and the Cosmos in Renaissance Philosophy*. New York, 1963.

Couliano, Ioan P. *Eros and Magic in the Renaissance*. Chicago, 1987.

Ficino, Marsilio. *Commentary on Plato's Symposium on Love*. Translated by Sears Jayne. Dallas, 1985.

———. *The Letters of Marsilio Ficino*. 8 vols. Translated by members of the Language Department of the School of Economic Science, London. London, 1975, etc.

French, Robert. "The Ancient Philosophers were Right: It is Friendship that Holds Organizations Together." EGOS Annual Colloquium, Barcelona, July 4–6, 2002.

Garin, Eugenio. *Portraits from the Quatrocento*. New York, 1972.

Klibansky, Raymond. *The Continuity of the Platonic Tradition during the Middle Ages*. London, 1939.

Kristeller, P. O. *Eight Philosophers of the Renaissance*. Stanford, 1966.

———. *The Philosophy of Marsilio Ficino*. New York, 1943.

———. *Renaissance Concepts of Man*. New York, 1972.

Lewis, C. S. *The Four Loves*. London, 1960.

McGuire, Brian Patrick. *Friendship and Community: The Monastic Experience 350–1250*. Kalamazoo, Mich., 1988.

Mandelstam, Osip. *Complete Critical Prose*. Ann Arbor, 1979.

Solnit, Rebecca. *Wanderlust, A History of Walking*. New York, 2000.

Thoreau, Henry David. *Excursions.* New York, 1962.

Walker, D. P. *Spiritual and Demonic Magic from Ficino to Campanella*. London, 1958.

Wind, Edgar. *Pagan Mysteries in the Renaissance*. Oxford, 1980.

11. The Magus of the North

Berlin, Isaiah. *The Magus of the North: J. G. Hamann and the Origins of Modern Irrationalism*. New York, 1993.

Corbin, Henry, *Hamann*. Paris, 1980.

Hamann, J. G. *Aesthetica in nuce: A Rhapsody in Kabbalistic Prose*. Translated by Joyce P. Crick, in H. B. Nisbet, ed., *German Aesthetic and Literary Criticism*. Cambridge, 1985.

———. *Golgotha and Shlebinini*. In Stephen N. Dunning, The *Tongues of Men: Hegel and Hamann on Religious Language*. Missoula, Mont., 1979.

————. *Socratic Memorabilia.* Translated by James C. O'Flaherty. Baltimore, 1967.

Hoffmanshal, Hugo von. *Selected Prose.* New York, 1952.

Leibrecht, Walter. *God and Man in the Thought of Hamann.* Philadelphia, 1966.

O'Flaherty, James. *Johann Georg Hamann.* Boston, 1979.

Smith, Ronald Gregor. *J. G. Hamann, 1730–1788: A Study in Christian Existence, With Selections from his Writings.* London, 1960.

Stahmer, Harold. *"Speak That I May See Thee": The Religious Significance of Language.* New York, 1968.

12. Becoming Novalis

Blanchot, Maurice. "The Athenaeum," in *The Infinite Conversation.* Translated by Susan Hanson. Minneapolis, 1993.

Dyck, Martin. *Novalis and Mathematics.* New York, 1969.

Hamburger, Michael. *Reason and Energy: Studies in German Literature.* London, 1957

Hiebel, Friedrich. *Novalis: German Poet, European Thinker, Christian Mystic.* New York, 1969.

Lacoue-Labarthe, Philippe, and Jean Luc Nancy. *The Literary Absolute: The Theory of Literature in German Romanticism.* Translated by P. Barnard and C. Lester. Albany, 1988.

Novalis. *Heinrich von Ofterdingen.* Translated by Palmer Hilty. New York, 1964.

————. *Hymns to the Night and Other Selected Writings.* Translated by Charles E. Passage. New York, 1960.

————. *Hymns to the Night.* Translated by Dick Higgins. New Paltz, 1984.

————. *Novellas: Two Tales and Sacred Songs.* Spring Valley, N.Y., 1978.

————. *The Novices at Sais.* Translated by Ralph Mannheim. New York, 1949.

————. *Pollen and Fragments.* Translated by Arthur Versluis. Grand Rapids, Mich., 1989.

————. *Werke.* 2 vols. Munich, 1978.

O'Brien, Wm. Actander. *Novalis: Signs of Revolution.* Durham, N.C., 1995.

Pfefferkorn, Kristin. *Novalis, a Romantic's Theory of Language.* New Haven, 1988.

Roder, Florian. *Novalis. Die Verwandlung des Menschen.* Stuttgart, 1992.

Schlegel, Friedrich. *Philosophical Fragments.* Translated by Peter Firchow. Minneapolis, 1991.

Spring, Powell. *Novalis, Pioneer of the Spirit.* Winter Park, Fla., 1944.

Von Molnar, Geza. *Romantic Vision, Ethical Context: Novalis and Artistic Autonomy.* Minneapolis, 1987.

13. Romanticism and the Evolution of Consciousness

Abrahams, M. H. *The Mirror and the Lamp: Romantic Theory and the Critical Tradition.* New York, 1953.

————. *Natural Supernaturalism: Tradition and Revolution in Romantic Literature.* New York, 1971.

Arber, Agnes. *The Manifold and the One.* London, 1957.

——. *The Mind and the Eye: A Study of the Biologist's Standpoint*. Cambridge, 1964.

——. *The Natural History of Plant Form*. Cambridge, 1950.

Barfield, Owen. *Poetic Diction*. Middletown, Conn., 1973.

——. *Romanticism Comes of Age*. London, 1966.

——. *Saving the Appearances, A Study in Idolatry*. New York, 1965.

——. *Speaker's Meaning*. London, 1967.

——. *What Coleridge Thought*. Middletown, Conn., 1971.

Bate, Walter Jackson. *John Keats*. Oxford, 1966.

Bennett, Benjamin. *Goethe's Theory of Poetry*. Ithaca, 1986.

Berdyaev, N. *The Beginning and the End*. London, 1952.

——. *The Destiny of Man*. London, 1948.

——. *Freedom and the Spirit*. New York, 1935.

——. *The Meaning of the Creative Act*. New York, 1946.

Blackstone, Bernard. *The Consecrated Urn: An Interpretation of Keats in terms of Growth and Form*. London, 1959.

Bortoft, Henri. *The Wholeness of Nature*. Hudson, N.Y., 1996.

Boyle, Nicholas. *Goethe, The Poet and the Age*. Oxford, 1991.

Cassirer, Ernst. *Rousseau, Kant, Goethe*. Princeton, 1945.

De Almedia. *Romantic Medicine and John Keats*. Oxford, 1991.

Engel, James. *The Creative Imagination: Enlightenment to Romanticism*. Cambridge, 1981.

Gode von Asch, Alexander. *Natural Science in German Romanticism*. New York, 1944.

Goethe, J. W. *Italian Journey*. Translated by W. H. Auden and Elizabeth Mayer. San Francisco, 1982.

——. *Tales for Transformation*. Translated by Scott Thompson. San Francisco, 1987.

——. *Theory of Color*. Translated by Charles Eastlake. Cambridge, Mass., 1970.

Gray, Ronald D. *Goethe the Alchemist*. Cambridge, 1952.

Heidegger, Martin. *Discourse on Thinking*. Translated by John M. Anderson and E. Hans Freund. New York, 1966.

——. *Early Greek Thinking*. Translated by David Krell and Frank Capuzzi. New York, 1975.

——. *The End of Philosophy*. Translated by Joan Stambaugh. New York, 1973.

——. *Identity and Difference*. Translated by Joan Stambaugh. New York, 1969.

——. *On Time and Being*. Translated by Joan Stambaugh. New York, 1972.

——. *Poetry, Language, Thought*. Translated by Alfred Hofstadter. New York, 1975.

——. *The Question Concerning Technology and Other Essays*. Translated by William Lovitt. New York, 1977.

——. *What Is Called Thinking*. Translated by J. Glenn Gray. New York, 1968.

Heller, Erich. *The Artist's Journey into the Interior and Other Essays*. New York, 1965.

——. *The Disinherited Mind*. New York, 1959.

——. *In the Age of Prose: Literary and Philosophical Essays*. Cambridge, 1984.

Jones, John. *John Keats's Dream of Truth*. London, 1969.

Keats, John. *The Letters of John Keats.* Cambridge, Mass., 1958.

Lehrs, Ernst. *Man or Matter.* London: Faber and Faber, 1958.

McFarland, Thomas. *Coleridge and the Pantheist Tradition.* Oxford, 1969.

———. *Romanticism and the Forms of Ruin.* Princeton, 1981.

Magnus, Rudolf. *Goethe as a Scientist.* New York, 1949.

Mueller, Bertha, trans. *Goethe's Botanical Writings.* Honolulu, 1952.

Murry, John Middleton. *Keats.* London, 1955.

———. *Keats and Shakespeare.* London, 1926.

Oxenford John, trans. *The Autobiography of Goethe.* Chicago, 1974.

———. *Conversations of Goethe with Eckermann.* London, 1913.

Raine, Kathleen. *Blake and the New Age.* London, 1979.

———. *Blake and Tradition.* 2 vols. Princeton, 1968.

Raphael, Alice. *Goethe and the Philosopher's Stone.* New York, 1965.

Riasanovsky, Nicholas V. *The Emergence of Romanticism.* Oxford, 1992.

Salm, Peter. *The Poem as Plant: A Biological View of Goethe's Faust.* Cleveland, 1971.

Schiller, Friedrich. *On the Aesthetic Education of Man.* Translated by Elizabeth M. Wilkinson and L. A. Willoughby. Oxford, 1967.

Sewell, E.. *The Orphic Voice: Poetry and Natural History.* New Haven, 1960.

Solovyov, Vladimir. *The Meaning of Love.* West Stockbridge, Mass., 1985.

Steiner, Rudolf. "The Aesthetics of Goethe's Worldview." In *Art as Spiritual Activity: Rudolf Steiner's Contribution to the Visual Arts.* Edited by Michael Howard. Hudson, N.Y., 1988.

———. *Goethe's World View.* Spring Valley, N.Y., 1985.

———. *Nature's Open Secret.* Edited by John Barnes. Great Barrington, 2001.

Todd, Ruthven. *Tracks in the Snow.* London, 1946.

Viëtor, Karl. *Goethe, The Thinker.* Cambridge, Mass., 1950.

14. Deserts and Gardens

Roberts, Karen Barbara. "The Influence of Rosary Devotion on Grünewald's Isenheim Altarpiece." Ph.D. dissertation, SUNY Binghampton, 1985.

Wilkins, Eithne. *The Rose Garden Game: The Symbolic Background to the European Prayer Beads.* London, 1969.

Winston-Allen, Anne. *Stories of the Rose, The Making of the Rosary in the Middle Ages.* University Park, Penn., 1997.

15. Washing the Feet

Colledge, E., trans. *Meister Eckhart, The Essential Sermons, Commentaries, Treatises etc.* New York, 1981.

McGinn, B., ed. *Meister Eckhart—Teacher and Preacher.* New York, 1986.

Maurer, A., trans. *Meister Eckhart: Parisian Questions and Prologues.* Toronto, 1974.

Schürmann, Reiner. *Wandering Joy: Meister Eckhart's Mystical Philosophy.* Great Barrington, 2001.